New Generation Political Activism in Ukraine

Individuals in the post-Communist Ukraine dealt with a political climate of stalled reforms and corruption, leading to a mass distrust of many political institutions. This had a demobilizing effect on a citizen's sense of capacity to effect social change. Therefore, the emergence of any individual to become an activist and involved in protest movements was a remarkable feat. So how does an individual become an activist in such a climate?

This book explains how socio-cultural experiences shape an individual's choices to become an activist in the authoritarian space of post-Soviet Ukraine by applying a cultural, actor-centred approach using qualitative methods of interviews and ethnography. The goal is to better understand the dynamics of individual decision-making between participants in collective protest actions under repressive conditions from the State using biographical narratives. The book covers multiple discussions with five young activists involved in the three largest protest events since Ukrainian independence in 1991: the Ukraine without Kuchma Movement of 2000–2001, the Orange Revolution of 2004, and the Euromaidan protests of 2014.

This is valuable reading for students and researchers interested in political sociology, social movements and Ukrainian politics, and how these Ukrainian protests can be related to wider European political movements.

Christine Emeran holds a PhD in Sociology from The New School for Social Research (New York), conducted post-doctoral research at the Université Paris Descartes (Sorbonne Paris Cité) and now works as an education policy consultant for an international organization. Her research interests include political sociology, social movements, Ukraine and higher education. She has been the recipient of the Fulbright U.S. Student Program and IREX Individual Advanced Research Opportunities Program fellowships in Ukraine.

Routledge Advances in Sociology

For a full list of titles in this series, please visit www.routledge.com/series/
SE0511.

212 **Homeownership, Renting and Society**
Historical and Comparative Perspectives
Sebastian Kohl

213 **Social Class and Transnational Human Capital**
How Middle and Upper Class Parents Prepare Their Children
for Globalization
Jürgen Gerhards, Silke Hans and Sören Carlson

214 **Transnational Social Policy**
Social Welfare in a World on the Move
Edited by Luann Good Gingrich and Stefan Köngeter

215 **Meta-Regulation in Practice**
Beyond Morality and Rationality
F.C. Simon

216 **The Sociology of Postmarxism**
Richard Howson

217 **The Precarious Generation**
A Political Economy of Young People
Judith Bessant Rys Farthing and Rob Watts

218 **Human Rights, Islam and the Failure of Cosmopolitanism**
June Edmunds

219 **New Generation Political Activism in Ukraine**
2000–2014
Christine Emeran

220 **Turkish National Identity and Its Outsiders**
Memories of State Violence in Dersim
Ozlem Goner

New Generation Political Activism in Ukraine
2000–2014

Christine Emeran

LONDON AND NEW YORK

First published 2017 by Routledge

2 Park Square, Milton Park, Abingdon, Oxfordshire OX14 4RN
711 Third Avenue, New York, NY 10017

Routledge is an imprint of the Taylor & Francis Group, an informa business

First issued in paperback 2018

Copyright © 2017 Christine Emeran

The right of Christine Emeran to be identified as author of this work has been asserted by her in accordance with sections 77 and 78 of the Copyright, Designs and Patents Act 1988.

All rights reserved. No part of this book may be reprinted or reproduced or utilised in any form or by any electronic, mechanical, or other means, now known or hereafter invented, including photocopying and recording, or in any information storage or retrieval system, without permission in writing from the publishers.

Notice:
Product or corporate names may be trademarks or registered trademarks, and are used only for identification and explanation without intent to infringe.

British Library Cataloguing-in-Publication Data
A catalogue record for this book is available from the British Library

Library of Congress Cataloging-in-Publication Data
Names: Emeran, Christine, author.
Title: New generation political activism in Ukraine: 2000–2014 / Christine Emeran.
Description: Milton Park, Abingdon, Oxon; New York, NY: Routledge, 2017. | Series: Routledge advances in sociology | Includes bibliographical references and index.
Identifiers: LCCN 2016055028 | ISBN 9781472482525 (hardback) | ISBN 9781315597966 (ebook)
Subjects: LCSH: Ukraine—Social conditions—1991– | Ukraine—Politics and government—1991– | Political activists— Ukraine—Biography. | Political participation—Ukraine. | Protest movements—Ukraine. | Post-communism—Ukraine.
Classification: LCC HN530.9.A8 E45 2017 | DDC 306.09477—dc23
LC record available at https://lccn.loc.gov/2016055028

ISBN: 978-1-4724-8252-5 (hbk)
ISBN: 978-1-138-34691-8 (pbk)

Typeset in Times New Roman
by codeMantra

Contents

List of interviewees		vi
List of abbreviations		vii
Foreword		viii
NADIA DIUK		
Acknowledgments		xiii
	Introduction	1
1	New generation and subjectivities	17
2	The emergence of an actor	44
3	Personalized expressions of activism	64
4	Professionalization of activists	76
5	Activists' self-organization of the Euromaidan protests, 2013–2014	96
6	Conclusion	117
	Index	131

List of interviewees

Activists and social movements

	2000	*2004*	*2013–14*
Andriy Shevtsiv	Committee "For Truth"	[black] Pora	Civic Sector of Euromaidan
Stanislav Kutsenko	N/A	"Student Wave" campaign	Ukrainian Youth Forum and Ukrainian Student Association
Andriy Kohut	Committee "For Truth"	[black] Pora	Civic Sector Euromaidan
Ostap Kryvydk	Committee "For Truth"	[yellow] Pora	Maidan Self-Defense
Volodymyr Ishchenko	"Ukraine without Kuchma"	N/A	Student strike meetings at the National University of Kyiv Mohyla Academy

List of abbreviations

CPU	Communist Party of Ukraine
DIY	Do-It-Yourself
EDS	European Democrat Students
EU AA	European Union Association Agreement
FNS	National Salvation Forum
IARO	Individual Advanced Research Opportunities Program
KGB	Committee for State Security for Soviet Union
MPs	Members of Parliament
NABU	National Anticorruption Bureau
NaUKMA	National University of Kyiv Mohyla Academy
NDPU	National Democratic Party of Ukraine
NGO	Non-Governmental Organization
NSF	National Salvation Forum
NSSR	New School for Social Research
OMON	The "Berkut" (special police force)
PORA-PRP	Reforms and Order Party
RPR	Reanimation Package of Reforms
SBU	Security Service of Ukraine
SDPU(O)	Social Democratic Party (United)
SNAU	Sumy National Agrarian University
SNUM	The Association of Independent Ukrainian Youth
SOCIS	Center for Social and Marketing Research
SUM	Union of Ukrainian Youth
UDAR	Ukrainian Democratic Alliance for Reform
UHU	Ukrainian Helsinki Union
UNU	Ukrainian Nationalist Union
USSR	Union of Soviet Socialist Republics
UWK	Ukraine without Kuchma

Foreword

Nadia Diuk

Historians and scholars throughout the ages have tried to understand what motivates people to behave the way they do and what brings people together to act collectively as a social or political movement that sometimes effects a major change in the course of history. The narrative in this book reaches back to the beginnings of Ukrainian independent statehood as the USSR dissolved and goes on a quarter century up to the present day. This turbulent time forms the backdrop to the author's investigation of the seminal protest movements that shaped that history; she focuses on the young people who took the lead. The main analysis is of the 2000 protests, the 2004 Orange Revolution, and the 2013–14 Maidan Revolution, with some reference to the first protests on the eve of independence in October 1990. The major theme explored in this book concerns the personal motivation that inspired individual actors in these events: their spur to participate and be involved in protests and their subsequent assessments of their own activities.

A turbulent twenty-five years

In the twenty-five years of independence since 1991, Ukraine has been faced with many challenges ranging from creating the institutions of an independent state where there were none, to bringing its citizens out of the Soviet era where neither politics nor free economic activity were allowed. The project of the past quarter century has been to create a nation of conscious and aware citizens. This would have been a tall order even in a completely peaceful and supportive international environment. Expectations held in the early 1990's that "the end of history" had arrived and that all the newly independent states of the former Soviet Union would naturally evolve along a path toward full liberal democracy and free market economy proved illusory, despite good faith efforts to support the newly established governments of the region.

The new Ukrainian state emerged in 1991 soon after massive protests spearheaded by students a year earlier. However, the fate of those protests established a precedent that would ensure that the pendulum of politics would swing between protest and passivity a few more times. The new, post-Soviet elite that suddenly became the government of the new

Foreword ix

independent Ukraine took note of the power of protest and especially the youth that had led them, and worked to undermine any youth participation in government. The 1990s were marked by the absence of young people in positions of leadership and power, nor were they welcomed into the political parties that started to form. At the same time, President Leonid Kuchma, who had distinguished himself by becoming the first President to win an election and accomplish a peaceful transfer of power in the non-Baltic post-Soviet region in 1994, was becoming increasingly authoritarian in his exercise of power—controlling the media, monopolizing power, and undermining all forms of opposition.

Perhaps we will never know how far Ukraine's governing institutions were still connected to Russia at that time, but it was clear that some elements around the top levels of government were not acting in Ukraine's best interests. The Gongadze murder brought everything to a head. Young people who had effectively been excluded from most institutions of government and politics took to protest as the only way to express their discontent.

The protests that followed showed the failure of the Ukrainian leadership to secure a level of security and prosperity for its citizens and it also showed that all channels that generally allow for the expression of discontent were blocked. The newspapers were controlled; publications censored, mass media were given a script to follow. There was no place for young people to forge a place for themselves as participants in determining their own future or the future of their country. This was epitomized by investigative journalist Heorhiy Gongadze's decision to create Ukrains'ka Pravda as an independent publication in 1999, out of reach of government control. As it turned out, he also created one of the first successful Internet publications that became a flagship for others. Gongadze's outspoken criticisms of corruption and control in government circles drew attention and in September 2000 has was abducted and murdered. The 2000 protests in this book first came together as a reaction to these events.

Why study youth?

Another of this book's themes is the focus on youth. Of all of the topics in political science and sociology and related areas of study, the study of youth is often the least covered. In situations where there is no extraordinary political situation, the study of youth is often relegated to an analysis of subcultures and human anthropology. The way youth are treated within a polity and how much access they have to decision-making and political processes can, however, reveal a lot about the nature of a state. A review of whether youth are the object of policy or whether they can conduct activities as subjects and actors in civic and political processes is a good indication of the level of democracy within a society. Young people have always been at the forefront of social and political protest, but it is the way a state deals with these protests that makes history.

x *Nadia Diuk*

The study of youth is often underestimated as a general predictor of future political developments. The influences and educational background of the generation is a factor that can illuminate how a social movement comes together and can provide explanations to help better understand the driving forces. For example, many of the leaders of the protests in 2000 had participated in the student hunger strikes and demonstrations of 1990. The euphoria of achieving independence gradually gave way to the realization that the entrenched political forces were not about to give up power. Young people were effectively blocked from real politics throughout the 1990s unless they joined in with the already established political formations. These same leaders made a success of the 2004 Orange Revolution, but again, the next generation of students became disillusioned by the inability of the leading elite to effect the changes in Ukraine that had been the driving force of the protests.

A study of the political environment at the time of the protests shows that governing institutions and political processes were still heavily drawn from the authoritarian arrangements of the Soviet system. Youth was considered an object of politics, with "youth ministries" and committees that handled any issues to do with youth on their behalf and often without any input from authentic youth movements, organizations, or voices. Even the nascent political parties were suspicious of young activists and often shunted them out of the way into "youth wings" of the main political party. The youth-led protests in 2000 and 2004 were perhaps the only way in which the younger generation could articulate their desires and aspirations in the absence of any channels that are afforded young people in more liberal political systems.

Despite the disappointments and disarray of the political landscape during the presidency of Viktor Yushchenko from 2005–2009, there was one area that benefitted from a liberal approach unexpectedly afforded by the otherwise weak administration—and that was the field of education. Benefitting from benign neglect in many cases, education in Ukraine was left to develop along relatively liberal lines. High school students were left to pursue their education unfettered by political control and were able to expand the area of studies from previous times. The educational institutions that were trying to institute quality education such as the Kyiv-Mohyla Academy in Kyiv and the newly re-established Ukrainian Catholic University in Lviv, did well during this period. This generation of students came out to support the Maidan protests in 2013. Allowed and encouraged to explore possibilities in Europe and further afield in their search for career opportunities throughout the Yushchenko period, the sudden reversal away from Europe by President Yanukovych in November 2013 hit them hard. They were supported by their elders: when asked why they were for Europe, their parents and grandparents often referred to the fact that even though it might be too late for them, they wanted their children and grandchildren to have the opportunities encapsulated in the idea of "Europe" and to have a better life.

From protest to politics

Another theme in this book is the author's main thesis, the exploration of what motivates a young person to become civically and politically active. There are many ways in which these protests can be compared with other youth led protests such as the Serbian protests against President Milosevic in 2000, the Arab Spring in 2011, and others, but there is a particular theme here that will be helpful to anyone studying the transition from Communism to democracy. One of the biggest challenges for states that have cast off the constraints of the Communist system is the absence of civil society; the lack of any independent organized groups or institutions that typically create the mediating fabric of a society. With a population that has been deprived of the possibility to take part in politics of any kind let alone voting for representative officials and government, the habits of passivity are difficult to cast off. Apathy reigns and the inability to formulate strategies and to organize is lost.

When the student protests and demonstrations for independence subsided in Ukraine in 1990–1991, there were few civic groups or organizations to conduct the civic life that is the lifeblood of an open democratic society. The old habits and mindset of assuming that the state authorities would take care of everything from cradle to grave persisted in many forms throughout the post-Soviet space. Gradually, and sometimes with international donor funding, civic groups began to emerge. But the interesting question for a researcher will always be, what prompted the individual to undertake the first step toward activism and what aspirations and objectives do individuals harbor when making those moves into civic and political life.

The civic groups and movements that were active in Ukraine during the 2004 Orange Revolution underwent something of a reversal once the new president Viktor Yushchenko was sworn in. The prevailing assumption was now that the "people's president" had won over the authoritarian, Russian-backed Viktor Yanukovych, the new government would take care of everything and the non-governmental groups that had formed felt a loss of purpose. As it turned out, the swift reversion to authoritarian rule by Yanukovych, when he won the 2010 election, took everyone by surprise and there were concerns that the previous five years of relative inactivity of the nascent civil society would be an obstacle to any renewed organization of protest actions. The mass turnout after the beating of young people on November 30, 2013 that launched the protests lasting three months, were not expected according to most public opinion polling that had been conducted immediately prior to those events.

There are now plenty of research materials that can be used to understand how and why young people joined the 2013–14 protests. Tracing the path from the initial act of protest and activism can be followed through to the self-organization on the Maidan. The next area for researchers to probe and understand will be to work out how and why civic activists, including investigative journalists and others, have had an aversion for entering politics. In many of the protest movements around the world, one of the main obstacles to proceeding through and acting on the ideals of the "revolution" has been the lack of a plan and lack of organization to follow up after the protests have dispersed. In the case of Ukraine, it was clear that an aversion to participating in the "dirty business" of politics was also an obstacle for many who saw their time on the Maidan as the fulfillment of a pure desire to defend and protect their future. However, another equally important imperative arose in the desire to secure the achievements of the protest and build on them, and not to allow the "victory" to slip away as it had in 2005.

For the first time in 2014, young people who had participated in the protests consciously and deliberately put aside their natural aversion to politics and joined various political parties running to support the newly elected post-Maidan president Petro Poroshenko. Around 30 of the activists that had been the leaders and organizers of the Maidan thus went into parliamentary politics, breaking the quarter century of precedent where activists and reforms were active primarily outside of the traditional institutions of governance. The next challenge for Ukraine will be to develop authentic grass-roots based political parties and to curb the influence of financial and oligarchical interests in the political sphere.

These past twenty-five years have seen the evolution of national identity in Ukraine and the post-Maidan emergence of a firmer sense of what it means to be a "citizen of Ukraine." This period has also coincided with a revolution in the way individuals communicate and the way social movements grow and develop. The advent of mobile technology and social media have both fuelled and been affected by the activism they have engendered. Each successive wave of protests has accelerated the use of some kind of digital media—from the establishment of the flagship Internet publication Ukrains'ka Pravda in 2000, to the innovations and creative use of Internet reporting by the newly established HromadskeTV and others that provided an uninterrupted stream of live coverage of the Maidan events through the turbulent three months of 2013–14.

In many ways the youth of Ukraine have taken a lead in organization, follow up, and channeling of protest that should provide instruction and lessons learned for any other movements so inclined. This book will help to provide an education for those who wish to pursue these themes further and will be a goldmine for historians in the future looking for eyewitness and first-hand accounts of important turning points in history.

Nadia Diuk, (D.Phil.) Vice President, Regional Programs
Europe, Eurasia, Africa, Latin America and the Caribbean
National Endowment for Democracy
Washington, D.C.

Acknowledgments

This book has been an ongoing labour of love and gratitude that began in 2007 and has been completed, at last, as a book in 2017.

On this journey, I would like to thank my graduate advisors at the New School for Social Research (NSSR) in New York, more notably, Jose Casanova and Terry Williams, for their constant support and belief in my dissertation project. Many thanks to my fellow students at the NSSR for our rich conversations and contributions, among them are Carol Garza, Rina Bliss, Ana Mallen, Veronica Alfaro Ahumada, and many more. I also thank my close friends and family from New York for their continued support throughout these years.

I send my gratitude and thanks to the Harriman Institute at Columbia University, in particular, the Department of Slavic Languages that worked hard to help me navigate and develop Ukrainian language skills. A special thanks is extended to Mark von Hagen, Rory Finnin, and Yuri Shevchuk. I also thank the Ukrainian-American diaspora in New York with their support with contacts in Ukraine.

This research would not have been possible without the external funding of two primary sources: The U.S. Fulbright Program's Fulbright Office in Ukraine and the IREX/Individual Advanced Research Opportunities (IARO) Program, Funded by the U.S. Department of State's Title VIII Program. I would like to thank them and the former director Myron Stachiw (Fulbright Ukraine) for providing me the resources to successfully complete my research.

In Ukraine, I would like to thank my host universities of affiliation: The National University of Kyiv Mohyla Academy (NauKMA) and the Ukrainian Catholic University in Lviv. I would like to thank the university rectors for their warm reception and their kind efforts to open their student community to me.

I thank all of those Ukrainian students, journalists, civic activists, politicians, and student groups (Opora, Student Wave, Black Pora, and Yellow Pora) that agreed to participate in my research and to contribute history with their personal stories. To all of you, I am indebted and humbled by your courage and strength to pursue social change in difficult conditions.

xiv *Acknowledgments*

I also thank the following Ukrainian students that helped with translations, they are Anastasiya Prymovych, Volodymyr Gushley, Olena Martynuk, Olena Synchak (who also helped with language classes), and last but not least, Olena and Katya Bondar who opened their homes and friendship to me.

To the Ukrainian researchers I met along the way and helped keep me grounded during the fieldwork, I thank with my heart, Phylissa Mitchell, Mayhill Fowler, Ksenia Nouril, Luda from NY, Alina Polynachuk, and many others.

In Paris, I would like to thank my host institution for my post-doctoral affiliation, at the Sorbonne, University Paris Descartes, Pr. Yves Charles Zarka and his research laboratory PHILéPOL (Philosophie, épistémologie et politique) and graduate students, for allowing me the opportunity to expand my knowledge within this intellectual space and to make this book possible. I also would like to thank students in my class, New Forms of Political Action at SciencesPO for their interest and stimulating discussions on my research and social movements.

I am thankful to Alice Mattoni for her sound advice on book publication, which worked! I also send gratitude to Cristina M. Flesher Fominaya for organizing this book panel at SciencesPo at the Council for European studies.

I would like to thank Claire Jarvis and Ashgate Publishing (now Routledge) for believing in my book proposal. I am also grateful to Neil Jordan and his editorial team at Routledge for their great work to finalize the copy for print.

I would like to also thank the following reviewers of this manuscript for their insightful commentaries, they are Laada Bilaniuk, Nadia Diuk, Geoffrey Pleyers, and Chantalle Verna. I also would like to thank a fellow sociologist in my book with her skills to help with editing, Sarah Fauer.

Many thanks to the activists that agreed to participate and share their protest experiences, this book has benefited from your contributions. I share my gratitude with you: Volodymyr Ishchenko, Andriy Kohut, Ostap Kryvydk, Stanislav Kutsenko, and Andriy Shevtsiv. A special thanks to Volodymyr Viatrovych for granting permission to use his image for the book's cover. I would also like to thank Alicia Mireles Juárez, my gifted friend in photography for her assistance on the book's cover.

I would also like to thank my mother and father, Ketly and George Emeran, for their patience and understanding as well as my sister, Kareen Emeran, for her unending support.

Lastly, a special mention to Giulia Reggiani for navigating me through Europe, and to all my friends and family in my life, thank you for always bringing out the best in me and inspiring me to reach new heights!

Introduction

The inspiration for this research arose from a profound interest in Ukrainian activists and their perceptions of agency in the wake of protest events. This book presents "The Ukraine Without Kuchma," Orange Revolution, and Euromaidan protests initiated by individual(s) relying on their own personal networks to coordinate a social movement. This research examines these individuals and their practices to understand the conditions that led them to adopt an activist role in a political climate of stalled reforms and corruption in the Ukrainian government. Individuals in the post-Communist Ukraine were more likely to have less trust in public institutions and to depend more on personal, friend networks or associations than the government (Rose-Ackerman, 2001). This had a demobilizing effect on a citizen's sense of capacity to effect social change. Therefore, the emergence of any individual to become an activist and involved in protest movements was a remarkable feat. This study places greater attention on the social transformation processes of an individual into activism in Ukraine. This approach considers actor reflexivity on politicization processes that are reflected in "personal storytelling" (Lichterman). These personal narratives are expressions of "...activists who see themselves as bearing their own, highly personalized commitments..." (Lichterman, 1996, p. 78).

This opening chapter presents some of the main actors involved in launching the first calls to collective action in three Ukrainian protest events (2000, 2004, 2013) featured in the book. This section is followed by a history of the opposition movement in Ukraine, research framework, and design, and concludes with a description of the book's chapters summarized by theme.

2000

The first case involved a return to December 2000, a period ripe with an unfolding political crisis due to the release of secret recordings that strengthened allegations connecting the Ukrainian president, Leonid Kuchma, with the kidnapping and murder of Heorhiy Gongadze, a well-respected investigative journalist and founder of online newspaper *Ukrainska Pravda* (Ukrainian Truth). Yet, as the scandal unfolded with incriminating evidence mounting

2   *Introduction*

against the president, it was remarkable that the public remained passive and did not mobilize. During that moment in late November, Oleh Levytsky—a lawyer who was frustrated by the absence of a public response over his friend's death—complained to his friend Myhailo Svystovych—a civic activist and founder of the Maidan website, an Internet hub of information for activists (www.maidan.ua)—and expressed an urgent appeal to organize a protest on Kyiv's Independence Square (*Maidan Nezalezhnosti* in Ukrainian, commonly referred to as Maidan) (Zubar, 2005). The following month, in early December 2000, Svystovych was offered the occasion on his birthday to mobilize old university friends into protest actions, since there was nothing organized on the grassroots level. Among his friends gathered near Kyiv's Independence Square, there were Yuriy Lutsenko, member of the Socialist Party of Ukraine, and Volodymyr Chemerys, a former politician and civic activist. In their conversation over dinner followed by a walk to Kyiv's Maidan, a tradition since the end of the student protests in the 1990s, Chemerys shared with the others reflections on his latest article from April 2000 about Ukraine at the brink of revolution. His anecdote served in hindsight as foreshadowing, since he did not realize that his words would come to fruition at that time (author's interview, Chemerys, 2008, Kyiv).

Despite the life events encountered—fatherhood for Lutsenko and resignation from employment from the National Bank for Svystovych—they decided together with Chemerys to plan and organize the "Ukraine without Kuchma" (UWK) protests. They reasoned that it was impossible to continue to live in this way; they wanted a European way of life (Shevchenko, 2003). Over the next few days, the UWK founders reached out to their friends in civil society and in politics for their participation in their protests. They were convinced that the people's anger over the disappearance of Gondadze would be the anchor to mobilize people to attend their first protest organized on 15 December 2000. On the protest day, UWK coordinators expected a turnout of 150 people; instead, they found a group of 50 people on Kyiv's Maidan to assist with the preparations for the protests. The organizers of protest were self-reflective in their deliberate decision to set up the tent camps to mirror the exact location, and use of similar methods as when they were student activists in the 1990 student hunger strikes, known as the "Revolution on the Granite" (Zubar 2005, author's interview, Chemerys, 2008, Kyiv).

A generational approach can help to explain "the formation of the post-Soviet generation" that emerged from the background of the "collapse of Communism and the subsequent social transformations" (Nikolayenko, 2007, p. 169). This generation had "political aspirations" that were important in "propelling political action" (Nikolayenko, 2007, p. 169). The organizers of UWK had thought more people would support their first action; their calls to protest attracted about 500 people. They quickly realized that mobilizing protest around Gondadze's murder was not sufficient. Chemerys later attributed the weak mobilization to the fact that they did not reach

Introduction 3

the cornerstone of the problem. This, for him, was rooted in the society's lingering doubt over President Leonid Kuchma's ability to obtain majority support in April's referendum to amend the Constitution and to expand the presidential powers ("Court deems," 2000; Chemerys, 2008, Kyiv).

2004

A few years later, on 21 November 2004, it was the eve of the second round of the presidential elections between Viktor Yushchenko representing "Our Ukraine" political party and Viktor Yanukovych and "The Party of Regions." Early election results released by Ukraine's Central Election Committee (CEC) suggested that Yanukovych had a lead over Yushchenko. The preliminary findings contradicted national exit polls by a significant enough margin to create alarm. In addition, there were media and international election monitor reports of gross irregularities in the voting process, pointing to fraudulent results. In Yushchenko's "Our Ukraine" headquarters, a contingent plan for fraud and public mobilization had already been underway for over a year and a half. Roman Bessmertny, deputy head of "Our Ukraine" election headquarters, was the campaign manager responsible for the organization of the protests on Kyiv's Maidan (author's interview, Stetskiv, 2008, Kyiv). He was in charge of delegating the coordination of the protests to the field commanders: Taras Stetskiv, Volodymyr Filenko, Mykola Tomenko, and Yuriy Lutsenko ("Orange Revolution," 2004).

The mobilization plan was activated in the early dawn of the following day at 2 AM; Yushchenko appeared on Ukrainian television Channel 5 to broadcast his lack of confidence in the CEC's projected election results, signaling a victory for Yanukovych. On air, Yushchenko urged the viewers to come to the streets and support him that morning at 9 AM on Kyiv's Maidan. In his TV appearance, he assured the public that the protests would be peaceful and lawful, according to the Constitution. His call to protest was repeated by Yulia Tymoshenko, who framed her appeals for political participation as necessary to protect Ukraine's future, which she stressed was highly dependent on massive popular mobilization ("ЮЩЕНКО НЕ," 2004). By 4 PM, 100,000 people gathered on Maidan, including those who arrived from the regions of Ukraine, and people who gathered there set up two tent camps with over 100 tents populated by students on surrounding streets off the main square ("НАМЕТИ НА МАЙДАНІ," 2004).

2014

The post-Soviet generation of young people mobilized in the Committee "For Truth" and a successive generation of student activists from the Orange Revolution rose in a new round of protests. On 21 November 2013, Mustafa Nayyem, a popular journalist and activist working for *Ukrainska Pravda* and a founder of online, independent television channel Hromadske.tv, was

4 *Introduction*

credited with launching the Euromaidan protests from Facebook. This was prior to Yanukovych's refusal to sign a trade agreement with the European Union (EU). Nayyem had originally thought that Yanukovych was holding back to negotiate more favorable terms of financing from the EU to address Ukraine's economic crisis. However, he remarked that Yanukovych's ultimate decision not to sign the agreement extinguished the Ukrainian people's aspirations for a European future. He described the people's mood as filled with disappointment and he observed this sentiment being virally expressed on Facebook. As Nayyem recalled,

> Facebook erupted with rage, people's posts dripping with venom. They were so disappointed after all the buildup. They had so little faith in their own institutions, in their ability to make their voices heard; many had come to see the EU as their chance to change everything.
>
> (Nayyem, 2014)

In the midst of his reflections on that experience, he remarked feeling a bittersweet emotion when he also realized that this day marked 10 years from the start of the Orange Revolution. This day had come to represent freedom for the activists involved until that time in 2013. His felt reaction to the injustice led him to conclude that "the outrage needed an outlet" (Ibid., 2014). In response, he went on his page on Facebook to put out the first call to protest on Kyiv's Maidan. He recounted events on that day. At 8 PM, he wrote a message on Facebook to motivate his friends to be prepared to move beyond the Internet activism of "liking" his post. Within an hour, he received more than 600 comments. In reply, he suggested a meeting place and time for them at 10.30 PM on Kyiv's Maidan near the monument (Ibid., 2014).

Nayyem's Facebook post on 21 November generated 3,200 likes, 1,356 comments, and 1,138 shares (https://www.facebook.com/Mustafanayyem/timeline). Newspapers in Kyiv reported that 2,000 people attended the Euromaidan rallies that evening ("EuroMaidan rallies," 2013).

What is noteworthy is that these forms of activism did not happen in isolation, but emerged from a context that is situational. In Ukraine, involved in this history were opposition actors who participated in anti-regime political movements during three key periods of social and political transformation discussed below.

Opposition actors and anti-regime protests

In the first period examined, from 1992–2001, the opposition consisted of two left political parties, the Communist Party (CPU, banned 1991 and reinstated in 1993) and the Socialist Party (outgrowth from a Soviet Communist Party). These political groups were opposed to Ukrainian independence and the Ukraine nation state, and desired a return to the system of Communism. The second period, in 1999, signified the rise of the oligarchs to political power.

Following independence, the former Communist *nomenklatura* represented the economic and business interests of the country. They purchased centrist political parties such as Social Democratic Party (United) (SDPU[O]), Green Party, and People's Democratic (NDPU) parties. These parties did not have a real political platform or proposed reforms; instead, they were tools to advance their interests using unlawful means. The rise of the business class of oligarchs signaled the decline in power of the CPU in the 1999 presidential elections (Kuzio, 2005, p. 118). The oligarchs supported the reelection of President Kuchma and were aligned against the left political parties. This election brought to power Viktor Yushchenko as Prime Minister. He led political and economic reforms which created opposition from the oligarchs in power whose interests had been adversely affected (Ibid., p. 119). This time was also marked by the Gondadze scandal and rise of protests—the largest since independence. Yushchenko and other politicians denounced the protests in 2001, resulting in the end of protests (Ibid., p. 120). Yushchenko was unpopular with the oligarchs in the Parliament who voted to dismiss him from power. This opened the door for the third period of change. At this time, Yushchenko created a new political party bloc "Our Ukraine" to mobilize against Kuchma's regime. The new bloc was divided and unable to mount an opposition against the government in power (Ibid., p. 121). New rounds of protests began in September 2002 and March 2003. In the latter, the organizers of "Rise Ukraine" anti-regime campaigns gathered over 50,000 people, as well as the support of the CPU and "Our Ukraine" parties. The opposition was unable to gain public support against Kuchma (Ibid., p. 122). The protests instead mobilized young people who underwent a "political awakening" from apathy. It was this young generation who formed the backbone for the organization of the Orange Revolution. Surveys conducted on the Ukrainian public in March 2003 found the majority of them supported change in Ukraine but none felt empowered to become the drivers of change (Ibid., p. 123).

Following the election of Viktor Yushchenko in 2005, the euphoria of the Orange Revolution quickly faded as a result of the government's inability to implement reform and improve the quality of life of its citizens. Yushchenko lost his reelection bid, and Viktor Yanukovych was elected president in 2010. This was also a period when citizens retreated from political life, grew disenchanted, and opposition forces reappeared again in larger numbers in new rounds of community-led protests. The largest of them appeared in 2010, when Yanukovych's government amended the tax code. This caused entrepreneurs to protest against the new tax code. This uprising greatly impacted the viability of small and mid-sized businesses. Activists formed a Tax Maidan protest movement to increase public interest in their cause of protesting in support of these businesses. The activists in this movement were subject to arrest for their participation in the protest events. The aim of organizers of the Tax Maidan was to mobilize sufficient public support to create a national strike. The protests ended in 2010 with the creation of a Ukrainian Trade Union of Market and Commerce Employees and Entrepreneurs (also known as Tax Maidan II)

6 *Introduction*

to protect the interests of small to middle sized businesses. However, this trade union did not gain much influence and suffered from an inability to mount a civil opposition. They were unable to succeed because of their exploitation by the political opposition who were solely motivated by their interest in controlling this new trade union as a means of gaining political power. At the same time, other protest campaigns emerged such as New Citizen organization with the support of 50 groups that openly organized protests against the government's language policy and residential code. Other activists mounted protests for local causes, among them, the NGO Self Help (Lviv), Unite Kyivites!, Kyiv Strength, and Kyiv for Kyivities (Pastukhova, 2011). These cases of citizen mobilization demonstrated the process where "...people [were] uniting around specific problems and finding solutions [it] is virtually the only way to prevent the domination of the government" (Ibid., 2011). The self-organization of citizens in local initiatives was a precursor to the mobilization structure that took shape a few years later in the Euromaidan protests.

Knowledge claims and gaps

This research places in conversation two theoretical schools of thought, to elucidate the knowledge gaps inherent when relying on theory to empirically study collective action in Ukraine. The first school, elaborated by Mancur Olson, represents rational choice applied to organizations. The second school, developed by W. Lance Bennett and Alexandra Segerberg, focuses on resource mobilization of digital networks to achieve objectives of collective action. In line with my book's central research question: Why is it that neither rational choice theory nor resource mobilization theory can fully explain Ukrainian students' social transformation into an activist?; I examine the self-organization of protests and an actor's repeated participation/ self-mobilization into activism in three protest events over a 14-year span of time. The competing approaches to collective action are illustrated below using the example of a theoretical debate between Mancur Olson's "collective" action and Bennett's and Segerberg's (2012) "connective" action theories.

Olson continues to be popular; however, his theory does not help us to understand Ukraine's movement, which operated under different organizing dynamics than those offered by him. Collection action as outlined Olson's (2002 edition) book titled *The Logic of Collective Action Public Goods and the Theories of Groups* continues to stir debate on rational choice theories applied to social movement studies (Udehn, 1993). In general, he believes rational actors do not participate in political action in order to reach common goals, thus an emphasis is placed on organizations that act on their behalf (Olson, 2002). As a result, Olson is interested in studying social organizations of groups and their conditions for cooperation based on furthering shared group interests (Ibid., pp. 6–7). However, Olson does not address how individuals organize collective action differently if they are not represented by an organized group, as was the case when a single actor launched the first call to protest in Ukraine's

Euromaidan (2014). Furthermore, his claim that people participate in politics when there is a low-cost "in relation to its benefit" gained, is also debatable when extended to Ukraine (Ibid., pp. 22–3). His thinking, when applied to Ukraine, is unable to explain people's long-term participation in Ukrainian protest when the risks involved in participating were heightened due to the political environment of fear and reprisals from the government (i.e., Ukraine with Kuchma, Orange Revolution, and Euromaidan).

In my research of Ukrainian activists, rational choice approach is insufficient since it does not analyze individual social action. Supporting this point of view is Hanson (1997) who argues against rational choice because, as an approach, it "rejects the importance of understanding subjective motivations and instead assumes all individual action can be analyzed as some variant of utility-maximizing behavior" (Hanson, 1997, p. 10). Other limits to Olson's approach are brought to light in the analysis of contemporary forms of protest that do not follow his organizational approach. This claim is supported by Bennett and Segerberg who observe a different model of organizing in their studies of recent protests in Spain's 15M, which can also be extended to the Occupy movement and Euromaidan. In their analysis of case studies of Spain's protest, they found differences in informal organization, including online, that "seemed to operate with surprisingly light involvement from conventional organizations" and also remarked that the protests' success seemed connected to their strategy in "keeping political parties, unions, and other powerful political organizations out" given that those groups were considered as the target of their oppositional struggle (Bennett and Segerberg, 2012, p. 741). Additionally, this example demonstrates how easily diverse people can work together in virtual spaces based on common interests, contrary to Olson's period of study when it was more difficult to find shared interests for building collective action.

Like Olson, Bennett and Segerberg are concerned with organizing behavior, albeit from different sources, in either organizations or social media network platforms. The point of divergence between them is the source of organizing of collective action. Olson focuses on established organizations, and Bennett and Segerberg privilege the collective impact of the personalized narratives supported by technology and people sharing on social media networks. Bennett and Segerberg argue that this aspect of personalization changes the dynamics of protest in terms of reach and diffusion of the movement's issues from the media into the public sphere.

However, resource mobilization theory also has limits when applied to social movements like Ukraine. As an example, Bennett and Segerberg (2012) introduce a theory of "connective" action defined as "personalized content sharing across media networks" that shape contemporary social movement-making processes (Bennett and Segerberg, 2012, p. 739). They make the claim that in collective action, the role of organizing has shifted from organizations to networks on "technology platforms and applications" (Ibid., 2012, p. 742). As an example, they discussed the Occupy movement's slogan "We are the 99 percent" and its global diffusion through the

8 *Introduction*

sharing of personalized narratives and photographs on social media networks (e.g., Twitter and Facebook) (Ibid., 2012, p. 742). A defining feature of such "digitally mediated action" movements that rely on technology for their organization is described by Bennett and Segerberg as "larger; have scaled up more quickly; and have been flexible in tracking moving political targets and bridging different issues" (Ibid., pp. 742–3). Overall, Bennett's and Segerberg's objective in their study of contemporary forms of collective action is to ascertain how the personalization of organizing takes place in digital networks (in the aforementioned case studies), is sustainable, and has a political impact.

Following the tendency of a personalized approach to collective action in contemporary social movements, Bennett and Segerberg do not go much farther than cite societal fragmentation and individualism as the underlying causes of this phenomenon, because they also stay focused on a personalized approach (Bennett and Segerberg, 2012, p. 743). They do not include an analysis of the agency effects of actors acting as agents of social change in their analysis. Instead, their research focuses on the causal effects of individual participation as no longer dependent on collective identity or ideological claims, but rather, collective action as materialized "through inclusive and diverse large-scale personal expression" (Ibid., p. 744). This view of mobilization did not follow mobilization patterns in Ukraine's Euromaidan protests in its early days. When we consider how the mobilization began in Ukraine, it clearly differed from Bennett and Segerberg's analytic framework. In the case of the Euromaidan protests, individuals were mobilized around identity claims for the European Union, and activists used the Internet to spread public opinion in support for Ukraine's signing of the Associated Agreement, a path towards European integration, which followed an ideology of Western Europe and democratization. Additional points of divergence from my case study derive from the functional approach taken by Bennett and Segerberg to explain the framing process of action of media networks. They explain the instrumental uses of "personal action frames" and the interactive process involved for people to "appropriate, shape, and share themes" on digital communication networks with other people. However, their analysis produces an instrumental view of individual communicative practices. This is a relational process that they interpret as a tool for organizing. In their words, "technologies and their use patterns often remain in place as organizational mechanisms" in collective action (Ibid., p. 746). In their analysis, they narrowed focus to the online communicative actions of individuals performing practices that illustrate the dynamics of organizing. In this process, the authors lose sight of the actor and his/her subjective process of producing these personalized frames that represent expressed, public opinions on protests. The collective sum of individual actions on digital networks are what matters for organizing contemporary collective action in their view. This perspective does not fully explain the early mobilization phase and why people start protests in the case of Ukraine's

Euromaidan protests. If we consider the call for protest in the Euromaidan, it was initiated by an individual acting alone and communicating to his own friends on his personal network (Facebook). An individual's action contributed to the launch of a collective action that later evolved into large-scale collective action of protests.

This type of call for protest by an individual can be understood as more than a mechanism of organizing supported by media technology. By redefining Bennett and Segerberg's concept of "personal action frames" to examine subjectivity, perhaps we can come closer to understanding why people self-mobilize. Such individualized frames may be relevant to explaining a person's participation in the first days of protest. The attendance of individuals and their interactions with others on the street was a type of linchpin that, once released, allowed for the self-mobilization of a larger group of individuals drawn from social ties formed on the ground with each other. First time attendance at the protest activity enabled the desire among participants to self-organize the unstructured protests, which were, in the beginning, spontaneous acts of individual citizens, and not organized by groups. This self-organization process involved personal contacts with old friends from past movements and so forth. Overlooked in Bennett and Segerberg's analysis is the reason why individuals contribute their personal pictures and stories on their own social media platforms in the first place. Underexplored are the multitude of reasons that have led individuals to share personal experiences on social networks, and the assessment of whether or not they are mindful of its impact on a social movement, indirectly or directly contributing to a growth in participation and/or diffusing the movement's issues. Social media networks have replaced the traditional role of social movement organizations for organizing collective action, as argued by Bennett and Segerberg. In their qualitative accounts of the user of technology through framing processes, their approach makes it possible to describe actor practices. However, at the same time, it remains difficult to explain the meaning and signification of an actor's behavior on digital networks, which in many cases, is not connected to a particular social movement organization in its early stages.

The task taken up by this research is to take Bennett and Segerberg's theory further in another direction, paying more attention to empirical aspects, including a perspective of an actor as an active subject. The aim is to shed more light on how organizing and communication channels in collective action have changed. In this research on Ukraine, the protests started as peaceful, nonviolent protest movements of social change as an alternative to an increasing authoritarian State of corruption. On the one hand, this aspect implied social action on the part of actors in the form of mounting campaigns of critiques about their social reality. In addition, on the other side, it displayed an actor's alternative vision of democratic social change. Additionally, this subjective approach may also uncover different aspects of self-mobilizing and self-organizing, and reach a closer understanding of what makes an activist remain politically active over a longer period of time.

10   *Introduction*

Research design

This research follows a methodology of John Creswell (2003). He provides a framework using ideas that draw inspiration from Michael Crotty's (1998) research methods (Creswell, 2003, p. 4). Creswell introduces four paradigms of knowledge claims: post-positivism, constructivism, advocacy/participatory, and pragmatism. Of these schools of thought, if one approach stood apart to apply to my research, it was constructivism (Berger and Luckmann, 1966) which Creswell describes as an interpretative strategy based on social construction with subjective meanings. The assumption underlying this perspective of research following Creswell's is "...that individuals seek understanding of the world in which they live and work. They develop subjective meanings of their experiences" (Ibid., p. 8). The objective of this knowledge claim is to "look for the complexity of views rather than narrowing meaning into a few categories or ideas" (Ibid., p. 8). The constructivist perspective observes multiple views from participants to understand the situation. The researcher following this inductive approach applies open-ended questions to ascertain subjective meanings "negotiated socially and historically" attached to life events. This is an interactionist approach that is used by researchers "to make sense of the meanings others have about the world" (Ibid., p. 9).

The research strategy for this qualitative study, selected from among many approaches, is the case study. The process characterizing this approach includes a detailed exploration of cases and data collected over a period of time. The research methods include interviews and open-ended questioning (Creswell, 2003, pp. 15–18). The goal is to better understand the dynamics of individual decision-making processes of the participants in collective protest actions under repressive conditions from the State and its constraints. This is usually a preferred research method "if a phenomenon needs to be understood because little research has been done on it" (Creswell, 2003, p. 23). This also follows Bromley's research strategy for case studies that arise from a "desire to derive an up-close or otherwise in-depth understanding of a style or small number of cases set in real-world contexts" (Bromley, 1986, p. 1). The case study method is best applied, according to Bromley, when research questions are descriptive or explanatory. Bromley explains how researchers following this approach depend on the natural environment for data collection through open-ended, non-structured interviews, archival research, secondary sources of information (media sources), and participant observations, for example.

The unit of analysis of this method is the case study of three protests (2000, 2004, 2013), which incorporates "time-series analyses" to arrange main events into chronological order as a research strategy (Bromley, 1986). My data was derived from a series of 90 interviews using a snowball sampling approach taken during my fieldwork in Ukraine from 2008–2009 on a U.S. Fulbright and IREX/IARO fellowships. The open-ended interviews were 90 minutes in length, digitally recorded and transcribed. For this book, there is intentional selection bias, I selected five individuals (from the

Introduction 11

group of interviews) to analyze as case studies who were very active in the network of activists during the 2004 Presidential Election campaigns and the Orange Revolution. The selection of activists is not meant to be statistically representative nor their experiences generalizable to all Ukrainians. They are meant to serve as an unique sample of individual processes of politicization. I had wanted to include women—I had met several in my interviews—but unfortunately, was unable to find one to participate in this study upon my request, thus, it is a limit of the research.

As I have followed the continued protests in Ukraine from 2013–2014, and because of the research I had already done, I decided to contact these activists to see what had become of them. I wanted to know if they had continued their activism for democratic political change in Ukraine after ten years. Out of the five activists, all but two originated from Lviv, in Western Ukraine. One comes from Kyiv and the other, Kirovohrad. The Central and Western regions are well-known for their civic activism, and for their support of Ukraine's democratic development arising from the historical experience of an anti-Soviet opposition movement (Kuzio, 2010). Four of the five activists share the same educational background: they have either an undergraduate or graduate degree from the National University of Kyiv Mohyla Academy, a university founded by dissidents in Kyiv in 1991. One activist in this research teaches as a lecturer in Sociology at this university. Overall, the activists selected have varied personal experiences, and following the Orange Revolution, they have advanced in their professional experiences as well. This book will examine each activist's point of entry into the first two protest events, based on their audio recorded interviews, which were transcribed. The majority of the interviews were conducted in English, with one exception: Andriy Shevtsiv's interview was transcribed from Ukrainian into English. I used a translator, since he does not speak well in English. The second round of interviews with these five activists took place in the summer of 2015 via Skype and Facebook. The interviews of three except Shevtsiv's were recorded and transcribed, and the interview with Shevtsiv was conducted with a translator. The fifth, Volodymyr Ishchenko, was interviewed through questions sent on Facebook messenger. The interviews ranged from 30 to 60 minutes in length. The questions were open-ended, concerning their activities in the Euromaidan protests. To address language issues and avoid misunderstanding, while I have a working knowlege of Ukrainian and the five activists have a good reading competency in English, they were all given the finalized manuscript to validate their experiences as told in the book. This data was supported by primary and secondary sources of information, including articles and books on the historical protest events for validation.

Structure of the book

The biographical narratives of five young activists are followed during the three largest protest events since Ukrainian independence in 1991. As subjects of analysis, these selected activists are relevant since they represented social, cultural, and structural dimensions of a new generation coming of

12 *Introduction*

age in a post-Soviet country with shared democratic values that align more closely to Western Europe than their predecessors. The protest events analyzed were the "Ukraine without Kuchma" movement of 2000–2001, the Orange Revolution of 2004, and the Euromaidan protest of 2014. The use of a timeline reminds us that political identification represents a progression of cultural practices and formative experiences of individuals that provide markers for what motivated them to protest over time. A time perspective also offers an explanation for the professionalization of the movement's actors and strategies in 2004 and 2014. This book is organized into the following chapters.

Chapter 1: New generation and subjectivities

This chapter investigates two areas: the first is student activism in the years preceding the fall of the Soviet Union and its direct connection to organizers in the three protests studied in this book. Included are two case studies that illustrate protest movements as social constructs of individuals in different fields of struggle (Sumy State University and National University of Kyiv Mohyla Academy). The former university culture was shaped by clientelistic patterns and the latter, more democratic spaces for free expression. As an alternative space to counteract the constraints on student freedom in state-controlled universities, I investigate student activists from Kyiv Mohyla University as an additional field that facilitates the struggle for student civil rights.

Chapter 2: The emergence of an actor

The initiators of collective action of protest are examined in this chapter as the emergent agent of social change in three protest events in Ukraine ("Ukraine without Kuchma" protests of 2000–2001, the Orange Revolution of 2004, and the Euromaidan protests of 2013–2014). Therefore, my objective is to follow the individuals' socialization process into activism through three social protests to better learn about the democratization process, civic participation, emotions and protest mobilization, protest experience, and political mobilization for subsequent civic activities.

Chapter 3: Personalized expressions of activism

The chapter focuses on introducing the five activists that will be the subjects of analysis and their processes of political socialization and protest mobilization. The objective was to investigate the micro aspects of this individualized form of activism. My purpose was to provide historical narratives to discover the ways in which individuals understood their first experience of political activity.

Introduction 13

Chapter 4: Professionalization of activists

This chapter builds on the previous chapter's discussion on self-mobilization processes to try to provide an understanding of an individual's participation and repeat activism, which reflects what Bennett labeled as "personalized politics" symbolizing "individually expressive personal action frames in many protest causes" (Bennett, 2012, p. 20). The chapter undertakes an analysis not of these frames, rather, it investigates the individualized process for frame-making or creating ideas to plan and execute new civic campaigns in newly formed groups.

Chapter 5: Activists' self-organization of the Euromaidan protests, 2013–2014

The last chapter examines an actor's subjectivity in relation to the sociocultural context and social change transformation to present alternative conditions for social movements to thrive. This final empirical chapter will return to the book's central interest in an activist's repeat participation, while observing a third case study of political protests in Ukraine.

Conclusion

Furthermore, the last objective is to redirect attention to and provide final comments on three critical areas that were revealed in this study on the individualized nature of protests in contemporary Ukraine. The first is to address the evolving forms of activism that were observed in the changing roles of an individual as a protester, volunteer, and eventually, coordinator of protest actions. The second point to underscore is the interaction between the individual's decision-making and preference for collective action of nonviolent protests and its effect of increasing participation, as observed in the protests studied. The third point to highlight is the social change effect of individual activists and their efforts to institutionalize civic campaigns into political structures following the end of protests.

Bibliography

Author's interview, Taras Stetskiv, former Member of Parliament "Our Ukraine" political party, November 19, 2008, Kyiv.

Author's interview, Volodymyr Chemerys, NGO Institute of Economic and Social Problems "Respublika," October 7, 2008, Kyiv.

Bandera, S. (2006). "The Role of the Internet and Ukraine's 2004 Presidential Elections." Development Associate Report.

Bauman, Z. (1992). *Intimations of postmodernity*. London: Routledge.

Beissinger, M. (2011). "Mechanisms of Maidan: The Structure of Contingency in the Making of the Orange Revolution." *Mobilization: An International Journal*, *16*(1), 25–43.

14 *Introduction*

Bennett, W. L. (2012). "The Personalization of Politics: Political Identity, Social Media, and Changing Patterns of Participation." *The Annals of the American Academy of Political and Social Science, 644*(1), 20–39.

Bennett, W. L., & Segerberg, A. (2012). "The Logic of Connective Action." *Information, Communication & Society, 15*(5), 739–768.

Berger, P. L., & Luckmann, T. (1966). *The social construction of reality; a treatise in the sociology of knowledge.* Garden City, NY: Doubleday.

Bromley, D. B. (1986). *The case-study method in psychology and related disciplines.* New York: John Wiley & Sons.

Bunce, V., & Wolchik, S. L. (2007). "Youth and Postcommunist Electoral Revolutions: Never Trust Anyone over 30?." *Reclaiming democracy: Civil society and electoral change in central and eastern Europe* (J. Forbrig & P. Demeš, Eds.). Washington, DC: The German Marshall Fund of the United States.

Cardoso, G. (2012). "Networked Life World: Four Dimensions of the Cultures of Networked Belonging." *Observatorio (OBS*) Journal*, Special issue "Networked belonging and networks of belonging" – COST ACTION ISO906 "Transforming Audiences, Transforming Societies," 197–205.

Castells, M. (2012). *Aftermath: The cultures of the economic crisis.* Oxford: Oxford University Press.

Castells, M. (2012b). *Networks of outrage and hope.* Cambridge: Polity Press.

Court deems Kuchma referendum bill constitutional. (2000, July 6). Retrieved September 22, 2015, from http://www.kyivpost.com/content/ukraine/court-deems-kuchma-referendum-bill-constitutional-3229.html.

Creswell, J. W. (2003). *Research design: Qualitative, quantitative, and mixed method approaches.* Thousand Oaks, CA: Sage Publications.

Dickinson, J. (2014). "Prosymo maksymal'nyi perepost! Tactical and Discursive Uses of Social Media in Ukraine's EuroMaidan." *Ab Imperio, 2014*(3), 75–93.

Diuk, N. (2012). *The next generation in Russia, Ukraine, and Azerbaijan: Youth, politics, identity, and change.* New York: Rowman & Littlefield.

Diuk, N. (2013). "Youth as an Agent for Change: The Next Generation in Ukraine." *Demokratizatsiya, 21*(2), 179–196.

Diuk, N. (2014). Finding Ukraine. *Journal of Democracy, 25*(3), 83–89.

EuroMaidan rallies in Ukraine-Nov. 21–23 coverage. (2013, November 25). Retrieved September 28, 2015, from http://www.kyivpost.com/content/ukraine/euromaidan-rallies-in-ukraine-nov-21-23-coverage-332423.html.

From Maidan camp to Maidan-sich: what has changed? (2014, February 3). Retrieved December 6, 2015, from http://www.kiis.com.ua/?lang=eng&cat=reports&id=226&page=15.

Giddens, A. (1991). *Modernity and self-identity: Self and society in the late modern age.* Stanford, CA: Stanford University Press.

НАМЕТИ НА МАЙДАНІ. Фоторепортаж. (2004, November 22). Retrieved September 22, 2015, from http://www.pravda.com.ua/news/2004/11/22/3004485/.

Hanson, S. E. (1997). *Time and revolution: Marxism and the design of Soviet institutions.* Chapel Hill, NC: University of North Carolina Press.

Helepololei, J. (2013, April). Manual Transmission: The Do-It-Yourself Theory of Occupy Wall Street and Spain's 15M. Poster presented at the On Protest Research Symposium, University of Massachusetts, Amherst, MA.

ЮЩЕНКО НЕ ДОВІРЯЄ ЦВК І ЗАКЛИКАЄ ВСІХ ПРИЙТИ НА МАЙДАН О 9 ГОДИНІ РАНКУ. (2004, November 22). Retrieved September 22, 2015, from http://www.pravda.com.ua/news/2004/11/22/3004451/.

Jasper, J. (1997). *The art of moral protest culture, biography, and creativity in social movements.* Chicago, IL: University of Chicago Press.

Juris, J. S., & Pleyers, G. (2009). "Alter-Activism: Emerging Cultures of Participation among Young Global Justice Activists." *Journal of Youth Studies, 12*(1), 57–75.

Kuzio, T. (2002, March 3). Ukraine debates the role of civil society (03/03/02). Retrieved February 28, 2016, from http://www.ukrweekly.com/old/archive/2002/090213.shtml.

Kuzio, T. (2005). "The Opposition's Road to Success." *Journal of Democracy, 16*(2), 117–130.

Kuzio, T. (2006a). "Ukraine Is Not Russia: Comparing Youth Political Activism." *SAIS Review, 26*(2), 67–83.

Kuzio, T. (2006b). "Civil Society, Youth and Societal Mobilization in Democratic Revolutions." *Communist and Post-Communist Studies, 39*(3), 365–386.

Kuzio, T. (2010). "Nationalism, Identity and Civil Society in Ukraine: Understanding the Orange Revolution." *Communist and Post-Communist Studies, 43*(3), 285–296.

Lichterman, P. (1996). *The search for political community: American activists reinventing commitment.* Cambridge: Cambridge University Press.

Maidan-2013. (2013, December 8). Retrieved December 6, 2015, from http://www.kiis.com.ua/?lang=eng&cat=reports&id=216&page=16.

Nayyem, M. (2014, April 4). Protests in Ukraine: It started with a Facebook message. Retrieved September 22, 2015, from https://www.opensocietyfoundations.org/voices/uprising-ukraine-how-it-all-began.

Nikolayenko, O. (2007). "The Revolt of the Post-Soviet Generation: Youth Movements in Serbia, Georgia, and Ukraine." *Comparative Politics, 39*(2), 169–188.

Olson, M. (1965). *The logic of collective action: Public goods and the theory of groups.* Cambridge, MA: Harvard University Press.

Onuch, O. (2014a). "Who Were the Protesters?" *Journal of Democracy, 25*(3), 44–51.

Onuch, O. (2014b). Social networks and social media in Ukrainian "Euromaidan" protests. *The Washington Post.* Retrieved May 11, 2014, from http://www.washingtonpost.com/blogs/monkey-cage/wp/2014/01/02/social-networks-and-social-media-in-ukrainian-euromaidan-protests-2/.

Orange Revolution Field Commanders Greet Maidan. (2005, November 22). Retrieved September 22, 2015, from http://www.ukrinform.ua/eng/news/orange_revolution_field_commanders_greet_maidan_61055.

Pastukhova, A. (2011, April 12). Rallying Non-Stop. Retrieved January 7, 2016, from http://ukrainianweek.com/Politics/20557.

Pleyers, G., & Glasius, M. *The resonance of «movements of 2011»: connections, emotions, values.* Socio n°2, "Révolutions, indignations, contestations", édited by Pénélope Larzillière and Boris Petric. Paris: Éditions de la Maison des sciences de l'homme, 16 décembre 2013, 376 p.

Polletta, F. (2014). "Participatory Democracy's Moment." *Journal of International Affairs,* Fall/Winter, *68*(1), 79–92.

Polletta, F., & Jasper, J. (2001). "Collective Identity and Social Movements." *Annual Review of Sociology, 27*, 283–305.

The readiness of the Ukrainian population to participate in actions of social protest (before 20 November 2013). (2013, November 20). Retrieved December 6, 2015, from http://www.kiis.com.ua/?lang=eng&cat=reports&id=214&page=16.

Rose-Ackerman, S. (2001). "Trust and Honesty in Post-Socialist Societies." *Kyklos, 54*(2–3), 415–443.

Shevchenko, A. (Director). (2003). *The Face of Protest* (Ukrainian: "Обличчя протесту" – "Oblytchia Protestu") [Motion picture]. Ukraine. TV documentary.

16 *Introduction*

Tilly, C., & Tarrow, S. G. (2007). *Contentious politics*. Boulder, CO: Paradigm.

Tucker, J. (2013). "How Ukrainian protestors are using Twitter and Facebook" – The Washington Post. Retrieved September 22, 2015, from http://www.washingtonpost.com/blogs/monkey-cage/wp/2013/12/04/strategic-use-of-facebook-and-twitter-in-ukrainian-protests/.

Udehn, L. (1993). "Twenty-Five Years with the Logic of Collective Action." *Acta Sociologica, 36*(3), 239–261.

Ukrainian Journalist Mustafa Nayyem to Receive 2014 Ion Ratiu Democracy Award. (2014, September 29). Retrieved September 22, 2015, from https://www.wilsoncenter.org/article/ukrainian-journalist-mustafa-nayyem-to-receive-2014-ion-ratiu-democracy-award.

Wilson, A. (2009). "Ukraine's Orange Revolution of 2004: The Paradox of negotiation." *Civil resistance and power politics: The experience of non-violent action from Gandhi to the present* (A. Roberts & T. G. Ash, Eds.). Oxford: Oxford University Press.

Woronowycz, R. (2001, February 18). Anti-Kuchma protests continue in Ukrainian capital (02/18/01). Retrieved February 28, 2016, from http://www.ukrweekly.com/old/archive/2001/070101.shtml.

Yin, R. K. (2003). *Applications of case study research*. Thousand Oaks, CA: Sage Publications.

Zubar, N. History of "Maidan": In the beginning was the word...(part I). (2005, December 5). Retrieved January 28, 2017, from http://world.maidan.org.ua/2005/history-of-maidan-in-the-beginning-was-the-word-part-i.

1 New generation and subjectivities

The section begins by discussing the conditions for young people's political transformation in the years preceding Ukrainian Independence. During the late 1980s, Communist Ukraine was undergoing social and political change as a result of Mikhail Gorbachev's policies of *perestroika* and *glasnost,* which will be discussed further below. These reforms had an effect on university students and their rejection of official student organizations set up by the Communist Party such as Komsomol. Students in Komsomol were "encouraged" to join as members and were presented with "authoritative discourse" (Yurchak, 2006, pp. 80–1). The purpose of these youth organizations was to mobilize young people "...for implementation of party politics, education, and training people in the spirit of communism" (Taylor, 2006, p. 25). The subversive action of one university student was influenced amidst these social changes. I am providing a description of his experience as an example to highlight the important role of alternative student associations and the strengthening of an opposition culture in the region of Western Ukraine. The student's narrative represents one account of many that I interviewed with similar experiences. It was for this reason that I chose to highlight it to more clearly illustrate the democratization processes occurring from within the State universities during a period of transition in the Soviet Union. The student actions described towards establishing alternative youth organizations mattered in their effects of empowering young people in opposition to the Marxist ideologies connected with the Komsomol organization. New youth associations such as the Student Brotherhood, introduced below, provided an alternative space, a Christian context, for students to transform politically and to create networks between new association groups. The network of these young people would be activated in the period of the 1990 student hunger strikes in Kyiv. The students tied to this student movement were also members of youth organizations that emerged in this period. The young people in the movement would also later reappear as civic activists in support of democratic change in the protests examined in the book following Ukrainian independence.

18 New generation and subjectivities

Ivan Franko National University of Lviv

This section will focus on the activities of a new generation and take a closer look into their founding of new youth organizations and their impact on challenging the control of the Ukrainian Communist Party's in universities. To take an example of how student associations were created as an alternative to official groups, we will look at a case for analysis. This one considers Taras Dubko's experience. In 1989, Dubko was a student at Ivan Franko National University of Lviv. He was a founding member of Student Brotherhood in his department at the university. He and his friends were already members of the larger Student Brotherhood in Lviv and wanted to create a Christian association in his faculty of mathematics and mechanics. He was attracted to the Student Brotherhood since it promoted itself "...as an alternative to all official student organizations at that time in the department" (author's interview, Taras Dubko, March 17, 2009). Dubko and others wanted to establish the Student Brotherhood as an official organization of the university and not an underground movement. In order to do so, Dubko and his friends went to the Dean and made a declaration about the existence of the Student Brotherhood association at their faculty. He recalled that the Dean of Students was open-minded and also understood the risks involved with a youth movement, especially during a period of time when the KGB was still operating in the USSR (Ibid., 2009).

Student Brotherhood functioned as a political group, and Dubko had participated in creating its structure at the university. To illustrate political activities, one example of the group's initiative was a public protest against the study of philosophy, which, at their university, was Marxism. The group convinced their Dean to cancel a philosophy class for second year students. The assistant to the Dean also agreed and the class was no longer considered a required course. The students staged similar actions to remove another class called Scientific Communism from the list of required classes, and over time it was no longer offered. The students also organized other larger protests in direct opposition to Komsomol. The primary reason for Dubko and other students' participation in Student Brotherhood was the organization's positioning as an alternative to Komsomol. As an act of protest against their membership in this official organization, Dubko and his friends held a public protest event to turn in their [Komsomol] membership cards. This event signaled a change in students' behavior displayed in overt acts of withdrawing from the official youth organization. Afterwards, Dubko remembered being approached by older members of Komsomol and receiving encouragement from them to apply the students' energy towards reviving the organization. Dubko explained his inner response to their request, which was conveyed in his words, "we believed this is not our mission to revive Komsomol. Other institutions should be instituted" (Ibid., 2009).

This period of time was active with protests and strikes in Lviv. A few events were organized to oppose the referendum to preserve the USSR.

New generation and subjectivities 19

Dubko also spoke about efforts by the authorities to silence the activists and the effect of these efforts to serve as an impetus that motivated more students to attend the strikes. In Student Brotherhood at his university, Dubko said that the students were quite independent to organize activities of protests. Students there did not need the university's approval for their actions. The students exercised independence from the university and the Communist Party. A good example that further demonstrated this change of mindset was a spontaneous music festival event organized by young people. Dubko and his friends from Student Brotherhood attended the second event of Chervona Ruta in Zaporizhia. It was promoted as an alternative to the official music contest of the Communist Party. At this event, Dubko got inspired by the young people's creativity expressed in the event, which produced for him a feeling that new consciousness was possible for students. Dubko attended the festival as "a way of opposing, a way of affirming that is there is some kind of new reality" (Ibid., 2009). Students like Dubko experienced a form of shared solidarity in this alternative music event. It was a symbolic period of transformation on the part of young people who were expressing their freedom in culture as an outlet to reject Communism.

1990

On 20–21 February 1990, Ukrainian university students organized a series of political strikes against the government authorities to put forth demands for education grants, a suspension of military education, the removal of Komsomol from education institutions, and an end to student repression. This anti-government movement took shape under the auspices of a congress in Lviv from 23–25 February 1990. At this congress, the students launched the Confederation of Student Organizations of Ukraine, "an umbrella group" that brought together for cooperation the Ukraine Students' Union and Student Brotherhood, a fraternity for students. The participants of the congress created a radical platform to vocalize support for the development of a student movement in Ukraine to build pressure for the closure of the Komsomol. The student movement promoted the use of national symbols to raise the national consciousness of young people. Student Brotherhood and Ukrainian Students' Union officially merged on 30–31 March 1991 into a single entity, the Union of Ukrainian Students (Kuzio and Wilson, 1994, p. 146; Emeran, 2011, p. 41). On 26–27 May 1990, a second inaugural congress was organized by the youth wing of Ukrainian Helsinki Union (UHU) and The Association of Independent Ukrainian Youth (SNUM) in Ivano Frankivsk. In attendance were 205 delegates and 2,000 representatives. This congress erupted in disputes between its radicals and moderate members, with the former separating in order to form the SNUM-nationalists and the Ukrainian Nationalist Union (UNU) six months later. Both groups joined Ukrainian Inter-Party Assembly and took control as the other groups

20 *New generation and subjectivities*

departed. SNUM was a political civic youth group, described as an alternative to Komsomol, which worked toward Ukrainian independence (Kuzio and Wilson, 1994, pp. 146–7). Another group established at this time was *Plast*, a scouting organization, which previously existed in pre-war Western Ukraine and persisted as an organization outside of Ukraine's border until independence. On 16 December 1989, *Plast* launched its inaugural congress (Kuzio and Wilson, 1994, p. 147).

Lviv Student Brotherhood and Kyiv's Ukrainian Students' Union, a total of 150 students, organized hunger strikes in Kyiv from 2–16 October 1990. The students put forth demands for the Prime Minister Masol's resignation, new parliamentary elections representing multiple parties, military service only in Ukraine, the nationalization of the property of CPU and Komsomol, and an opposition to Union Treaty with Moscow. The authorities grew aware of their activities when the hunger strikes were initiated. Ukrainian Student Union's Kyiv branch had received the public's support during the occupation of Kyiv's central Square of the October Revolution (renamed by the opposition as Independence Square) and staged hunger strikes in October 1990 (Revolution on the Granite). The students' political activity attracted the attention of the Communist Party's hardliners who did not seek to appease the students; rather they followed a strategy of force to remove them. Cultural figures, democrats, and Kyiv's members of city council responded in support of the students. Even Ministry of Internal Affairs, General Nedryhailo set up meetings with the students on strike and gave them assurances of police support and protection against their forced dispersal (Kuzio and Wilson, 1994, p. 161; Emeran, 2011, pp. 42–3). Student efforts to mobilize were assisted by invitations to address parliament and media coverage. The ability of students to disrupt the "political deadlock" was marked by an address of their leader, Oles Donii, to Ukrainian parliament and on television. He made pleas to urge students to go on strike and to occupy university buildings. Later that evening, in solidarity, the students from Kyiv University occupied the main building on its campus and "raised a blue and yellow flag over it" (author's interview, Gusak, 2008, Kyiv; Emeran, 2011, p. 43).

The political problem of student strikes and their consolidation of public support was the subject of a closed meeting of the CPU. Documents from the CPU reported that the Party had realized that by not negotiating with the students, they had "lost an important battle" (author's interview, Gusak, 2008, Kyiv; Emeran, 2011, p. 44). In hindsight, the authorities missed their opportunity to negotiate that may have prevented the students from "…mobiliz [ing] mass public support" (Nahaylo, 1999, p. 315; Emeran, 2011, p. 45). As for the student activists, they were successful in getting most of their demands met, except for Parliament's dissolution. Overall, student activists felt that the Communist Party betrayed them when the student movement was at its peak. Students expressed that they might have had an opportunity to change the Communist elite system into a new one. Overall,

New generation and subjectivities 21

this realization of a partial defeat continued to disappoint them years later (author's interview, Gusak, 2008, Kyiv). As summarized by Markian Rushchyshyn, a supporter of the revolution:

> We did not reach what we needed. We did not bring new quality to the politic at that time. We just had a small victory. We passed our victory to people who cannot manage. Then our gains disappeared. On the other hand, without this revolution, I can say for certain that we would not have the result of independence for Ukraine. With this revolution [on the Granite] we forced people out of their fear into creating something out of Moscow's putsch. People already knew that there were forces that want independence for Ukraine. They could decide to connect to them or to help them. But showed them that young people are 100 percent for the independence of Ukraine. There is no other way for development of Ukraine.
>
> (author's interview, Rushchyshyn, 2009,
> Lviv; Emeran, 2011, p. 44)

A knowledge of this history of youth as an opposition force was important to understanding the processes that led former students from the 1990 student hunger strikes to reemerge as leaders in the "Ukraine without Kuchma" protest. This campaign of protest was structured into four main groups. One group was represented by Volodymyr Cherymyrs, Yuriy Lutsenko, and Mykailo Svystovych. A second group was led by Viacheslav Kyrylenko, a leader in the youth wing of political party Ukrainian People's Party, which was called "Youth Party of Ukraine." A third group was coordinated by Oles Donii with the political party "Bativshchyna" of Yulia Tymoshenko. The last was made up of a political party named "Party of Reforms and Order," which included Vladyslav Kaskiv with his Freedom of Choice Coalition of Ukrainian NGOs. This last group was composed of mobilized students in the "All Ukrainian Public Resistance Committee for Truth." All the meetings of the Committee "For Truth" were held in the offices of "Party of Reforms and Order." Lastly, the leaders of these groups were former students who had participated in the 1990 student hunger strikes in Kyiv (author's interview, Kryvdyk, 2008, Kyiv).

New generation activists

The actors that I traced in the first wave of protests (2000–2001) were veteran activists from the 1990 student hunger strikes ("Revolution on Granite") in Kyiv ("Lenin Square" later renamed "Independence Square" after the fall of the Soviet Union). The activists were products of the era of *glasnost* and Perestroika that shaped their lived experiences. During that period, some young people got mobilized in political activism and were supporters of a political opposition for Ukrainian Independence. The period of *glasnost*

22 New generation and subjectivities

produced in Ukraine a revival of ethno and civic nationalism (Hrycak, 1997). The latter, civic nationalism, was also a cultural phenomenon, as Hrycak explained, in the Ukrainian youth subcultures, that involved the rejection of a Soviet identity and appropriation of Western identity. Civic and political actors such as Rukh activists (the People's Movement of Ukraine for Reconstruction, established in 1989) were involved in the process of redefining Ukrainian culture by employing strategies that "...imperceptibly co-opted institutionally organized activities targeting young people" (Hrycak, 1997, p. 65). Their protest actions were "high-risk" since they involved the "subversion of official frames and adoption of Western youth culture" in the era of *glasnost* (Hrycak, 1997, p. 65).

Following Ukraine's independence, young people's subjectivity continued to be connected to Western culture. This was evident in young people's lived experiences, including, as Hrycak found, their attendance in large numbers at a national festival "*Vyvykh*-92" held in Lviv, Ukraine in 1992. This festival was unique, as Hrycak described, for its "inversion of rituals" that applied strategies of subversion, satire, and parodies in its cultural performances. To illustrate, featured at that event was a popular rock opera, "The Chrysler Imperial," that expressed a subjectivity, which was non-conformist and favored Western popular music culture. It was a transformational experience for young people. As Hrycak explained, "through its use of rock music and inversion of historical narratives, this festival self-consciously sought to lead young people to question the official establishment that had organized the city's previous youth festivals and other public celebrations" (Hrycak, 1997, p. 67). High attendance at this event suggested that the cultural performances resonated with the subjectivities of young Ukrainians. Subjectivity, in the example presented, was framed in terms of resistance, and followed the dimensions of the alter-globalization activists whom, as Pleyers described, "...construct themselves as actors through performances and lived experience" (Pleyers, 2010, p. 35). In Ukraine, cultural performances with a political message were one method for activists to publicly express their subjectivity and "...their opposition to myth, conformism, and homogeneity" displayed in official, public events (Hrycak, 1997, p. 79). For the Ukrainian activist, cultural performance as a mode of political action, in association with alter-activism practices, mattered because it "represent[ed] a call for personal freedom against the logics of power" (Pleyers, 2010, p. 37). This sense of autonomy to mount an opposition against the regime would be experienced differently by a new post-Soviet generation of young activists in the next protest.

In 2001, young people (from the 1990s student hunger strikes) stood up to actively mobilize a new generation of students to protest against the death of a popular journalist in the "For Truth" Committee (within the larger "Ukraine without Kuchma" protest movement). Among these activists, as Kuzio described, "young people and students participated in the 'Ukraine without Kuchma' movement and the 'For Truth' civic group that grew out of

New generation and subjectivities 23

Kuchmagate.' Many of the young leaders of both of these groups were well-known activists from the 1990–1991 student movement..." (Kuzio, 2002). The repeat activism of young people can be explained by a generational theoretical approach that argued "dramatic social changes experience[d] by individuals during their formative years will exert long-lasting effects on their political dispositions" (Nikolayenko, 2007, p. 175). The young newcomers were recruited to protest because they "...dreamt and worked towards living in a 'normal' European country" (Kuzio, 2006b, p. 374). Young people participated in the "tent city protests" and pickets, as described by Diuk, with the objective of removing the president (Diuk, 2012, p. 51). Young activists lived in tent camps that signified "new spaces of experiences" for "actors to live according to their own principles, to knit different social relations and to express their subjectivity" (Pleyers, 2010, p. 37). This was visible in the protest movement where "the tent city [had] become the center of the 'Ukraine Without Kuchma' movement with hundreds of Ukrainians gathering in and around the tents daily to debate or simply gawk" (Woronowycz, 2001). The atmosphere of friendship and mutual understanding in tent camps was depicted in the film *The Faces of Protest*. The protesters were filmed dancing, singing songs, and sharing a cup of tea. The festive nature of protests and tent cities was ephemeral, but it also provided, as Pleyers said, a logic of action in its organization of "...daily life, a social centre... [that became] spaces where alternative practices are tried out and lived" (Pleyers, 2010, p. 39). Nonviolence as a key concept of social change was adopted as a principle of organization for the movement, and reflected the subjectivity of the activists. Unfortunately, their vision of non-violence was unsustainable, as Wilson explained, because of the more radical factions in the group that advocated for violence as a protest tactic, resulting in the failure of the protests (Wilson, 2009, p. 338). While the protests did not produce regime change as the activists had hoped, they did leave a mark on young people's subjectivity. Kuzio described the transformational process as "...a profound change did take place in people's hearts and minds" (Kuzio, 2006b, p. 374). The effect was radicalization, the "Ukraine without Kuchma" protests developed "a hard core of young activists and dedicated civil society volunteers, reduced apathy among young people, and helped convince many Ukrainians that it was time for change. These changes in society created the backdrop for the Orange Revolution" (Kuzio, 2006a, p. 71). This generation of activists and the successive generation of young people would intersect and be placed at "forefront of mobilization" for the subsequent protest event in 2004 (Kuzio, 2006a).

By 2004, there were different conditions for young people to express their subjectivity in a context that Bandera described as "...a country where society was weary, hopeless, and cynical" (Bandera, 2006, p. 44). This generation labeled "Generation Orange" (Kuzio, 2006b) had distinct experiences from its predecessors in terms of expanded opportunities for travel "abroad to work, for holidays or on scholarships" and increased contact with a "globalized world through satellite television and the Internet" that

24 *New generation and subjectivities*

informed them about their alternatives to Kuchma's regime (Kuzio, 2006, p. 374). These young people, like the older generation, wanted to improve their material conditions of life and "to live in a 'normal' country," were acutely aware that the regime was to blame for this situation. As young people, they grew "tired of the limited possibilities they faced at home and became active because they wanted to register their dissatisfaction with the impossibility of obtaining a decent job and the lack of opportunity for professional advancement" (Bunce and Wolchik, 2007, p. 20).

These differences in terms of a generational effect were visible in the organization of two different types of activist groups in preparation for the presidential elections. The first group, Yellow Pora, was a civic campaign organized from a coalition of NGOs with "professional radicals"—leaders from the 1990 student hunger strike (Kuzio, 2006b, p. 370; Bunce and Wolchik, 2007, p. 196). The second group, Black Pora, "'closer' in age and spirit to students" (Bandera, 2006, p. 39), adopted tactics of "non-violent resistance" and "horizontal, leaderless structures working autonomously in decentralized networks with no leaders" (Kuzio, 2006b, p. 370). Black Pora "conducted more hands-on work with the student population" (Bandera, 2006, p. 39). Generational activism was identified in "the way of organizing the movement" that offered visions that "reflect the alternative values of the way of subjectivity: horizontal organization, strong participation…" (Pleyers, 2010, p. 43). The organizers in the group employed information communications technology, such as mobile phones, text messaging, and the Internet, which permitted them "to develop inter-activist communications networks facilitating the coordination of their activities and the dissemination of campaign materials" (Bandera, 2006, p. 28). New information technologies were important for both Pora campaigns since they allowed them to "to organize legal and successful protest actions against undemocratic regimes" and "circumvent the authorities" (Bandera, 2006, p. 44; Kuzio, 2006b, p. 374). Both campaigns "employed a form of branding meant to appeal to youth, such as the use of t-shirts, stickers, logos, rock concerts, and a ubiquitous humor" (Beissinger, 2011, p. 31). The latter played an important role in the mobilization process, Kuzio explained that "humor and ridicule were crucial in undermining fear of the authorities with young people playing a central role in promoting them" (Kuzio, 2006b, p. 375). Young people attended Pora's events in large numbers, which, for most represented "their first significant political experience," and had a long-term impact on the "Generation Orange" "…who valued fun and pleasure and those who valued loyalty to friends were more likely to participate in protests in Ukraine in 2004" (Beissinger, 2011, p. 31). The pre-election mobilization efforts of Pora produced an "opposition youth culture in the months leading up to the electoral campaign" that resulted in their participation in the elections, Diuk argued that "young people were the leading force in election monitoring groups such as the Committee of Voters and exit polling efforts…" (Ibid., 2011, p. 31; Diuk, 2013, p. 185).

Spaces for the expression of subjectivities in universities: case study post-Soviet Ukraine

National University of Kyiv Mohyla Academy: Dr. Vyacheslav Bryukhovetsky

In this section, I selected the National University of Kyiv Mohyla Academy for analysis. It was founded by a dissident (from the Ukrainian independence movement) and the university's students are known for their activism in the three protests studied in the book. This university also presented an alternative to the clientelist system in place at state universities and its founders provided legal protection through its political ties to opposition parties for its student activists. This university was a place where students could experience and exercise democracy in their everyday interactions with the community established on campus. While there were no political groups on campus, there were students who were activists and took active roles in the three cycles of protest examined in this book. That is the reason this section delves further into the practices of this university; its structure permitted students to experience freedom and participate in social movements for democratic and social change.

Dr. Vyacheslav Bryukhovetsky, the former rector of the National University of Kyiv Mohyla Academy, was active in political life and one of the founders of The People's Movement of Ukraine (Narodnyi Rukh Ukrajiny) political party in 1989. His role in the political party was self-described as an "ideologist," he wrote the political party's program for Rukh and his apartment was the center for the party's activities (author's interview, Bryukhovetsky, Kyiv, 2008). This nationalist political party appeared in the context of Mikhail Gorbachev's reforms as a popular oppositional front to the Communist Party of Ukraine (CPU). The leadership in the party included former political prisoners and the cultural intelligentsia. By 1990, Rukh became more radical in its positions and its leadership spoke publicly about Ukrainian independence and its opposition to Gorbachev's Union Treaty for the republics. During Rukh's second Congress, in October 1990, it officially declared itself as a movement in the midst of mass demonstrations and student hunger strikes taking place in Kyiv (Wilson, 1996, p. 68). At this Congress, Rukh announced a new plan for national independence and democracy for Ukraine (Kuzio, 2000, pp. 148–9).

When Ukraine gained independence, Bryukhovetsky decided to reopen Kyiv Mohyla Academy along with a small group of five people without any financial or material resources. In his office at Kyiv Mohyla Academy, Bryukhovetsky proudly pointed to his office desk, explaining it was the same one that he used to write the party's program for Rukh and the project proposal for re-establishing Kyiv Mohyla Academy in 1991. He wanted to create a free and independent university with an emphasis placed on the personal development of talented, young people to become the future

26 *New generation and subjectivities*

elites of the nation. As a structure for the university, he sought to combine the best examples of American and Ukrainian systems of education. At that time, he recounted that he was well-known in political circles and that State bureaucrats and members of Parliament were not interested in creating conflict with him and allowed him to open a university. He recalled, "the time was interesting, almost everything was allowed" (author's interview, Bryukhovetsky, Kyiv, 2008). He received permission from the Ukrainian Parliament and Viktor Kravchuk, Ukraine's first president at that time. Upon approval, Bryukhovetsky sought out ways to launch his idea, but he did not have a legal entity. He explained that there was no money and no space; there was nothing. On 16 October 1991, Bryukhovetsky wrote the first order for Kyiv Mohyla Academy, which did not exist, for him to assume work as rector of the university. He admitted that it was probably illegal, but nobody attempted to dispute him (author's interview, Bryukhovetsky, Kyiv, 2008). Kyiv Mohyla Academy was different from other universities in Ukraine in a few important ways. First, Bryukhovetsky explained that the principles of freedom were emphasized as the main goal of their educational policy for students and professors. This was unlike other Ukrainian state universities that had rampant corruption and students oftentimes paid bribes to professors and for admission. Second, the university was tolerant and permitted opposing views, he said that unlike a corporation with disciplinary actions, their university's role, instead was "the only place for young people to discuss, find new ways, to make mistakes and to correct mistakes" (Ibid., 2008). Third, the university allowed students to be involved in political life. The only exception was that political parties as a student organization on campus were not allowed, but they could be members of political groups outside of the university (Ibid., 2008).

In terms of protests and student political engagement, Bryukhovetsky discussed that his students were very active in the "Ukraine without Kuchma" protests. He explained that many students from Kyiv Mohyla Academy participated in the anti-regime protests (Ibid., 2008). Its students reflected a segment of Ukrainian society that was against Kuchma's power and the State under Kuchma (author's interview, Serhiy Kvit, 2008, Kyiv). Bryukhovetsky was very pessimistic at that time because he thought that the protest's goals were impossible to achieve success. He thought that the protest actions did not have the critical mass of young people who supported the idea; therefore, it was impossible to change them. Bryukhovetsky participated in the demonstrations and was interviewed several times. He expressed publicly his opinion that he did not believe that it was possible to remove Kuchma from office. Despite his view, he supported the protests and students. He was a member of Yulia Tymoshenko's Committee of National Salvation and in terms of personal political position, he defended Viktor Yushchenko. He acknowledged that two or three years later, social transformation arrived. He explained that the "demographic situation had changed in Ukraine, a mass, a big amount of young people that needed change in Ukraine appeared" (author's interview, Bryukhovetsky, Kyiv, 2008). He mentioned that students were living in an unstable political situation since 2000. This produced conditions for the rise of a growing opposition as a political force at the university. This was visible in students' cultural productions such as the founding of an unofficial underground newsletter, called the *Maidan* (initiated in 2003). The articles transmitted political ideas about student life at the university and the political situation in 2003–2004. The authors wrote fictional accounts to describe the political situation and to attract student readers to reflect on Ukrainian politics. The published articles presented an analogy of the political situation for students to make connections between an imagined world and their social reality. Konstyantyn said the paper was well-received by students who were "open to the new ideas and they are not biased by those political things" (author's interview, Konstyantyn Peresiedov, Kyiv, 2008). Konstyantyn Peresiedov, a student, wrote for the paper and understood its structure. The paper had three or four active editors to manage the newsletter, and they received articles from a main group of authors who submitted articles regularly. The paper sold 100 to 150 copies in a week, he said (Ibid., 2008). During the 2004 presidential elections, he said, "the percentage of articles was becoming higher than before. It was an influence on students because it was the only newspaper available in the university that was read and bought by students" (Ibid., 2008). As a result, they enjoyed some sort of influence. He felt that their activities were like "executing the functions of leaders" (Ibid., 2008). He felt their role was as "opinion leaders, we wanted to protest against that [mass media censorship and the regime]. We were at the front line" (Ibid., 2008).

In the 2004 presidential elections campaigns, Bryukhovetsky thought since he had students in political science and economics at the university, that it would be interesting for them to observe the elections. For this reason, the university allowed the press center of the headquarters of "Our Ukraine" to be on-campus and for students to get political education for future activities. To justify their presence at the university, he explained that they did not receive any money from the political party. They invited the political party for the benefit of teaching the students, but recalled that "no one believed me" (author's interview, Bryukhovetsky, Kyiv, 2008). The political party's presence on campus also directed the government's attention to the university and targeted the university students' activism. Bryukhovetsky discussed that during the elections, the government authorities had made several preliminary arrests of their students. He recounted a story that took place during the week of student holidays: the police came to the university on allegations that there were weapons and drugs on campus. His first response was to refuse entry on campus to the police to search the premises. A few days later, he recalled that students returned from the holiday break and had heard about the police attempts to search the campus from television. That prompted action by the university's student strike

28 *New generation and subjectivities*

committee, a student member, Iryna Fartukh discussed their response to the situation. It provided the group a first encounter with the university president Bryukhovetsky to discuss organizing a strike at the university. The group wanted to avoid a conflict with the administration and felt confident that the university would support them. Bryukhovetsky agreed to let them organize a strike but not on a study day. The university president helped students to organize meetings for the strike to take the form of a human chain around the perimeter of the campus. Iryna was involved in the organization of this protest event, a 30-minute strike, to be held in late September or early October. The student strike committee wanted to show the students at the university that they were prepared to react to the government's aggression. With the president's approval, students felt free to participate and it made a difference, she recalled. In her words, "it was the best advertising to us and a lot of people went, the press wrote about it and people saw this. Our main aim at that time was met" (author's interview, Fartukh, Kyiv, 2009). It was during the protest action, that the slogan *Razom Nas Bahato, Nas Ne Podalty* (in English: Together we are many, we will not be defeated) was first used, Bryukhovetsky said (author's interview, Bryukhovetsky, Kyiv, 2008). The lyrics later became converted into a protest anthem song by Greenjolly for the Orange Revolution.

In contrast, student activism was different at Bryukhovetsky's alma mater, Taras Shevchenko National University of Kyiv, where the university rector closed the university to prevent students from participating in the Orange Revolution demonstrations. He described that the rector of that university had "firm control" over the students. Bryukhovetsky explained that Kyiv Mohyla Academy was different and as a result provided the necessary environment for their students to be the first to initiate a university strike in Kyiv (Ibid., 2008–). When the election results of the second round were falsified, Kyiv Mohyla Academy went on political strike in support of free elections (Ibid., 2008). It was a shared collective decision taken in the university's square between students and faculty to strike (author's interview, Serhiy Kvit, 2008, Kyiv). Bryukhovetsky explained that the university went on strike against the fraud in the elections and their slogan was "Kyiv Mohlya Academy on Strike" (author's interview, Bryukhovetsky, Kyiv, 2008). The university created a special strike committee and would convene with a daily meeting between the faculty and students to decide on the day's protest action in Kyiv. The special committee would meet twice a day, once early in the morning and once in the evening. In the latter, they would plan for the next day's event and determine needs. They prepared flags, slogans, and materials. Each member of the committee—one part faculty and the other students—were organizers or responsible as coordinators of the activities. The group held brief meetings and went to the university square and discussed proposals with the university students and faculty members in order to reach a decision about the day's protest activities. All the students went together to protest as a group on Kyiv's Maidan. Serhiy Kvit, rector, cited as examples, some protest actions that were held near different ministry buildings, the Russian Embassy, and pro-Kuchma Ukrainian television channels. The university also hosted other students from outside Kyiv and provided them with food and shelter. Kvit explained that "our university was a revolution camp" (author's interview, Serhiy Kvit, 2008, Kyiv). Kyiv Mohyla Academy acquired a reputation and its appropriations of the social movement were reflected in his words, "[the university] is well-known as a Ukrainian university affiliated with Ukrainian culture, language, traditions, and the Orange Revolution: it was our revolution" (Ibid., 2008).

This example served to illustrate the influence of an actor's subjectivity on the founding of a university. Bryukhovetsky created a university community based on his personal worldview of democracy, which integrated western values and free critical thought into student life. This perspective was depicted in the lived university culture that extolled his principles, in his words, of a "free society" characterized as "another State on this territory [of Ukraine]" (author's interview, Bryukhovetsky, Kyiv, 2008). Bryukhovetsky, in his self-reflections, interpreted that his university was more autonomous than other universities in Ukraine. This was demonstrated when the university leaders were able to divert the police from conducting searches of its students on campus during the 2004 presidential campaigns. In relation to Sumy University, the university administrators at Kyiv Mohyla Academy had more freedom to self-govern and transmit the university's values to students. In the next case, students from Sumy were acting out of a historical situation to resist the state control over its university. In its performance of protests, students elaborated an alternative vision of university, autonomous and respectful of student's rights to protest against perceived wrongs. At Kyiv Mohyla Academy, the university supported the students against the government's repression (on students). The university provided students with the freedom to create protest actions to demonstrate in cases where students' rights were violated. This permitted conditions for students to experiment and create their own spaces to discuss political issues, as in the case of the *Maidan* newspaper. This paper was an exercise of freedom for students to develop and disseminate its own political culture in the student body. These ideas took the form of an unofficial paper that published articles using fictional narratives to subtly transmit their political ideas to an open-minded audience, which was receptive demonstrated by the 150 sales per week.

The paper had two important functions. Firstly, it was a form of political action that raised the political consciousness of students in the months preceding the Orange Revolution. Secondly, it demonstrated the capacity of students to be reflexive to form their own political opinions and propose alternative visions to the existing political life.

These actions can be compared to students' activism at the university in 2013 where, with the participation of diverse civic actors, the evolution of actors and their practices was observed with greater visibility

30 *New generation and subjectivities*

(national/international) and strategic orientation than previously seen. The recent protests, once again, put students from the university at the forefront as strategic actors to initiate the first political strikes and to make an appeal for other students at different universities in Ukraine to join them to protest against Yanukovych's decision not to sign the EU's Association Agreement. In contrast to 2004, the student engagement in the period of the Euromaidan included the following self-productions illustrated as political activities at the university: 1) Stop Fake, begun by journalism students to provide uncensored information about the protest actions in Ukraine and international volunteers contributed to the overall digital project in Russian and English languages; 2) Ukraine Crisis Media Center, provided 24-hour objective news coverage on events; 3) E-Maidan, information experts in cooperation with Civic Sector of Euromaidan launched E-Maidan as a digital project to evaluate transparency in decision-makers and that it reflects the views of civil society professionals; 4) EuroRevolution, Kyiv Mohyla Academy in partnership with Civic Sector of Maidan to advocate for political and economic reform; and 6) CyberBatalion, partnership with Ukrainian internet activists ("we dreamed," 2014). Additionally, the students from Kyiv Mohyla Academy re-appropriated tactics used by the former student strike committee [from its university] in the Orange Revolution. In 2004, the committee and faculty had organized a series of demonstrations to target key ministries and media outlets with political messages (as described above by Kvit). In 2013, these actions were reinterpreted by university students and adapted to the political situation. The effects of the action were measurable in the first case and in the third instance, they gained publicity for their protest actions. In the recent instance, the students re-appropriated earlier forms of protest actions to demonstrate in front of the Ministry of Education, the Russian Embassy, and media channels. In a particular case that illustrates this point, students organized a protest in front of the Ministry of Education demanding the Minister's resignation for pressuring students involved in political activism. These protests resulted in the Minister signing a decree to permit students to participate in protests free from persecution. The second action that they organized was a demonstration in front of the Russian Embassy to protest against Russia's interference and its open support of Yanukovych's government. Lastly, as a result of their political actions, they received publicity from the television station Channel 5. This was one of few uncensored television stations at that time. The students were interviewed about their political activities and they voiced their resolve to protest until the end despite government pressure ("we dreamed," 2014).

In the section below, we consider the student experiences of protest activism at a public university in the region of Sumy.

SUMY University

> "It's a quiet and completely apolitical place," Liliya Hryhorovych, an "Our Ukraine" deputy from the Sumy region said, "to force students and their supporters into the street, there had to have been a serious abuse of people's rights."
>
> ("student protest," 2004)

In 2004, the changing nature of the practices of clientelism was evident in the growing capacity of universities to increase their level of protest actions against the administration. In many Ukrainian universities, the practices of patronage existed, and the result was that politicians tended to distribute favors to universities to manage the elections to their advantage. The practice of universities engaging in relations of patronage with politicians was not new, and it had the result of discouraging students' interest in politics. The conditions of clientelism in election periods operated as a reciprocal relation between university rectors and politicians who would exchange votes for the ruling party for stipends and keeping their positions at the university. Taras Kuzio (2005) used a concept of "partial delegative democracy" to describe ruling elites in a "competitive authoritarian regime." The role of elites was to control a passive citizenry that fostered what he called a "neo-Soviet patrimonial culture," that fragmented by suppressing citizens who wished to mobilize. He cited as evidence the practice of politicians in eastern Ukraine utilizing political favors and financial incentives to gain votes in the region (Kuzio, 2005, p. 169).

The case of Sumy demonstrated how citizens (students, journalists, and university professors) became a counterforce to oppose the government's system of corruption, and had the capacity to propose independent universities as an alternative vision. The victory was achieved on the annulment of the reunification of the universities. This protest in Sumy inspired many students that I interviewed in the Pora movement; it taught them that social change was possible. Many of the Pora activists got involved to help Sumy students and this activism experience would later be applied in the fall's political events. The Sumy protests ended late summer, but they were considered by young activists as a practice run for the presidential campaigns in the fall. In the section below, we consider the student experiences of protest activism at a private university in the capital of Kyiv. The purpose is to see how the structure of a university can assist or impede students in the activism against social or political injustice.

When a student protest movement erupted in Ukraine prior to the Orange revolution, the university illustrated the process of awakening political consciousness among students. SUMY State University came into being from a political decision made by the government to bring three local universities (merging Sumy State University, Sumy Pedagogical University, and Sumy

32   *New generation and subjectivities*

National Agrarian University into the Sumy National University) under its control in an election year. It was public information that the university merger was most likely politically motivated in order to guarantee the student vote for the pro-government candidate in the upcoming 2004 presidential elections ("student protest," 2004). These views were expressed in the media in an interview by Oleh Medunytsia, leader of the protest committee and the Youth Nationalist Congress. He said that "this could have been done to bring the students into one place under Oleksandr Tsarenko's control, and to utilize a huge administrative resource" ("student protest," 2004). The universities combined would total 40,000 students and 4,000 professors ("student protest," 2004). Tsarenko, the president of Sumy National Agrarian University (SNAU) and Ukrainian Parliament deputy in Social Democratic Party of Ukraine (united) political party, endorsed the presidential candidate Prime Minister Viktor Yanukovych ("Sumy students," 2004). This was controversial since Tsarenko was notorious for encouraging a culture of corruption; his university was ranked the most corrupt by NGO Partnership for Transparent Society Program. The NGO reported that "official bribery flourished and student labor was exploited" ("partnership for," 2004, p. 48). Students at this university (SNAU) filed several complaints with the Union of Ukrainian Youth (SUM) about the administration's abuse, but they refused to go further. The report detailed,

> unfortunately, most of the plaintiffs were not willing to openly testify against the Administration. They expressed the fear that they would be put under pressure, and they refused to give their last names, which made it difficult to counteract the negative phenomena at the university ("partnership for," 2004, p. 48).

Local NGOs responded by initiating a campaign in 2003 to educate students on their rights. Their efforts "familiarized the local communities with the illegal activities within the walls of SNAU through the media and the Coalition paper, *"Your Right"* ("partnership for," 2004, p. 48).

These underlying conditions at the university also provided valid explanations for the strong student and faculty backlash against the unification proposed the following year. "I heard a long time the talks about this unification, but it was bad news for us when our president signed it," said Leonid Melnyk, a faculty member in the department of economics at SUMY University (author's interview, Leonid Melnyk, 2009). He remembered that the process of unification was initiated by the Cabinet of Ministers and the Ministry of Education without any formality; President Kuchma had signed in April and the Prime Minister Yanukovych submitted his signature for implementation in June 2004. In August, students met with Melnyk and other faculty members to declare a protest against the decision. Melnyk supported his students' protest action at the university and even participated in the events. Melnyk and other professors lived with

New generation and subjectivities 33

the students in the tent cities that they created and occupied near campus (Ibid., 2009).

As a participant, Leonid explained that the protests had three stages. The first one was a protest action planned in the center of the city on Ukraine's Constitution Day. It was not a coordinated action between students and faculty. A day earlier, the faculty learned of student plans to protest and met with them to discuss their strategy. Through the night, Melnyk helped them to plan a legal protest event and hoped for a positive outcome that would result in the university president's refusal to sign the formal agreement to unify the universities. Melnyk thought and believed that their university president was intelligent and also courageous to refuse the decision for unification. Their protest actions were "absolutely positive and very aggressive" in their tactics (Ibid., 2009). On Ukraine's Constitution Day, the students planned a town meeting on Sumy's Shevchenko Square with their university professors. Melnyk explained, that as organizers of protest, it was essential to reach other professors for support, since it was very likely once the universities unified that some faculty would lose their positions. In terms of strategy, Melnyk explained different forms of protest participation by professors in activities like petition signing. He worked with students to write a complaint letter to the university president with approximately 1,000 professors' and students' signatures. He remembered that only two professors and around seven students did not participate. It felt to him like a victory that they obtained over 950 signatures of support to reject the unification decision. Speaking for the university community, he described that day as "full of victory" and "a successful meeting" (Ibid., 2009).

The second phrase of protest arrived a month later when the living conditions grew difficult in the tent cities. Leonid described that the period was filled with many attacks and pressure from the authorities and the governor. He spoke of the authorities that used terrible smelling gas on the students. Leonid recalled that they responded by sending letters translated in English to their international research network of economics and ecology scientists seeking support for their university students. This included countries such as the U.S., Canada, Poland, Czech Republic, Italy, and foreign embassies in Ukraine. In the third stage, he said, the students decided to organize a demonstration march that involved walking over 400 kilometers from Sumy to Kyiv. The authorities, he recalled, were angry and the police attacked them. He described it as a "real military action, more than a few hundred policemen with weapons, it was terrible" (Ibid., 2009). The police reacted to their march by raiding the tent cities in Sumy. Oleksandra Vesnych, a leader of the protest committee, recalled, "at 2 a.m. on Aug. 1 around 50 militiamen swarmed the tent city on Sumy's Shevchenko Square, pulling students out of tents and shoving them into cars before conducting a search of the grounds" ("Sumy students," 2004). It resulted in fourteen arrests of students for resisting the police, and two were charged

34 *New generation and subjectivities*

with drug and firearms possession. The students claimed that the weapons were planted in the tents by the authorities. The following day, representatives from the Parliament's human rights committee, Socialist deputy Yuriy Lutsenko, and politicians from Yushchenko's "Our Ukraine" headquarters came to the aid of the student protesters. The students detained were eventually released (Ibid., 2004). The march continued and the students were stopped a few times before completing their march to Kyiv. Leonid recalled that when the students reached the halfway point, the authorities grew fearful or were afraid of the bad consequences that could be produced from this event. They came close to failure, Melnyk said, but "the student protesters remained in mass numbers" (author's interview, Leonid Melnyk, 2009). This march to Kyiv was also highlighted by Eugene Pology, who was the chief editor of Sumy's *Panorama* newspaper, as a success, since their governor, Volodymyr Sherban, went after the students with the police and tried to arrest them. The students, he said, did not make any political demands. This attracted the attention of Ukrainian television channels that wanted to know why the students were demonstrating. The student protests became the number one news story, he said, on ICTV and Channel Five, national television stations. When the students reached Kyiv, they became symbols. He said, "So maybe they are heroes. We didn't do anything like this, so we have to support them." He thought that the case of Sumy represented a "good example of how to achieve one's own goals" (author's interview, Eugene Pology, 2009).

At that time, Melnyk described the atmosphere: the city was in motion as a result of the students. He described it as "electromagnetic energy. It was like energy charging all the city, citizens, and parties" (author's interview, Leonid Melnyk, 2009). The people of Sumy, he said, were trying to save their own universities from political party interests. He remembered that the protests gained the support of nearly all the Ukrainian television channels except for some local channels in Sumy. The latter broadcast that their students were bad students who used drugs and alcohol. To the contrary, Leonid said, "almost all of them were excellent students and one got a scholarship prize by the Cabinet of Ministry. They were clever students and many of them were [notable] individuals" (Ibid., 2009). The student protests were met with widespread approval and Sumy residents came to support the students. Melnyk credited the students as leaders and his role as their advisor. All the principal decision-making came from the students with the support of faculty. He saw these students differently, "I felt that they see further than adults or teacher people. It was a crucial and critical moment because of the new generation. In this critical moment, they did not make a mistake" (Ibid., 2009).

When the process of unification was implemented, the students saw the university's symbols being taken off the building and the students started to fight the removal of the logos. Leonid felt the removal of university symbols was a mistake; it produced a negative attitude, and students started to behave aggressively because they and the faculty opposed the unification. He admitted that there are many universities in Ukraine and perhaps that number should be reduced, but using different means. In this process, he remarked that there was an absence of communication and consideration of public opinion in the university. He did not like that the unification was imposed and decided without discussion. From his view, it looked like "occupants came and started to ruin the university, and that is why there [was] mass disappointment at that time" (Ibid., 2009). As response, the different faculty members and departments started to fight and display a negative attitude towards the unification. He participated to give strength to the protests as a citizen of Ukraine. He did not like pressure and expressed his personal opinion against this. He was aware that his stance was not without consequences. While all the professors supported the student movement, they were aware that doing so was not easy since they put themselves at risk of losing their university positions with the new university administration. The student protests ended in August with the reversal of the decision; Kuchma cancelled the decree to unify the universities in Sumy. Leonid attributed the victory not only to the students but also to the Academy of Sciences that advised the administration to change its policy and refrain from restricting students' participation in protest. He reasoned that the support was given to the university since other students at different universities in Ukraine could freely join the student movement. Leonid felt the Academy's decision had an impact on President Kuchma's understanding of what could develop (more protests) and perhaps that was why he changed his position (Ibid., 2009).

Sumy protests: Alexandra's perspective

Alain Touraine reminds us that in social movements there are two sides: an offensive and a defensive position. The offensive position, he describes as negotiable. He elaborates "the actor's capacity to define a project, a vision or a utopia and, on the basis of a strong identity, to put forward an alternative conception of community life" (Wieviorka, 2005, p. 12). The latter, a defensive side, considers the aspects of an actor's self-preservation from forces that subjugate his existence (Ibid., p. 12). Upon examining the personal narrative of Alexandra (presented below), I found many similarities to connect with Touraine's conception of a social movement actor from the subjective perspective. These aspects were visible in Alexandra's articulations of three protest activities: 1) creating a website for the protest movement; 2) petitioning; and 3) demonstrating in a political march.

During the period of conflict over the unification of universities in Sumy, Alexandra was a second-year university student at SUMY university and journalist of a local newspaper named *Panorama*. This paper was owned by Eugene Pology. The journalists described the paper's mission as being to provide objective accounts of the student protest events. These journalists

36   *New generation and subjectivities*

also participated in the movement (author's interview, Eugene Pology, 2009). Her work at the newspaper brought to her attention the proposed merger of three universities in Sumy, it also contributed to providing visibility for the student movement and presenting the issues for the struggle from the exterior. This was six months before the protests erupted. She was assigned to write an article about the situation, which evoked emotions of anger in her and produced action. She got involved with other students in writing letters to their professors to verify whether the process of unification was actually taking place, and to question whether it would actually be implemented within six months. Alexandra's political engagement continued with a discussion with her editor-in-chief, Pology, who suggested and wrote an open letter to the Ministry and Ukraine's President to inform them that they were aware of their plans for unification. Alexandra was assigned the task of obtaining signatures for this letter from the university. She was not confident in her activism. These emotions were reflected in her thoughts about this action, "I felt like a fool going to the halls of the university asking for signatures with surnames" (author's interview, Alexandra, 2009). Despite Alexandra's initial doubts, the petitioning enabled the expansion of her social networks and produced positive effects on enlarging the student struggle. In the course of gathering signatures, she met a student rector in the university administration that supported the students' position in opposing the unification (Ibid., 2009). In total, the students obtained over 1,000 signatures for their initiative; they sent their letter to the Ministry and did not receive any response. It seemed to Alexandra that no one was interested in talking with the students or intellectuals, so it led them to make the decision to create street protests. She explained that the university's response to student activism was varied but in general, she said, "if they were not with us, they were not disturbing us" (Ibid., 2009).

The students were granted autonomy from the university to develop political actions. Within the SUMY university community, the students created a website (*Bezpective*) as a forum for students to write about the bad situation and their experiences concerning the unification. Students were able to freely express their opinions since the posts in the online forum were intentionally created to be anonymous. It produced student solidarity and created an affinity group of sympathizers from which to plan future protest actions. Alexandra was a subscriber to this website and received messages from students who wanted to organize a political meeting near Sumy State University. The students also invited other members of the student administration to the meeting. She remembered approximately 500 to 1,000 students stood on the square. In her words, "nobody knew what to do, no one had a megaphone, nobody shouted. It was a silent process. After that, the student administration decided to be leader of this process" (Ibid, 2009). The student administration had the approval of the university to organize a meeting with the students. Alexandra went to the two-hour scheduled meeting and was asked to leave since she was from a different faculty of

New generation and subjectivities 37

humanities. However, she found other ways to participate in the student protests. Alexandra was selected to be an anonymous speaker at a meeting on 12 May 2004. In attendance on the square were her friends who wore black kerchiefs to cover their faces. She described the uncertainty surrounding this event: "we didn't know what to say, my speech was awful, it was the first experience" (Ibid., 2009). Alexandra's experience demonstrates the reflexivity of the social movement actor that emphasized the aspect that they did not want to be a visible face of the protest at the beginning. It also presented a challenge to the methods to publicly articulate a vision for the movement when its actors adopted anonymous identities. This vision of activism as anonymous actors changed for Alexandra over time when she assumed a visible role as speaker for the protests when interviewed by the media in the demonstration march to Kyiv.

The student movement gained more visibility and publicity with the demonstration march from Sumy to Kyiv by student activists. Alexandra participated in planning the march to Kyiv. She explained that they invited students from the Pora civic campaign to provide them protection in the march. In addition, she described that the students requested political and financial support from political parties, including "Our Ukraine" and the Party of Regions. Their request for funding was approved by "Our Ukraine" political party. They also contributed logistical support in terms of transport by bus, cameras, and funds for meals. Other local parties like the Communist party and nationalist parties agreed to march with them. Alexandra was interviewed on television by Andriy Shevchenko from Ukraine's Channel 5 about the protest. When the president cancelled his decree the next day, she recounted her feelings of victory for the student movement, which ended the student protests in Sumy. Alexandra was surprised by the protest outcome. She admitted that, "we did not believe we could do it" (Ibid., 2009). When she heard the news, she thought it was a mistake. It was not expected. Furthermore, she said, "the thing is we didn't believe in victory, but we believed we're doing the right thing. We didn't want to say that we are afraid because we believed in our truths of our thoughts not victory" (Ibid., 2009). The effect of the protests coincided with the resignations of Deputy Tsarenko from his position of president at Sumy National Agrarian University, as well as the new president of the proposed unified university. The merger of universities was annulled through a decree issued by Ukrainian president Kuchma ("partnership for," 2004, p. 48).

The grievance that led the students to initiate the protests was student opposition to the merger of Sumy State University to bring universities into the administration's fold. Suddenly, Sumy State University became a space for political development of consciousness of student rights in Ukraine. The apolitical students in Sumy awoke to revive their political awareness of student rights. This was due in large part to the pressure exerted by government on the state universities in the campaign period for the 2004 presidential elections. The protests unified students together with faculty, local NGOs, local

38 New generation and subjectivities

media, and ordinary citizens. The students created a resistance front in their tent city occupations and garnered more support from opposition politicians during the violent police raid. They also caught the attention of youth civic campaign Pora that offered support during their demonstration march from Sumy region to Kyiv. Universities' institutions remained vital arenas for instilling democratic values and cultivating civic life among university students living in post-Soviet Ukraine. As illustrated by Kyiv Mohyla Academy, the new private universities were founded by former dissidents with a democratic vision. They set out to establish universities to develop national and political consciousness; the students embodied the democratic life of freedom on campus. These universities had a positive effect in cultivating and supporting students' political participation especially in 2004. Students that were members of civic campaigns or university strike committees were part of a university community that enabled free thought and new associations, which generated more willingness from students in this community to participate in political action. This was illustrated in the vote to strike that the university rector presented to his students, which would decide collectively whether or not to strike in the early days of the Orange Revolution. The effect in terms of its contribution to the creation of lifelong activists will be examined in the chapters to follow on its alumni's continued activism in Euromaidan.

2013

Nearly 10 years later, a nationwide survey in Ukraine, conducted on 9–20 November 2013 by Democratic initiatives and Kiev International Institute of Sociology, found that 56 percent of those surveyed were not ready to participate in mass protests and only 22 percent answered in the affirmative that they were ready for social protests ("The Readiness," 2013). The protests began by late November 2013 and main reasons Diuk cited were "...an uprising against the corruption and dictatorship that had been eroding peoples' dignity on a mundane level, as well as in their spiritual lives" (Diuk, 2014, p. 83). Among the Maidan protesters surveyed, from 7–8 December 2013 by Democratic initiatives and Kiev International Institute of Sociology, during the nonviolent phase of protest, the study found that the two main reasons for popular mobilization were Yanukovych's refusal to sign the Associated Agreement and the student beatings on 30 November. This suggested that the protesters' subjectivity about the political situation guided their decision-making to participate. Among the Maidan protesters surveyed, 38 percent were from 15–29 years old and 49 percent were 30–54 years old. In addition, in terms of profile of the protesters, 63 percent of them had higher education degrees. These protesters were also asked what kind of collective actions they would be willing to participate in. The three most popular responses were "authorized meetings and demonstrations," "participation in election campaign," and "participation in strikes." The survey found among participants that only 13.8 percent supported the occupation of buildings, and 15 percent

New generation and subjectivities 39

of them would participate in the "creation of armed force, independent from authorities" ("Maidan," 2013). In the second phase of protests, the two most common responses for participation were mobilization because of the violent repression of the students and desire of social change for Ukraine. In terms of demographics during this second phase, the surveys of Maidan protesters conducted by Democratic initiatives and Kiev International Institute of Sociology in February 2014 found that the average age for protesters was 37 years old (33 percent between 18–29 years old and 56 percent 30–54 years old) and 88 percent of inhabitants on the Maidan were men ("From Maidan," 2014). This shift in population and attitudes in the tent camps was also reflected in national surveys performed 24 January to 1 February 2014 by the Center for Social and Marketing Research "SOCIS" and Kiev International Institute of Sociology. The survey found that citizen support for the protests was at 47 percent. When asked how protesters should act to defend their rights, 63 percent supported protesters' negotiations with authority, while only 20 percent supported continuing with peaceful protests, and 11 percent advocated for more decisive actions using force ("Intentions of," 2014).

During the early days of protests, there was a pessimism about the new generation and its capacity to mobilize, expressed by veteran activists from the Orange Revolution. This sentiment was expressed by Nayyem and Diuk, who captured his thoughts. She described Nayyem as a 33-year old journalist that was disillusioned about the "wired" younger generation connected to new technology like laptops and smartphones. He did not believe that young people would be capable to self-mobilize and "to undertake civic activism in real life." (Diuk, 2014, p. 85) However, Diuk explains that young people who traveled to Europe had aspirations for Ukraine to create deeper relations with the West. However, when their president Yanukovych stopped the negotiations with the EU, the young people felt that their future had been stolen from them (Ibid., 2014, p. 85).

As a result, young people did mobilize and they "...focused first on foreign relations, advocating a 'European future' for Ukraine—a goal not as widely supported by citizens in 2013 as clean elections had been nine years earlier. Protest rhetoric then moved on to attack the regime for corruption, repressiveness, and rights violations" (Onuch, 2014a, p. 46). Diuk describes how the young people that had participated in the protests of 2004 had grown up into adults. These young adults were very concerned that the EuroMaidan produce results in the end unlike the Orange Revolution, which failed to do so. To achieve this outcome, these young adults prepared themselves in the following way:

> They were using their skills in civic organizing to bring their self-help networks to the Maidan, and reporting qualitative leaps in capacity and effectiveness. They were eager to put these new capabilities and assets to use in building a new post-Maidan, post-Yanukovych democracy.
>
> (Diuk, 2014, p. 87)

40 *New generation and subjectivities*

Euromaidan protesters, like the alter-activist, embodied a *"way of subjectivity"* that represented "...an appeal to personal and collective freedom against the logics of power... to a desire for autonomy in the face of the domination exercised over different aspects of life" (Pleyers, 2010, p. 46). In the Euromaidan, political action had a physical dimension of tent camps and occupation on the city's square, as well as a virtual aspect to exercise freedom to speak out on social media networks. Euromaidan was also notable for its integration of social media in its protest strategies (Tucker, 2014; Onuch, 2014b; Lokot, 2014). In the Euromaidan protests, social media helped sustain activism, Dickinson conceded that "the international reach of both Facebook and Twitter as well as the widespread availability of livestream feeds of violent clashes between Maidan protesters and government forces have proved central to the long-term viability of Maidan social networks" (Dickinson, 2014, p. 80). That placed Ukraine's recent protest alongside other global movements (Arab Spring, 15M movement Spain, and Occupy Wall Street), which incorporated social media practices into their protest strategies. These movements followed the concept of *cultures of networked belonging* (Cardoso, 2012) where individualist cultures had changed their values and were no longer focused on pure self-interest, but creating openness (i.e., "cloud cultures," Cardoso, 2012, p. 198). This *social networking culture* created a new identity by "combining mediated environment and non-mediated environment in networks of relationship" (Ibid., 2012, p. 198). These *cultures of belonging* included membership in online communities, civic and political participation, and sharing among members, for example on Facebook. It also helped to explain the conditions of autonomy that enabled Nayyem's activation into protest on Facebook that went viral. His sense of freedom to put the first call to protest captured a "transformative force... by reclaiming the space of the city for its citizens" (Castells, 2012b, p. 225) to initiate protest. These types of interactions described a "new spatial form of networked social movement" that consisted of "horizontal, multimodal networks" on the Internet and in physical sites (Castells, 2012). This hybrid network provides a "space of autonomy" to increase an individual's potential for participation in the movement "given that these are open-ended networks without defined boundaries always reconfiguring themselves accordingly to the level of involvement of the population at large" (Castells, 2012, pp. 221–2).

The Ukrainian case studies speak about individual transformation into subjectivities from emotional responses—in particular, of indignation. This resulted in actors' freedom or feeling of empowerment, which had a long-term effect on spreading ideas of democracy. This was enabled by the open culture and practices in the "movements of places" at the level of networks (Pleyers and Glasius, 2013). It is a narrative that will analyze new forms of activism that have transformed a new generation of Ukrainians supporting a democratic future for their country.

New generation and subjectivities 41

Bibliography

Author's interview, Alexandra, writer at Panorama newspaper and student at Sumy State University, June 24, 2009, Sumy.

Author's interview, Andriy Gusak, former [yellow] Pora, October 17, 2008, Kyiv.

Author's interview, Eugene Pology, editor of Panorama newspaper, June 24, 2009, Sumy.

Author's interview, Iryna Fartukh, university student at National University of Kyiv Mohyla Academy and member of Kyiv Mohyla student strike committee, March 12, 2009, Kyiv.

Author's interview, Konstyantyn Peresiedov, university student and editor of Maidan student newsletter at National University of Kyiv Mohyla Academy, Sept 10, 2008, Kyiv.

Author's interview, Leonid Melnyk, Professor, Sumy State University, June 24, 2009, Sumy.

Author's interview, Markian Rushchyshyn, businessman, March 21, 2009, Lviv.

Author's interview, Ostap Kryvdyk, Committee "For Truth", September 10, 2008, Kyiv.

Author's interview, Serhiy Svit, university rector at National University of Kyiv Mohyla Academy, October 8, 2008, Kyiv.

Author's interview, Taras Dubko, Sr. Vice Rector Ukrainian Catholic University, March 17, 2009, Lviv.

Author's interview, Vyacheslav Bryukhovetsky, first rector and founder of the National University of Kyiv Mohyla Academy, September 1, 2008, Kyiv.

Bandera, S. (2006). "The Role of the Internet and Ukraine's 2004 Presidential Elections." Development Associate Report.

Beissinger, M. (2011). "Mechanisms of Maidan: The Structure of Contingency in the Making of the Orange Revolution." *Mobilization: An International Journal, 16*(1), 25–43.

Bunce, V., & Sharon L. Wolchik. (2007). "Youth and Postcommunist Electoral Revolutions: Never Trust Anyone over 30?." *Reclaiming democracy: Civil society and electoral change in central and eastern Europe* (J. Forbrig & P. Demeš, Eds.). Washington, DC: The German Marshall Fund of the United States.

Cardoso, G. (2012). "Networked Life World: Four Dimensions of the Cultures of Networked Belonging." *Observatorio (OBS*) Journal*, Special issue "Networked belonging and networks of belonging" – COST ACTION ISO906 "Transforming Audiences, Transforming Societies," 197–205.

Castells, M. (2012). *Aftermath: The cultures of the economic crisis.* Oxford: Oxford University Press.

Castells, M. (2012b). *Networks of outrage and hope.* Cambridge: Polity Press.

Dickinson, J. (2014). "Prosymo maksymal'nyi perepost! Tactical and Discursive Uses of Social Media in Ukraine's EuroMaidan." *Ab Imperio, 2014*(3), 75–93.

Diuk, N. (2012). *The next generation in Russia, Ukraine, and Azerbaijan: Youth, politics, identity, and change.* Plymouth: Rowman & Littlefield.

Diuk, N. (2013). "Youth as an Agent for Change: The Next Generation in Ukraine." *Demokratizatsiya, 21*(2), 179–196.

Diuk, N. (2014). "Finding Ukraine." *Journal of Democracy, 25*(3), 83–89.

Dyczok, M. (2000). *Ukraine: Movement without change, change without movement.* Harwood Academic Publishers, Amsterdam 2000, p. 59.

42 New generation and subjectivities

Emeran, C. (2011). "Transforming Opposition Networks into a Movement: Case Studies from Ukraine's Independence Movement to the 2004 Presidential Elections." ProQuest dissertation database.

From Maidan camp to Maidan-sich: what has changed? (2014, February 3). Retrieved December 6, 2015, from http://www.kiis.com.ua/?lang=eng&cat=reports&id=226&page=15.

Hrycak, A. (1997). "The Coming of 'Chrysler Imperial': Ukrainian Youth and Rituals of Resistance," *Harvard Ukrainian Studies, 21*(1997), 63–91.

"Intentions of Ukraine"–Results of conjoint nationwide sociological survey kiis and socis. (2014, February 7). Retrieved July 31, 2016, from http://www.kiis.com.ua/?lang=eng.

Kuzio, T. (2002, March 3). Ukraine debates the role of civil society (03/03/02). Retrieved February 28, 2016, from http://www.ukrweekly.com/old/archive/2002/090213.shtml.

Kuzio, T. (2005). "The Opposition's Road to Success." *Journal of Democracy, 16*(2), 117–130.

Kuzio, T. (2006a). "Ukraine Is Not Russia: Comparing Youth Political Activism." *SAIS Review, 26*(2), 67–83.

Kuzio, T. (2006b). "Civil Society, Youth and Societal Mobilization in Democratic Revolutions." *Communist and Post-Communist Studies, 39*(3), 365–386.

Kuzio, T., & Magocsi, P. R. (2014). *Theoretical and comparative perspectives on nationalism: New directions in cross-cultural and post-communist studies.* Stuttgart, Germany: ibid.em-Verlag.

Kuzio, T., & Wilson, A. (1994). *Ukraine: Perestroika to independence.* New York: St. Martin's Press.

Lokot, Tetyana. "Ukrainian #DigitalMaidan Activism Takes Twitter's Trending Topics by Storm." *GlobalVoices*, January 27, 2014. Accessed May 11, 2014. http://globalvoicesonline.org/2014/01/27/ukrainian-digitalmaidan-protests-twittertrending-topics-storm/.

MAIDAN-2013. (2013, December 8). Retrieved December 6, 2015, from http://www.kiis.com.ua/?lang=eng&cat=reports&id=216&page=16.

Mcadam, D., & Paulsen, R. (1993). "Specifying the Relationship between Social Ties and Activism." *American Journal of Sociology, 99*(3), 640–640.

Nahaylo, B. (1999). *The Ukrainian Resurgence.* Toronto: University of Toronto Press.

Nikolayenko, O. (2007). "The Revolt of the Post-Soviet Generation: Youth Movements in Serbia, Georgia, and Ukraine." *Comparative Politics, 39*(2), 169–188.

Onuch, O. (2014a). Who Were the Protesters? *Journal of Democracy, 25*(3), 44–51.

Onuch, O. (2014b). "Social networks and social media in Ukrainian "Euromaidan" protests." *The Washington Post.* Retrieved from http://www.washingtonpost.com/blogs/monkey-cage/wp/2014/01/02/social-networks-and-social-media-in-ukrainian-euromaidan-protests-2/.

Partnership for a Transparent Society program. (2004, May 1). Retrieved November 16, 2015, from http://pdf.usaid.gov/pdf_docs/Pdacf060.pdf.

Pleyers, G. (2010). *Alter-globalization: becoming actors in the global age.* Cambridge: Polity Press.

Pleyers, G., & Glasius, M. *The resonance of movements of 2011: connections, emotions, values.* Socio n°2, "Révolutions, indignations, contestations", edited by Pénélope Larzillière and Boris Petric. Paris: Éditions de la Maison des sciences de l'homme, 16 décembre 2013, 376 p.

Porta, D. D., & Diani, M. (2006). *Social movements: An introduction.* Malden, MA: Blackwell Publishing.

The readiness of the Ukrainian population to participate in actions of social protest (before 20 November 2013). (2013, November 20). Retrieved December 6, 2015, from http://www.kiis.com.ua/?lang=eng&cat=reports&id=214&page=16.

Student protest in Sumy continues. (2004, July 8). Retrieved November 16, 2015, from https://www.kyivpost.com/content/ukraine/student-protest-in-sumy-continues-21335.html?flavour=mobile.

Taylor, K. (2006). *Let's twist again: Youth and leisure in socialist Bulgaria.* Wien: Lit.

Tucker, J. (2013). "How Ukrainian protestors are using Twitter and Facebook." *The Washington Post.* Retrieved from http://www.washingtonpost.com/blogs/monkey-cage/wp/2013/12/04/strategic-use-of-facebook-and-twitter-in-ukrainian-protests/.

Wieviorka, M. (2005). "After New Social Movements." *Social Movement Studies,* *4*(1), 1–19.

Wilson, Andrew. (1996). *Ukrainian nationalism in the 1990s: A minority faith.* Cambridge: Cambridge University Press.

Wilson, A. (2009). "Ukraine's Orange Revolution of 2004: The Paradox of negotiation." *Civil resistance and power politics: The experience of non-violent action from Gandhi to the present* (A. Roberts & T. G. Ash, Eds.). Oxford: Oxford University Press.

Woronowycz, R. (2001, February 18). Anti-Kuchma protests continue in Ukrainian capital (02/18/01). Retrieved February 28, 2016, from http://www.ukrweekly.com/old/archive/2001/070101.shtml.

Yurchak, A. (2006). *Everything was forever, until it was no more: The last Soviet generation.* Princeton, NJ: Princeton University Press.

2 The emergence of an actor

In this chapter, I examine the initiators of collective action of protest as an emergent actor of social change in three protest events in Ukraine ("Ukraine without Kuchma" protests of 2000–2001, the Orange Revolution of 2004, and the Euromaidan protests of 2013–2014). The main purpose was to investigate the mechanisms involved in the social construction of protest from the individual level. This meant explaining individual actions that preceded social movement identity formation. The latter emerged, according to Jasper, when individuals or groups were transformed into subjects as activists and obtained self-reflexivity about their ability to bring about social change from collective action (Jasper, 1997, p. 86). In this chapter, this form of subjectivity was a critical to the process of activating an individual into contentious politics.

"Ukraine without Kuchma" (UWK) and "For Truth" protests of 2000–2001

To illustrate the social processes preceding the emergence of social movement culture in Ukraine, I analyzed the case study of the construction of the UWK protests through the personal narratives of co-founder Volodymyr Chemerys, and Taras Stetskiv, who co-founded the "For Truth" campaign. The latter mobilized young people into the larger UWK protests. As explained earlier, the initial idea to protest against President Kuchma's corrupted regime caught Chemerys's attention at a friend's birthday party. The following evening, as Chemerys recounted, he received a phone call from Yuriy Lutsenko, the press secretary in the Socialist Party, who had been at the party. Lutsenko spoke to him about a conversation that he had earlier with Oleksandr Moroz, the Socialist Party leader. Lutsenko told Chemerys that Moroz had confided in him about Kuchma's guilt[1] and was astonished that no one was protesting. Moroz expressed to Lutsenko the need for some initiative to take action to express discontent. This conversation prompted Chemerys and his friends to start the protests. They decided to seize on the public outcry created by the political scandal to organize demonstrations. Their personal motivations to get involved were to protest against the fact that journalists were killed under the regime. In cases like Chemerys, his call to action was connected to deteriorating social conditions. That period, as Chemerys recalled, was fraught with tension. In his words, he and his friends were like a match whose flames lit a powder keg. They understood that protesting was the only possible means to resolve the political crisis. He reasoned that momentum was in their favor, given the impetus for mobilizing supporters with Gondadze's case, which served as a sufficient condition to spur large-scale protest. They gathered initial support from a group of friends and personal supporters that extended to members of the Socialist Party, which offered them security. To illustrate, in one incident, they received politicians' protection in the period when the police authorities were threatening the removal of their tent cities. The members of Parliament (MPs) were protected from government persecution through their immunity powers. Later on, other individual deputies of Parliament from nationalist parties joined them independently from their political parties. Even with the participation of representatives from nationalist and socialist parties, the UWK began as a protest movement with no overt political party influence. The groups shared political vision on democracy was what motivated most to participate (author's interview, Chemerys, Kyiv, 2008). The UWK protest was notable as the first attempt to protest against Kuchma's regime. It began as a form of "moral protest" (Jasper) after Gongadze's death when the regime was blamed for involvement in his murder. The protest actions gained some radical traits in spite of the fact that the movement would have stood a chance of gaining widespread support after it narrowed its aim to the removal of Kuchma. Despite narrowing its aim, UWK did not gain the widespread public support anticipated, perhaps as a result of the use of radical tactics (author's interview, Stetskiv, 2008).

First stage: launch of protests – Friday, 15 December 2000

On this day, Ukrainian President Kuchma attended the historic closing of the Chernobyl nuclear plant. International efforts had succeeded in pressuring President Kuchma to close the site of the largest nuclear disaster ("Chernobyl," 2000). While international attention was placed on Ukraine, it was also the day when the UWK protests began in Kyiv's Maidan and attracted about a hundred people ("Youth groups," 2000). The majority in attendance were the friends of the founders. This was the first public demonstration since independence and it was not organized; the people came on their own. Chemerys' first impression of that protest was that he felt like animals in a zoo for apathetic people to watch (author's interview, Chemerys, Kyiv, 2008). The early days of protest grew from an informal gathering of protesters to more organized protests/demonstrations in Kyiv with each subsequent event attracting from a hundred to tens of thousands at its peak. This mobilization triggered a fearful reaction from Kuchma, Chemerys reasoned. It seemed to him that the president's administration

46 *The emergence of an actor*

reacted quickly to create an anti-crisis headquarters and used media outlets like ICTV to broadcast its messages (author's interview, Chemerys, Kyiv, 2008). ICTV, a national television group, was owned by Viktor Pinchuk, wealthy businessman, and son-in-law of president Kuchma; he was a supporter of the Labor Ukraine political party in Parliament. On ICTV, journalists played the role of questioning the motives of protesters, and spread doubt about the origins of taped recordings about Gondadze from the president, which were attributed as the cause for bringing protesters to the street (Bachynsky, 2000). Media bias was also discussed in a weekly program on Ukrainian television channel Studio 1+1 that discussed the tape scandal. They also highlighted in this program the connection between leaders of anti-Kuchma protests and their earlier role as former student strikers of the 1990 student hunger strikes, which drove Prime Minister Vitali Masol to resign from power. The media drew the conclusion that people were willing to risk all in protests if the authorities ignored their pleas (Bachynsky, 2000). Through the media, Chemerys remembered that the information presented about the UWK activists on Maidan was distorted. They presented the protesters as including participants from the extreme right and extreme left (author's interview, Chemerys, Kyiv, 2008).

The protest events became more reccurent beginning in 17 December 2000. On that day, protest organizers planned a two-day anti-Kuchma protests with tents placed on Kyiv's Maidan (Independence Square). Among the protesters were young people and youth organizations, as well as people who were not formally involved with a specific group totaling about 100 ("Youth groups," 2007). The following day, 18 December, the number of tents on the square increased as 250 protesters arrived to hear politicians' speeches from Oleksandr Moroz, the leader of the Socialist Party; Anatolii Matvienko, Sobor Party; and Levko Lukianenko, Chairman of the Ukrainian Republican Party (Bachynsky, 2000). Mykhailo Svystovych, a founder of the protests, published online (on his Maidan website) a call to protest planned on a larger scale for 19 December 2001 at 11 AM on Kyiv's Maidan ("Youth groups," 2007). In the morning of protest, on the main square, the supporters of the Communist Party came out to hear speeches from Petro Symonenko, CPU First Secretary. Symonenko appealed to the people to unite and to reclaim power from the regime of Kuchma (Bachynsky, 2000). On that day, the protest coordinators organized a march from the city's central square to the Parliament building (Verkhovna Rada). The demands expressed in slogans included, "Kuchma Kaput!," "Kuchma! If you go away, you will save Ukraine," "Heorhiy, you are with us," and "The Criminal Kuchma-to prison" ("Youth groups," 2007). Their demands were for the resignations of government officials involved in the Gondadze scandal such as Interior Minister, Yuri Kravchenko; Head of Security Service of Ukraine, Leonid Derkach; and President Leonid Kuchma ("Ukraine without," 2000). Among their list of demands was a call for an independent investigation into the tapes affair and Gondadze's case ("Ukraine Without," 2000). At noon, approximately 5,000–8,000 anti-Kuchma protesters left Kyiv's Maidan and marched to Ukraine's Parliament. There were minor infractions between protesters who broke through the police barricades to enter the Parliament. The Chairman of the Parliament, Ivan Pliusch, made a speech and communicated that Volodymyr Chemerys, a founder of UWK protests, would address Parliament later that day at 4 PM pending the approval of the MPs. The day passed and the resolution did not manage to obtain necessary votes to allow Chemerys to speak in the Parliament. Pliusch also made assurances that Volodymyr Lytvyn, Presidential head, would meet representatives of the UWK protests in the evening. At 5 PM, the anti-Kuchma protesters marched to the presidential administration, and they did not meet with Lytvyn. Instead, the deputy head, Oleh Diomin, met with Yuriy Lutsenko who delivered the protest movement's list of demands for him to transfer their message to the president. Following this meeting, the protesters dispersed with the intention to meet again tomorrow and to start a hunger strike if the president refused to meet them (Bachynsky, 2000). Meanwhile, on that day, they encountered at Parliament 1,000 pro-Kuchma supporters who organized a separate counter-demonstration. The theme was "In support of Constitutional order" (Ibid., 2000). In attendance were politicians from Rukh for Union and others including the former Ukrainian president Leonid Kravchuk. Students numbering 300 also attended; however, they spoke of getting paid to attend plus receiving free refreshments. The protesters held posters with messages that strongly implied Western countries or Russians were involved in producing the Gondadze scandal (Ibid., 2000).

The next day, 20 December, the protesters at the tent camp continued to increase in numbers and at noon President Kuchma met with UWK founders Chemerys and Lutsenko. In the meeting, the president refused to resign. He said he would consider the request for the resignation of ministers if it came from the Prime Minister Viktor Yushchenko. Kuchma said that he would allow an independent investigation into the tapes and Gondadze matter. He would contact Pliusch to see if they would allow time in the legistature for them to speak in Parliament. In return, Chemerys and Lutsenko would agree to remove the tents from the square and suspend any further protest action. Afterwards, Chemerys and Lutsenko had a debriefing meeting with over 1,000 demonstrators to discuss the outcome (Bachynsky, 2000). Also that day, a group of 500 anti-Kuchma protesters marched to Cabinet of Ministers and met with the Prime Minister, Viktor Yushchenko. He promised them that he would consider the issue of Kravchenko and Derkach in an upcoming meeting. The day ended and the tent city was still in place, and Kyiv's Maidan was filled with people. The Parliament was reviewing the law on special investigative commissions that was vetoed by Kuchma. On 21 December, there were 2,000 anti-Kuchma protesters gathered by the Parliament, along with 1,000 pro-Kuchma supporters, including National Democratic party, SDP(U), and Labor Ukraine. They cried out "Kuchma is our President" while their opponents yelled "Ukraine without

48   *The emergence of an actor*

Kuchma" across police barricades. Chemerys made a speech to address the Parliament for five minutes and reiterated their demands. He also continued to advocate for an independent investigation on the tapes and insisted that Gondadze's case be handled by the Council of Europe. The tent city increased to 50 tents for the anti-Kuchma side and six tents for the pro-Kuchma supporters (Ibid., 2000).

Due to the approaching Christmas holidays and New Year, which preoccupied people, the organizers decided to end the protests around 27 December. They left behind a symbolic tent on the Maidan. They waited for the New Year to arrive, and on 10 January 2001, they made an attempt to form a counter-demonstration to one organized by Kuchma's people, which was a failure since people were forced to participate in the protest. This date also represented a failure for Kuchma to implement a referendum to increase the presidential powers into Ukrainian law, the Parliament rejected the draft law. That day was memorable for Chemerys because Parliament's decision saved Ukraine from becoming an authoritarian republic (author's interview, Chemerys, Kyiv, 2008). Later that month on 30 January, the second stage of protest began in defense of Kyiv's mayor's decision to close Kyiv's Maidan for renovation. This prevented the protesters from putting tents on the main square. Instead, the area was fenced off. The activists brought tools and created a hole in the fence for them to reach the main street Kreshchatyk off the square. During this stage, several large actions were held with 70,000 to 100,000 people participating (Ibid., 2008). The following month on 6 February 2000, a full day of demonstrations was planned, and tents were reestablished on the square. At noon, a group of 7,000 protesters marched through the square to the Parliament and presidential administration building waving Ukrainian flags and shouting "Kuchma Out!" and "Ukraine without Kuchma." There were minor incidents with 300 youths from anarchist groups that attacked their tent cities (Woronowycz, 2001a). The protests continued on 11 February 2001 with demonstrators numbering 5,000. They created a mile-long human chain from the central square to the Presidential administration building. Protesters shouted "Kuchma Out" and held a caricature of Kuchma inscribed "Kuchma Kaput" (Ibid., 2001a). In their demonstrations, they displayed symbols such as a 60-foot Ukrainian flag, and banners representing 20 political parties and youth organizations. The day ended with a candlelight vigil on the square (Ibid., 2001b). The next day, on 12 February 2001, Kyiv courts ordered the removal of the tents from the city's central square for the following day. Public officials had grown aware that the tent city "has become the center of the Ukraine without Kuchma movement with hundreds of Ukrainians gathering in and around the tents daily to debate or simply gawk" (Ibid., 2001b). Later that month, on 21 February 2001, Maidan was closed for renovation. City workers began construction to renovate the city's square in preparation for the 10th anniversary of Ukrainian independence. The UWK protesters put posters on the construction site such as "Prison for Bandits" and made

The emergence of an actor   49

demands for the resignation of the president and other officials. Instead of continuing the "Ukraine without Kuchma" campaign, other protesters proposed a new initiative of "Ukraine For Truth" (Ibid., 2001b).

The Committee "For Truth" was organized with a council consisting of nine members acting independently from the UWK protests. The Committee "For Truth" organized its tactics and protest actions daily until early March (author's interview, Stetskiv, 2008). On 1 March 2001, the police raided the tent camp and detained, and later released, 44 activists (Mann and Dougherty, 2001). The media outlet CNN broadcasted an interview on 2 March 2001 with key figures in the protest, following the raid on the tent city the previous night. CNN online published a transcript of an interview with President Kuchma, who said, "the authorities showed today that government power exists, and I consider that an absolutely correct decision. Everybody should know that in the future" (Ibid., 2001). Lutsenko, who was interviewed, replied, "We realize what kind of machine we're dealing with here. While the criminals in power continue to give orders to police, our resistance will only increase" (Ibid., 2001). He informed potential protesters about new protests for 9 March (Ibid., 2001). Moroz responded that the reasons for the crisis were not only the tapes. He explained the political crisis was a result of the suspected death of a journalist named Gondadze. For him, the tapes served as a form of evidence on the president's role to place pressure on the media, violate human rights, and to persecute journalists (Ibid, 2001).

Later that month, on 9 March 2001, 10,000 people took to the streets in Kyiv and demanded the president's resignation. Kuchma's response was use of "psychological warfare," based on a "direct threat to Ukraine's national security" serving as justification for the authorities to mobilize security forces to defend constitutional order in their country (Ibid., 2001).

The second stage ended on 9 March when the riots broke out between the demonstrators and militia. The prior images of the protests were peaceful demonstrations, since the UWK activists knew that violence would result in failure for their opposition movement. But the riots that occurred that day were provoked by the imprisonment of the deputy Prime Minister Yulia Tymoshenko. The riots resulted in 18 people being imprisoned. After that the movement began to end. President Kuchma, Prime Minister Yushchenko, and the speaker of Parliament had denunced the protests and activists as fascists. Yet, the UWK protests left a deep impression on the minds of the people. While they lacked resources at the beginning of protests, the activists were motivated by pure enthusiasm. But even that sort of feeling ends sooner or later, as Chemerys reflected. That was the start of the third and final stage of protest, the declining phase he said. The demonstrations continued to occur, but they were more sporadic, with the last one taking place on 26 April 2001. This protest demonstration was against Yushchenko's removal from his position as Prime Minister. Chemerys remarked his disappointment that this demonstration organized by Tymoshenko and

50 *The emergence of an actor*

Yushchenko had been the first time people were paid for their participation. The deputies and state administration participants came for the purpose of earning money, not standing their ground. For Chemerys, that was a kind of finishing point in the action of UWK. He explained that the main reason for failure was that the leadership of the movement was now in the hands of politicians who were mostly preoccupied with the perception of their employment, rather than the idea that started the protest (author's interview, Chemerys, Kyiv, 2008).

The reasons why UWK failed were political ones. From the beginning of UWK, Chemerys remarked that they had only one politician supporting them, and it was Moroz. Political leaders such as Yushchenko and Tymoshenko sat in their chairs observing the protests from a distance (author's interview, Chemerys, Kyiv, 2008). The opposition parties could not reach people's hearts. They were unable to show people the future without Kuchma. Tymoshenko's arrest only contributed to the narrowing of opposition's orientation, and people's support was also weakening with the increase in violence in the protest's support (author's interview, Stetskiv, 2008). At risk of losing the support of the people, the opposition had to use radical measures—and even go to extreme protests actions—which resulted in the events of 9 March. In one or two months, the politicians changed their minds, and Tymoshenko, who was accused by Kuchma of corruption, joined them and she wanted to take the lead and become leader of the movement, Chemerys recalled (author's interview, Chemerys, Kyiv, 2008). The movement was now taken over by radical forces, which actually wanted this violence with the government, as Chemerys recounted. These radicalized forces thought that if the state used violence on participants, it would raise the attention of other people and gain large-scale support. At that time, Stetskiv remembered that he represented the minority view of those against using violence in the protest movement. For him, Tymoshenko represented the radical part. Her point of view became dominant and it failed. That was why the UWK movement died, in Stetskiv's opinion (author's interview, Stetskiv, 2008). Chemerys spoke of Tymoshenko's failure: her presence, he felt, did more harm than good to UWK. He observed that as soon as politicians emerged in the protest movement, that was when political bargaining appeared. Activists knew that a temporary government would form. Tymoshenko founded the National Salvation Forum (NSF). At that time, Chemerys realized that their socialist movement had been absorbed by the interests of politicians. He remarked that their aim to change the political system instead turned into a demand for seats in Parliament (author's interview, Chemerys, Kyiv, 2008).

2004: Our Ukraine

Ukrainian politics and social relations under President Kuchma were described by Paul D'Anieri (2006) as a semi-authoritarian regime operating through a political machine of reciprocity that was particularly visible

The emergence of an actor 51

during elections. Given that Ukraine was not a fully consolidated authoritarian state, and held competitive elections, winning votes was the regime's strategy to stay in power. To do so, the regime used a system of rewards and exchanges to control the elections and to make attempts to gain the majority power in the Parliament. The 2004 Ukrainian presidential election campaign was no different. The regime employed its previous coercive tactics alongside more extreme measures of partisan politics, such as media bias, media censorship, negative political ads, and overt harassment of journalists (D'Anieri, 2006, p. 233; IMI Official News, 10/12/2004; Pavlyuk, 2005, p. 254). These were some examples of political strategies used by the incumbent Kuchma to assure that the pro-government candidate, Viktor Yanukovych, representing the Party of Regions, got elected president. Yanukovych was the acting Prime Minister and former Governor of Donetsk from the Eastern region. He had a colored past with a criminal record, and was known to be an unpolished speaker with his usage of street slang. Among the public, an opinion circulated that Yanukovych did not measure up as a presidential candidate; the people perceived him as an unacceptable choice (D'Anieri, 2006, p. 240). The regime's target was the opposition presidential candidate Viktor Yushchenko, the former Prime Minister under Kuchma and previous director of the National Bank. Yushchenko had popular appeal; he signified to the public "a new image of a politician: energetic, professional, and Western-looking" (Tudoroiu, 2007, p. 327). He ran on a political platform of change, including vowing "...to draw Ukraine closer to Europe, [and] to fight corruption" (Harasymiw, 2005, p. 207).

The administration used the media to represent Yushchenko as "a radical nationalist and fascist, an agent of the United States" (Harasymiw, 2005, p. 207). This effort was unsuccessful. Kuchma's regime realized that it was no easy feat to diminish Yushchenko's popularity, and instead resorted to extraordinary means and made an attempt on Yushchenko's life. Yushchenko suffered dioxin poisoning and disfigurement following a dinner with the director of the Ukrainian Security Service (Tudoroiu, 2007, p. 328). The regime denied any wrongdoings in Yushchenko's poisoning. In his political rhetoric, Yushchenko was quoted as saying, "...you will not poison us, you will not destroy us" (Sumar, 2004), clearly implying that the regime was responsible for his previous poisoning. One repercussion of Yushchenko's poisoning was that it had a positive effect on gaining public sympathy, which was reflected in the first round of elections, where Yushchenko gained the lead with 39.9 percent of the vote, compared to Yanukovych's 39.3 percent. On 21 November, the run-off election was observed by international observers corroborated by conflicting results of national exit polls that declared massive vote fraud, with the election commission's declaration of Yanukovych's victory with 49.5 of the vote to Yushchenko's 46.6 percent (Tudoroiu, 2007, p. 328; Harasymiw, 2005, p. 208). The civic NGO, Committee of Voters of Ukraine, observing the presidential elections with over 10,000 volunteers, reported violations in election registers and voter list data ("Report of," 2005).

52 *The emergence of an actor*

The implausible increase in Yanukovych votes totaling "three-quarters of a million" was linked to voting irregularities from Yanukovych's region of Donetsk that resulted in his 2.9 percent lead in votes, which suggested voter fraud (Arel, 2005, p. 2).

This brought out hundreds of thousands to the streets of Kyiv and in the regions of Ukraine to demonstrate against the election fraud in what became the Orange Revolution. Parliament passed a resolution to invalidate the election results of 21 November (Tudoroiu, 2007, p. 328; Harasymiw, 2005, p. 209). On 25 November, the Supreme Court announced that the results were not valid until they heard Yushchenko's appeal. On 26 November, 15 members of the CEC removed their signatures from the official results of the presidential election. On the same day, closed-door negotiations took place with Yanukovych and Yushchenko. In attendance were President Leonid Kuchma, European Union Javier Solana, Polish president Aleksander Kwasniewski, Lithuanian President Valdas Adamkus, and Boris Gryzlow, Russian Parliament speaker (Newsletter, 27/11/04). On 3 December, the Supreme Court rendered the vote invalid due to election violations and ordered a repeat vote of the second round re-run for 26 December (Newsletter, 12/6/04). Yushchenko won the vote with 52 percent and was elected Ukrainian president and inaugurated on 20 January 2005 (Tudoroiu, 2007, p. 328).

Yushchenko's campaign strategy for mobilization

Taras Stetskiv, deputy of Parliament, "Our Ukraine," was responsible for creating a mobilization strategy for Yushchenko's campaign. In the headquarters of "Our Ukraine," they had created a special structure—a department for mass demonstrations coordination—and Stetskiv was appointed the leader of this department. The decision-making process shifted from taking place in the headquarters to taking place in the regional offices. Stetskiv remembered that it was well-organized, and the system worked because they were motivated and convinced that they were doing a good deed by bringing Yushchenko to power. There were two main objectives of their mass mobilization plan: the first was to train young activists to take charge of protest actions and the second, to create a plan for citizen mobilization on the streets to defend voting rights in the event of election fraud (Diuk, 2006). The strategic plan for revolution was prepared a year and a half in advance of the 2004 presidential elections. The goal was to make people believe that mass demonstrations would succeed (author's interview, Stetskiv, 2008). In the pre-election phase, Stetskiv held somewhere between 10 or 20 training seminars for at least 5,000 activists that participated in these seminars. During the training, Stetskiv explained to the activists the mistakes they made in the UWK protests and lessons learned from the experience. He taught them how to avoid their mistakes in the future, and gave them information about how to participate in

The emergence of an actor   53

and organize mass demonstrations. They also adapted, as examples, the patterns of revolution from Yugoslavia, Serbia, and Georgia to specific Ukrainian conditions. They realized that they needed to use these examples and multiply by 10 to win; they succeeded, since over 1 million gathered on the Maidan. The colored revolutions were influential factors that the government should not have taken for granted in the view of Stetskiv (Ibid., 2008).

Stetskiv was responsible for the Student Wave campaign and the Yellow Pora's activists, who numbered around 15,000 activists ready for the action from the very first day. They held several student demonstrations, and their main contribution was the work to mobilize students in universities in Kyiv. On the first day of revolution, they organized student strikes in practically all the universities in Kyiv. Their tactics applied a method of rise and fall in waves to gather supporters to Yushchenko's campaign. They started small with political events attracting 10,000 to 20,000 people to grow larger on 3 July 2004 with the official launch of Yushchenko's campaign proclaiming him as the "people's president" at Spivoche Pole in Kyiv with 50,000 participants. It was among the largest gathering for a political candidate in Kyiv's contemporary history (Woronowycz, August 15, 2004). Other strategies of rising tide were applied to demonstrations in small towns and then in big cities. Stetskiv described it as a heartbeat method that functioned to move and rock in order to increase the empowerment of people. Stetskiv used these political events to teach people to come onto the streets and speak out while blocking the state institutions. They created mass demonstrations on a rising scale, and afterwards they started to bring people from different regions to make more demonstrations involving more people. He admitted that the majority of people who were coming to participate in the demonstrations were self-oriented and came on their own. The main contribution to the pre-mobilization stage was aided by the efforts of Stetskiv and those student groups working with him. Their major achievement was to raise people's spirits. Once accomplished, they were able to stage events and choose the orange color as a symbol for the campaign. The most important contribution, in Stetskiv's point of view, was that their actions trained people on how to raise their voices. His training had resulted in a victory (author's interview, Stetskiv, 2008).

Following the launch of the the second phase to begin the Orange Revolution, strategists in the Yushchenko camp were focused on taking power, and to enable that Yushchenko became president. However, unlike in the UWK movement that failed due to violent tactics against the state, Stetskiv recalled that they were mindful in their strategy of refusing physical violence in their planned struggle. Instead, they chose collective protest actions of mass demonstrations and the blocking of state administration buildings to paralyze the functioning of the government. They were not motivated by hatred to the State, rather a political dislike of Kuchma and his supporters represented in state institutions (Ibid., 2008).

54 *The emergence of an actor*

Protesting the election fraud

The Yellow Pora's ("It's Time!") informational and educational campaign launched in April 2004 as part of the "Wave of Freedom" program. It featured in its leadership Vladyslav Kaskiv from the coalition "Freedom of Choice," and Taras Stetskiv, member of "Our Ukraine" campaign as Yellow Pora's coordinators. Overall, they had a "high-profiled leadership and structured membership, in favor of local initiatives and central coordinators, relying on veterans of the earlier protests to recruit like-minded people" (Morgan, 2004; Vilkos, 2004; Bandera, 2006, pp. 34–5). Their group functioned more like a movement than an organization (CIUS Press Release). The Yellow Pora civic campaign built a nationwide network of young people as recruits, totaling approximately 9,000 registered mobile volunteers. It began as a politically independent civic campaign (Bezverkha, 2004b). Their stated goals from a press release were to "assert the democratic development of Ukrainian society, to reinforce the reform process, to contribute to transparency of political process and power structures, and to highlight the importance of Ukraine's Euro-Atlantic integration" (Ibid., 2004b).

Yellow Pora became a "forum for activists and leaders of the student movement of the early 90s" for them to unite in protest. They were self-described as "...the product of our time. The new post-Soviet, post-Communist generation...essentially, uniform, with similar principles, approaches, corporate culture, shared values, common interests and business aspirations" (Kaskiv, 2006). The activists were driven to change the socio-political conditions of average Ukrainians that were "characterized by authoritarianism, and a systematic oppression of basic rights and freedoms" (Newsletter, 31/08/04). The 2004 presidential elections for the Ukrainian society presented an opportunity to make a democratic choice through fair and free elections (Newsletter, 31/08/04). The pre-election campaign's activities aimed to increase young citizens' participation in the presidential elections by providing information to educate young voters on how to protect their rights (Bezverkha, 2004). On 16 September, Yellow Pora's civic campaign announced that 10,000 of its members would participate in the observation of the first and second rounds of the presidential elections (Newsletter, 26/9/2004). The planned civic initiatives for the elections were to "educate voters, monitor pre-election campaigns and electoral process, mobilize citizens to participate in the elections, and watch the legitimacy of their results" (Bezverkhna, 2005). To reach the young people, Yellow Pora incorporated creative methods of political performances used to draw their attention to current issues related to the elections. To further illustrate this point, on 4 October, Yellow Pora organized a collective action named "An egg is not a hard metal object!" for their activists to perform in front of the Council of Ministers Building in Kyiv. It was a theatrical performance called "Traveling Egg" that was meant to demonstrate how Yanukovych was manipulating the public, and had overblown attention to the incident that occurred on 24 September. He collapsed after

The emergence of an actor 55

being hit by an egg thrown by a student in Ivano-Frankivsk while campaigning; he had hoped to exploit media attention to obtain public sympathy as Yushchenko had following his dioxin poisoning (Newsletter, 10/8/04).

Yellow Pora's grassroots activity also drew the increased attention of the authorities who started to closely monitor them. By September, more than 50 activists were arrested in different regions of Ukraine, and 25 cases of student repressions from their universities were recorded since the start of their campaign. The regime's hostility to their campaign resonated even in the Parliament, to quote from Yellow Pora's newsletter the deputy, Ihor Shurma of the Social Democrats (United) party: "tell me who will react to the distribution of leaflets among students, leaflets of that civil campaign PORA, to the wearing of yellow t-shirts. They call for actions of civil protest, taking as their example Georgia, Serbia, and Belarus. The office of the General Prosecutor has to react to that immediately..." (Newsletter, 31/08/04).

More repressions in terms of searches, arrests, and harassment were escalated on activists from National University of Kyiv-Mohyla Academy on 17 October 2004. In addition, on 22 October, Myhailo Svystovych, Yellow Pora's coordinator and the founder of the Maidan website, a central network of exchange for civic activists (it had over tens of millions of site views a month and a "free forum" for event information on 2004 presidential elections, online discussions with politicians). His apartment was searched by special police forces of SBU National Security Services looking for explosives. Criminal charges were filed against Pora for terrorism and possession of illegal weapons (Newsletter, 26/10/04; PORA website, 19/10/04). This reached the attention of Amnesty International, which on 25 October expressed "concern about recent reports that activists of the Yellow Pora's campaign for voter information and education had been illegally arrested and prevented from expressing their opinions," and also pleaded to the government for release of its activists (Newsletter, 30/10/04).

During the elections, Yellow Pora "distributed more than 70 million copies of printed materials, directly communicated with 25 million Ukrainians, held more than 750 regional pickets and public events, and created the website www.pora.org.ua which became the 5th most popular web site in Ukraine" (PORA website, 19/04/05). Following the first round of elections, on 1 November, Yellow Pora civic campaign organized a mass demonstration of students nationwide of nonviolent resistance on Kyiv's Independence Square against voting irregularities that took place, and on 2 November, 3,000 students gathered in a student rally at Kyiv's Kontraktova Plosha near the university Kyiv Mohyla Academy with the theme "Do not let them steal your victory!" co-organized by Yellow Pora and two other student civic initiatives called "Clean Ukraine" and "Student Wave" (Newsletter, 2/11/04; Newsletter, 15/10/04). On 4 November, Yellow Pora activists gathered at the Central Elections Committee to enact a satirical performance entitled "Great Laundry" which entailed volunteers demonstrating public voting by

56 *The emergence of an actor*

submitting their ballots into a washing machine. The ballots in their sketch represented the CEC and "how the electoral process launders 'people's mistakes'" (Newsletter, 11/10/04). Yellow Pora decided between the first and second rounds to cooperate through shared agreement on collective actions with Yushchenko's "Our Ukraine" since they knew that the regime would abuse its power to manipulate the votes in favor of Yanukovych (author's interview, Kutsenko, 2008). They cooperated with the opposition based on shared values for fair elections and also were "Our Ukraine" deputies to call upon for help when their activists' apartment had been raided by police (Vilkos, 2004).

As a response to the large-scale vote rigging, in Kyiv, on 22 November, orange-clad supporters of Yushchenko gathered on Kyiv's Maidan from the regions of Ukraine. Yellow Pora's activists were first responders on the main square. There were two tent cities with 136 tents, one on the main square and the other encampment occupied by Yellow Pora was the tent city off the square on nearby Khreshchatyk Street, inhabited with young people under the age of 25 ("Tents on," 22 November 2004). They were well-organized, and newspapers reported the following about their logistics know-how:

> within minutes they pitched tents, posted unarmed sentries, and produced mounds of food and winter clothing. Within hours they set up field kitchens and medical aid stations, circulated broadsheets outlining details of disobedience and urging the police not to shoot, and passed out a seemingly endless supply of posters.
>
> (Chivers, 28/11/04)

The tent camps on Maidan—called "territory of freedom" by Yellow Pora activists—quickly grew to 2,000 tents with over 7,000 people living there from the universities and all regions, media, and NGOs (Newsletter, 27/11/04). Yellow Pora's tent city would grow to 1,546 tents with 15,000 people (PORA website, 19/04/05). The protesters on the main square were described as students, intellectuals, West-oriented citizens of cities, war veterans, professionals, some police, and retired people (Chivers, 28/11/04). The local community from Kyiv supported the activists with donations of food, drink, and clothing. The total participants in the 17-day protest numbered over 700,000 (Newsletter, 27/11/04). Yellow Pora also contributed to blocking access to the Presidential Administration buildings, Parliament (Verkhovna Rada), and Kuchma's residence outside Kyiv. Concerning the latter, they felt its presence contributed to conditions for Kuchma's regime to surrender (PORA website, 19/04/05).

2013–2014 Euromaidan protests

November's 2013 peaceful and nonviolent European movement, organized first by students, recalling the Orange Revolution and people power (Karatnycky, 2005) strength in numbers, was a protest against the

The emergence of an actor   57

government's failure under pressure from Russia ("Accord," 2013) to sign a trade accord with the EU ("Ukraine's Black," 2014). The protest movement in Ukraine evolved into a political crisis, partially resulting from the strategy chosen by political leaders in the regime to maintain its stronghold ("Birth of," 2013) and on the part of the opposition in their bittersweet quest for regime change ("A Kiev," 2014). Beginning in January 2014, it was clear that the revival of protest actions had signaled a new phase in the movement ("Signs of," 2013; "Ukraine protests," 2014). The once proclaimed apolitical movement had been taken over by opposition parties with competing collective strategies of action (such as nonviolence/violence, all or nothing approach to negotiations, and/or forced takeovers of centers of power-regional ministries ("Ukraine: en," 2014) to achieve their shared goals, namely, of regime change, amnesty for activists imprisoned, repeal of anti-protest laws, and the signing of a trade agreement with the EU ("Defiant Ukraine," 2014).

The opposing collective action strategies used by the opposition revealed power limits in its use of street protests as a bargaining tool with the authorities, in contrast to the Orange Revolution ("Le president," 2014; Emeran, 2011). In 2004, the massive street protests worked to pressure both candidates into a roundtable discussion with Western leaders to negotiate the outcome, which led to a cancellation of the second round vote by the Ukrainian Parliament and a revote of the second round vote on 26 December 2004. By contrast, in the Euromaidan, the usurping of the people power movement by the opposition political groups had severe outcomes. This produced a change in the authorities' response to the mass movement that they considered as a threat to their power. It also provided justification for them to arrest, detain, and harass activists tied to the movement. Additionally, it gave them cause to clear out the occupied spaces of Kyiv's Independent Square, albeit in a violent manner, and to impose repressive sanctions, including the dismantling of protest camps and controversial rolling back of the civil liberties of free speech and the right to street protests ("En Ukraine, la," 2014; "L'Ukraine," 2014). This law was canceled by the Parliament and replaced by a conditional law to offer amnesty to those activists imprisoned, if the opposition ended the street protests and occupation of ministries within 15 days. This offer was rejected ("Back from," 2014; "A Kiev, des," 2013). The authorities' authoritarian strategies to end protests with the use of force ("Activist's torture," 2014; "Ukraine protests," 2014) had the opposite effect of escalating the violence, especially among some members of the opposition (among them the extreme far-right) (Shekhovtsov, 2014). These individuals were now willing to justify the use of violence to achieve their aim of opposing the government's brutality against protesters ("Clashes in," 2014). It also had the unintended consequence of generating more attention from international communities and world leaders from, for example, the U.S. and EU, and these world leaders were concerned about the Ukrainian government's forceful response to the street protests ("Ukraine Protesters," 2013).

58 *The emergence of an actor*

While the authorities did not like being exposed to external pressure, it was being imposed on them from the West ("En temps, 2014; "Ukraine leader," 2014; "Yanukovych tells," 2014), the government's legitimacy rests largely with oligarchs in South and East Ukraine ("En Ukraine, le clan," 2014). The regime shifted strategies to pursue internal negotiations with the two key leaders representing different opposition parties, Arseniy Yatensnyuk (Fatherland Party) and Vitali Klitschko (Udar Party). The government offered Yatensnyuk the position of Prime Minister, and Klitschko the position of Deputy Prime Minister. They both declined ("Ukraine, le geste," 2014; "Ukraine opposition," 2014). The attempts at a negotiated resolution failed; the proposals made by the authorities to end the conflict did not meet satisfactory conditions for the opposition or the protesters to accept. There were defections in the government, most noteworthy, the resignation of the Prime Minister, Mykola Azarov and the Ukrainian Army's announcement that it would not intervene unless Parliament directed it to do so ("Ukraine opposition rejects," 2014). The prolonged political instability had serious consequences on Russia's offer to buy Ukraine debt ("Ukrainian standoff," 2014), which was deferred, pending the formation of a new government ("Ukraine President," 2014). In the meantime, the opposition forced a political stalemate, unwilling to accept a compromise to share power with the president. At the same time, the movement activists pursued a strategy of seizure and occupation of municipal buildings, which gathered strength in the regions of Ukraine ("Ukraine protests spread," 2014).

The European Union chief, Catherine Ashton, failed in an attempt to end Ukraine's political crisis on 5 February ("En Ukraine," 2014; "Russia offers," 2014). She met with opposition leaders to offer financial support, once the crisis was over. Later that month, on 17 February, the opposition was offered an amnesty deal for those protesters imprisoned. These activists would be released from prison when the protesters evacuated Kyiv's city hall, a site of occupation ("Europe-Ukraine," 2014). The fighting increased on 18 February with over 25 protesters dead, and president Yanukovych responded by blaming the opposition for the protester's death. He met with the opposition leaders to request they remove the protesters from Kyiv's Maidan. The following day, Yanukovych ordered an anti-terrorist operation. The riot police stormed the tent camps to gain control over the square, which escalated the violence. The authorities had the authority to use snipers and live ammunition on the protesters. In 72 hours of fighting, the result was a death toll of 100 and 562 wounded. This resulted in defections in Parliament from the pro-government side. They voted to remove the Interior Ministry troops from the central square and to ban the use of live weapons on the protesters. The Parliament had removed Yanukovych's right to call a state of emergency. On 22 February, Parliament voted to remove Yanukovych and approved a new call for elections, while Yanukovych fled to Kharkiv in Eastern Ukraine ("Ukraine Crisis," 2014). On 23 February,

The emergence of an actor 59

the Parliament speaker Aleksandr Turchynov was voted as interim president to Ukraine ("Ukraine speaker," 2014).

This chapter introduced the socio-historical conditions from which individuals arose into three waves of anti-government protests. The individual narratives described a context of struggle, contradictions, and conditions for renewed oppositional activity and protest. The outcome would impact the process of politicalization of citizens who would become involved in activism for social change. The following chapter will continue an investigation into the processes that influenced five young people to become political and join three protest movements, beginning with the "Ukraine without Kuchma" and youth movement "For Truth" described above.

Note

1 Moroz was the politician who publicly released secret tapes implicating Kuchma in ordering the disappearance of Gondadze (Kuzio, 2005).

Bibliography

Accord d'association: l'UE propose à l'Ukraine une feuille de route. Retrieved February 2, 2014, from http://www.lemonde.fr/europe/article/2013/12/12/accord-d-association-l-ue-propose-a-l-ukraine-une-feuille-de-route_4333684_3214.html.

Activist's torture shines harsh new spotlight on embattled Ukraine – CNN.com. Retrieved February 2, 2014, from http://edition.cnn.com/2014/01/31/world/europe/ukraine-unrest/index.html.

A Kiev, des manifestants racontent la brutalité policière. Retrieved February 3, 2014, from http://www.lemonde.fr/europe/article/2014/01/23/a-kiev-des-manifestants-racontent-la-brutalite-policiere_4353672_3214.html.

A Kiev, les révoltés de Maïdan s'attendent au pire. Le Monde.fr. Retrieved February 2, 2014, from http://www.lemonde.fr/europe/article/2013/12/14/les-revoltes-du-maydan-s-attendent-au-pire_4334542_3214.html.

Arel, D. (2005). The "Orange Revolution" Analysis and Implications of the 2004 Presidential Election in Ukraine. Third Annual Stasiuk-Cambridge Lecture on Contemporary Ukraine. Cambridge University. February 25, 2005.

Author's interview, Serhiy Kutsensko, September 25, 2008, Kyiv.

Author's interview, Taras Stetskiv, Our Ukraine, November 19, 2008, Kyiv.

Author's interview, Volodymyr Chemerys, founder NGO Institute of Economic and Social Problems "Respublika," October 7, 2008, Kyiv.

Bachynsky, Y. (2000, December 24). Protesters erect tent towns in Kyiv as Gongadze scandal continues. Retrieved June 28, 2007, from http://www.ukrweekly.com/Archive/2000/52003.shtml.

Back from the brink in Ukraine? – Al Jazeera English. Retrieved February 2, 2014, from http://m.aljazeera.com/story/20141299141932862.

Bandera, S. (2006). "The role of the Internet and Ukraine's 2004 Presidential elections." Report, Development Associates (July).

BBC News – Defiant Ukraine opposition continues pro-EU rallies. Retrieved February 2, 2014, from http://www.bbc.co.uk/news/world-europe-25486887.

60   *The emergence of an actor*

BBC News – Russia offers Ukraine major economic assistance. Retrieved February 2, 2014, from http://www.bbc.co.uk/news/world-europe-25411118.

BBC News – Ukraine President Viktor Yanukovych defiant amid turmoil. Retrieved February 2, 2014, from http://www.bbc.co.uk/news/world-europe-25966962.

BBC News – Ukraine protests spread into Russia-influenced east. Retrieved February 2, 2014, from http://www.bbc.co.uk/news/world-europe-25905031.

BBC News – Yanukovych tells West to keep out of Ukraine crisis. Retrieved February 2, 2014, from http://www.bbc.co.uk/news/world-europe-25423808.

Bennett, W. L., & Segerberg, A. (2012). "The Logic of Connective Action." *Information, Communication & Society, 15*(5), 739–768.

Bezverkha, A. (2004). (Issue #1, 31 August). "Civil Society and the Presidential Elections in Ukraine 2004." Newsletter "Times of Change" www.pora.org.ua.

Bezverkha, A. (2004). (Issue #2, 26 September). "Civil Society and the Presidential Elections in Ukraine 2004." Newsletter "Times of Change" www.pora.org.ua.

Bezverkha, A. (2004). (Issue #3, 8 October) "Civil Society and the Presidential Elections in Ukraine 2004." Newsletter "Times of Change" www.pora.org.ua.

Bezverkha, A. (2004). (Issue #4, 15 October). "Civil Society and the Presidential Elections in Ukraine 2004." Newsletter "Times of Change" www.pora.org.ua.

Bezverkha, A. (2004). (Issue #6, 26 October). "Civil Society and the Presidential Elections in Ukraine 2004." Newsletter "Times of Change" www.pora.org.ua.

Bezverkha, A. (2004). (Issue #7, 30 October). "Civil Society and the Presidential Elections in Ukraine 2004." Newsletter "Times of Change" www.pora.org.ua.

Bezverkha, A. (2004). (Issue #8, 2 November). "Civil Society and the Presidential Elections in Ukraine 2004." Newsletter "Times of Change" www.pora.org.ua.

Bezverkha, A. (2004). (Issue #9, 10 November). "Civil Society and the Presidential Elections in Ukraine 2004." Newsletter "Times of Change" www.pora.org.ua.

Bezverkha, A. (2004). (Issue #11, 27 November). "Civil Society and the Presidential Elections in Ukraine 2004." Newsletter "Times of Change" www.pora.org.ua.

Bezverkha, A. (2004). (Issue #12, 6 December). "Civil Society and the Presidential Elections in Ukraine 2004." Newsletter "Times of Change" www.pora.org.ua.

Bezverkha, A. (2004b). Pora–It's Time. National, Information, Education, and Mobilization Campaign. Pora Newsletter. http://trends.gmfus.org/doc/PORA%20Newsletter.pdf.

Chernobyl shut down for good. (2000, December 15). Retrieved December 1, 2015, from http://news.bbc.co.uk/2/hi/europe/1071344.stm.

Chivers, C. (2004, November 28). Youth Movement Underlies the Opposition in Ukraine. Retrieved December 1, 2015, from http://www.nytimes.com/2004/11/28/world/europe/youth-movement-underlies-the-opposition-in-ukraine.html?_r=0.

CIUS Press Release. (2005, April 21). PORA Coordinator, Vladyslav Kaskiv, Speaks in Edmonton on the Invitation of CIUS (Canadian Institute of Ukrainian Studies).

Clashes in Kiev after protest ban. (2014, January 19) – BBC News. Retrieved February 2, 2014, from http://www.bbc.co.uk/news/world-europe-25798320.

D'anieri, P. (2006). "Explaining the Success and Failure of Post-communist Revolutions." *Communist and Post-Communist Studies, 39*, 331–350.

Diuk, N. (2006). "The Triumph of Civil Society." *Revolution in Orange* (A. Aslund & M. McFaul, Eds.). Washington, DC: Carnegie Endowment, pp. 69–83.

Emeran, C. (2011). "Transforming Opposition Networks into a Movement: Case Studies from Ukraine's Independence Movement to the 2004 Presidential Elections." UMI/ProQuest.

En temps de crise, Ianoukovitch veut agir comme Poutine. Le Monde.fr. Retrieved February 2, 2014, from http://www.lemonde.fr/europe/article/2014/01/23/en-temps-de-crise-ianoukovitch-veut-agir-comme-poutine_4353545_3214.html.

En Ukraine, Ashton s'entretient avec les deux camps. (2014, February 5). Retrieved December 1, 2015, from http://www.lemonde.fr/europe/article/2014/02/05/ashton-rencontre-le-president-ukrainien-somme-de-mettre-fin-a-la-dictature_4360241_3214.html.

En Ukraine, la loi restreignant les manifestations promulguée. Retrieved February 2, 2014, from http://www.lemonde.fr/europe/article/2014/01/17/ukraine-les-lois-restreignant-les-manifestations-critiquees_4350233_3214.html.

En Ukraine, le clan Ianoukovitch se porte bien. Retrieved February 2, 2014, from http://www.lemonde.fr/europe/article/2013/12/11/ukraine-la-famille-se-porte-bien_3529274_3214.html.

Europe-Ukraine protesters evacuate Kiev City Hall. (2014, February 16). Retrieved December 1, 2015, from http://m.france24.com/en/20140216-ukraine-protesters-evacuate-kiev-city-hall?ns_campaign=editorial&ns_source=twitter&ns_mchannel=reseaux_sociaux&ns_fee=0&ns_linkname=20140216_ukraine_protesters_evacuate_kiev_city_hall.

Harasymiw, B. (2005). "Elections in Post-Communist Ukraine, 1994–2004: An Overview." *Canadian Slavonic Papers*, 47(3–4), 191–239.

IMI Official News. (2004, September–October). Digest of Freedom of Expression-Related Developments in Ukraine. Retrieved June 5, 2006, from http://eng.imi.org.ua/?id=read&n=124&cy=2004&m=thm.

Jasper, J. (1997). *The art of moral protest culture, biography, and creativity in social movements*. Chicago, IL: University of Chicago Press.

Karatnycky, A. (2005). "Ukraine's Orange Revolution." *Foreign Affairs, 84*, 35–52.

Kaskiv, V. (2006, March 4). The Goals of Parties that Formed Orange Coalition are Different. Civic Party "Pora." Retrieved December 6, 2015, from http://pora.org.ua/eng.

Kuzio, T. (2005). "The Opposition's Road to Success." *Journal of Democracy, 16*(2), 117–130.

Le président Ianoukovitch se joue des revendications de la rue. Retrieved February 2, 2014, from http://www.lemonde.fr/europe/article/2013/12/15/le-president-ianoukovitch-se-joue-des-revendications-de-la-rue_4334617_3214.html.

Lichterman, P. (1996). *The search for political community: American activists reinventing commitment*. Cambridge: Cambridge University Press.

L'Ukraine vote une loi draconienne contre les manifestations. Retrieved February 2, 2014, from http://www.lemonde.fr/europe/article/2014/01/16/le-parlement-ukrainien-vote-une-loi-contre-les-manifestations_4349624_3214.html.

Mann, J., & Dougherty, J. (2001, March 2). One Dead Man, One Defiant Leader In Ukraine. Retrieved September 6, 2007, from http://www.cnn.com/TRANSCRIPTS/0103/02/i_ins.00.html.

Morgan, M. (2004, December 23). Analysis: Ukraine's youths rise up. Retrieved December 1, 2015, from http://news.bbc.co.uk/2/hi/europe/4122485.stm.

Pavlyuk, L. (2005, September-December). "Extreme Rhetoric in the 2004 Presidential Campaign: Images of Geopolitical and Regional Division." *Canadian Slavonic Papers*, pp. 293–316.

Pora – civic campaign. (2004, October 19). Of the civic campaign Pora. Retrieved May 6, 2005, from http://pora.org.ua/en/index2.php?option=content&task=view&id=302&pop=1&page=0.

62 *The emergence of an actor*

Pora – civic campaign (2005, April 19). "Pora before and during the orange revolution." Retrieved May 13, 2005, from http://pora.org.ua/en/index2.php?option=content&task=view&id=776&pop=1&page=0.

Report of the Commitee of Voters of Ukraine on results of work during the presidential elections in Ukraine in 2004. (2005). Retrieved February 24, 2006, from http://www.cvu.org.ua/?menu=yreport&po=doc&doc_type=654&lang=eng&date_.

Shekhovtso, Anton. blog: What the West should know about the Euromaidan's far right element. Retrieved February 2, 2014, from http://anton-shekhovtsov.blogspot.fr/2014/01/what-west-should-know-about-euromaidans.html.

Signs of Momentum Shifting to Protesters in Ukraine – NYTimes.com. Retrieved February 2, 2014, from http://www.nytimes.com/2013/12/15/world/europe/struggle-in-ukraine-reflects-a-larger-battle-between-europe-and-russia.html?smid=tw-share&_r=1&.

Sumar, V. (2004, 20 September). IMI Official News. "I want to tell to authorities-you will not poison us."

"Tents on the Square." *Ukrainska Pravda*. 22 November 2004. Translated by The Ukrainian List (UKL) team.

The birth of the nation? (2013, December). The Economist. Retrieved February 2, 2014, from http://www.economist.com/news/europe/21591642-viktor-yanukovychs-botched-crackdown-protests-maidan-seemed-defy-common sense?fsrc=scn/tw_ec/the_birth_of_the_nation_.

Touraine, A. (2000) "A Method for Studying Social Actors." *Journal of World-Systems Research*, 6(3), 900–918.

Tudoroiu, T. (2007). "Rose, Orange, and Tulip: The Failed Post-Soviet Revolutions." *Communist and Post-Communist Studies*, 40, 315–342.

Ukraine crisis: Police storm main Kiev "Maidan" protest camp – BBC News. (2014, February 19). Retrieved December 1, 2015, from http://www.bbc.com/news/world-europe-26249330.

Ukraine's Black Saturday – openDemocracy. Retrieved February 2, 2014, from http://www.opendemocracy.net/od-russia/andrey-chernikov/ukraines-black-saturday.

Ukraine: en province, des bâtiments gouvernementaux pris d'assaut. Retrieved February 2, 2014, from http://www.lemonde.fr/europe/video/2014/01/24/ukraine-en-province-des-batiments-gouvernementaux-pris-d-assaut_4354136_3214.html.

Ukraine leader intends to sign EU deal, diplomat says – CNN.com. Retrieved February 2, 2014, from http://edition.cnn.com/2013/12/12/world/europe/ukraine-protests/index.html.

Ukraine: le geste du président Ianoukovitch, cadeau empoisonné pour l'opposition. Retrieved February 3, 2014, from http://www.lemonde.fr/europe/article/2014/01/26/ukraine-le-geste-du-president-ianoukovitch-cadeau-empoisonne-pour-l-opposition_4354637_3214.html.

Ukraine opposition rejects president's offer; protester mourned – CNN.com. Retrieved February 2, 2014, from http://www.cnn.com/2014/01/26/world/europe/ukraine-protests/index.html.

Ukraine opposition rejects offers. (2014, January 26) – BBC News. Retrieved February 2, 2014, from http://www.bbc.co.uk/news/world-europe-25900267.

Ukraine's Orange Revolution – Foreign Affairs. Retrieved February 2, 2014, from http://www.foreignaffairs.com/articles/60620/adrian-karatnycky/ukraines-orange-revolution.

The emergence of an actor 63

Ukraine: Speaker Oleksandr Turchynov named interim president – BBC News. (2014, February 23). Retrieved December 1, 2015, from http://www.bbc.com/news/world-europe-26312008.

Ukraine Protesters Reclaim City Center After Police Raids – Bloomberg. Retrieved February 2, 2014, from http://www.bloomberg.com/news/2013-12-11/ukraine-riot-police-flood-anti-government-protest-camp.html.

Ukraine Protests: Anti-Government Demonstrators Clash With Police In Kiev (VIDEO). *Huffington Post*. Retrieved February 2, 2014, from http://www.huffingtonpost.com/2014/01/21/ukraine-protests_n_4635120.html?ncid=edlinkusaolp00000003.

"Ukraine Without Kuchma" protest action gains momentum (2000, December 19). Retrieved October 16, 2015, from http://www.brama.com/news/press/001219anti-kuchma-protest.html.

Ukrainian Standoff – NYTimes.com. Retrieved February 2, 2014, from http://www.nytimes.com/2014/01/23/opinion/ukrainian-standoff.html.

Vilkos, Y. (2004, November 11). "Pora: We'll Get Half a Million onto the Streets." *Kyiv Post*, *11*(45).

Woronowycz, R. (2001a, February 11). "Ukraine without Kuchma" protests intensify. Retrieved September 6, 2007, from http://www.ukrweekly.com/Archive/2001/060101.shtml.

Woronowycz, R. (2001b, February 18). Anti-Kuchma protests continue in Ukrainian capital. Retrieved September 6, 2007, from http://www.ukrweekly.com/Archive/2001/070101.shtml.

Woronowycz, R. (2004, August 15). ROUGH DRAFT: The Chestnut Revolution (08/15/04). Retrieved December 1, 2015, from http://www.ukrweekly.com/old/archive/2004/330418.shtml.

Youth groups hold anti-Kuchma rally in Ukraine. (2000, December 17). Retrieved October 16, 2015, from http://www.brama.com/news/press/001216anti-kuchma-rally.html.

3 Personalized expressions of activism

The chapter focuses on introducing the five activists who will be the subjects of analysis, and their processes of political socialization and protest mobilization. Their personal accounts are retold through a descriptive method, with the intended purpose of capturing the actor's voice and point of view.

2000–2003 political mobilization: an actor's perspective

I selected the timeframe from 2000–2003 for its connection to events that politicized the five activists featured in the book. The research was set in two Ukrainian cities, Lviv (Western Ukraine) and Kyiv (the capital, in Central Ukraine). Students were primarily mobilized into the structure of the Committee "For Truth" campaign tied to the larger "Ukraine without Kuchma" (UWK) movement. For many of these young people, it was their first protest event. Their participation in these protests had the effect of transforming some of them into lifelong activists. The personal narratives of five individuals trace the origins of a youth movement and the recruitment process for young people in the movement organization of the Committee "For Truth." The participants in the UWK campaign were primarily students like the five individuals who will be introduced in this section.

We will now turn our attention to the case studies of five activists and analyze the dynamics of protest recruitment in Ukraine. The purpose of this study is for the community-at-large to begin thinking about how individuals are introduced to social movements, and how a person chooses to become a protester. We begin by discussing Andriy, a 13-year old junior high school student and activist from Lviv, Ukraine.

Andriy Shevtsiv, Lviv, Ukraine

At the early age of 13, he became involved with the anti-government Committee "For Truth," in his city of Lviv in 2000. His participation as a minor, over time, brought more risks for the movement. This was made more evident upon his arrest in a political event organized by the group in the capital of Kyiv. As he recounted his experience on 9 March 2001, "there were mass

Personalized expressions of activism 65

riots that day in Kyiv and these riot police were persecuting students at the railway station. I was detained for my political activity" (Shevtsiv, 2009). The group grew concerned about Andriy's whereabouts on that particular day and soon after, they could no longer assume the risks if it were publicly known that they had an underage minor in the movement. In order to mitigate the group's risk, he was told that they no longer needed him as an activist in the movement.

But his participation in these protests had lasting effects; it permitted Andriy to develop a political awakening. He said that his participation in Committee "For Truth" enabled him to gain a consciousness to make the decision to become committed as an activist. This was at the same time when he was also taking part in the cultural organization *Moloda Prosvita* ("Young Enlightenment") that held nightly poetry and literary events. With his release by the organizers of the Committee "For Truth," he no longer divided his time between the two groups. He was now able to devote more time to this new organization. As a participant, he was able to pursue cultural interests and to contribute his writings of poetry. In his cultural pursuits, Andriy made new acquaintances with others who were politically minded. As a result, Andriy's interest in political activism did not remain dormant for very long. At these events, Andriy met a group of young people who were interested, not only in culture and art, but also in politics. In particular, he recalled attending a poetry event and meeting, again, a young man familiar with this group. The young man approached Andriy and invited him to take part in an organized hunger strike of protest to support Viktor Yushchenko, who had been dismissed as Prime Minister by Kuchma's government (author's interview, Shevtsiv, 2009). As he recalled the encounter, Andriy shared the following: "I agreed and that night I sat on the train to Kyiv. It's how I met Volodymyr Viatrovych (who became a Pora coordinator in Kyiv's tent cities in the Orange Revolution) and a few other people with whom I would work later in Pora in 2004" (Ibid., 2009).

Moreover, this example served to demonstrate the process of recruitment on the individual level from shared social groups. In Andriy's case, the mobilization structures were from affinity groups. These processes followed recruitment theories of Bedford Snow and others, cited by Jeff Goodwin and James Jasper, that affirmed the important role of social networks for recruitment, and more importantly, its function as a "predictor of who will join" (Goodwin and Jasper, 2003, p. 54).

The next objective in the analysis was to measure the effects of personal, weak links (Granovetter) on Andriy's engagement beyond participation in a singular event. Andriy's commitment to new forms of political action could be seen in his willingness to establish a new political organization with the same activists. This was a form of reactivation that followed Doug McAdam's idea that activists could recruit people known from former protest events for new protest actions (Ibid., 2003, p. 59). In Andriy's situation, he received another invitation from Vitrovych, with whom he had participated

66 *Personalized expressions of activism*

in an earlier protest, to get involved in the formation of serious political activity. He described his recruitment into a new organization as follows: "I agreed without knowing them. I joined them in creating a student committee of *Opir Molodi* (Young Resistance, a youth association)" (author's interview, Shevtsiv, 2009). The processes at work for Andriy's recruitment into a new group were twofold, it was the result of knowing someone from past participation in shared group activities, as well as already attending a protest with them. While Andriy did not consider them friends yet—he hardly knew them, in his words—it was still sufficient for him to be recruited into new protest activity. His involvement in creating a new organization marked a period in Andriy's transformation as an activist. He gained valuable skills in terms of organizing people and political events. This experience was also self-affirming. It was "...an opportunity to educate myself, and understand what I should work for in the future" (author's interview, Shevtsiv, 2009).

This organization would become the breeding ground for future members of civic campaign Pora (2004) to meet and later form their group together. Andriy's encounters with the group, he said, "was not an accidental case, my participation was within a process that later created Pora. It involved two critical phrases, *Moloda Prosvita* (2001–2003) and 2003 *Opir Molody*" (author's interview, Shevtsiv, 2009). Andriy explained that emerging from the activists of *Moloda Prosvita*, the *Opir Molody* was an independent civic structure for Pora. Andriy said that the goal of the new group was oriented toward public political activity, as compared to *Moloda Prosvita*, which was only involved in cultural activity (author's interview, Shetsiv, 2009).

Stanislav Kutsenko, Kirovohrad, Ukraine

In our second case, Stanislav Kutsenko was a third-year undergraduate student when his interest in politics shifted towards political activism in 2003. He was active in associational life, as a member and chair of student government at his university, the National University of Kyiv Mohyla Academy. His university was founded by dissidents who supported democratic development for Ukraine. At times, the university president hosted events for politicians he knew from the opposition political parties (author's interview, Kutsenko, 2008, Kyiv). Its effects were visible on Stanislav. His university provided opportunities to introduce him to political activities in on-campus events with politicians. The university served as what Florence Passy called a "structural connection," further explained by Porta and Diani as being where "social networks create opportunities for transforming predispositions into action" (Porta and Diani, 2006, p. 119). Stanislav attended on these occasions and was surprised that these meetings were not organized for political purposes. He observed that these politicians were there to discuss other issues and to develop relationships with the students (author's interview, Kutsenko, 2008, Kyiv). At one of these events, Stanislav, like other students, made the acquaintance of one of the politicians from Yushchenko's

"Our Ukraine" political party, who would transform him into an activist the following year. This was the context where Stanislav was mobilized.

Upon his return from a summer work and study trip to the U.S. in 2004, Stanislav was contacted by the politician he met earlier and invited to chair one branch of the "Student Wave" campaign in coordination with "Our Ukraine" political party headquarters. These campaigns were meant to prepare for large-scale student mobilization to participate and vote in the 2004 presidential elections (author's interview, Kutsenko, 2008, Kyiv). Again, his experience of recruitment illustrated Passy's findings that mobilization, at times, occurred through social connections created in particular contexts (Porta and Diani, 2006, p. 124). Stanislav's experience also corroborated the findings of Donatella Della Porta and Mario Diani. They concluded that people did not only form social ties as members of organizations, and that these kinds of relations could develop among participants in other social events (Ibid., 2006, p. 117).

Andriy Kohut, Lviv, Ukraine

In the third case, Andriy Kohut's socialization into activism was connected to his participation in the youth organization of the Committee "For Truth" in 2000. He was involved in organizing anti-Kuchma protests. Over time, he and others in the group concluded that their protest activities would not produce social change, as expected. Andriy observed the negative effects of these views on activist behaviors, which curtailed any final hope of achieving success (author's interview, Kohut, 2007, Kyiv). Despite the movement's failures, Andriy continued his activism. This outcome could be explained by Porta and Diani who drew from Passy's work to explain that "sustained involvement in collective action may also be facilitated by the participation, not necessarily planned or anticipated, in events that turn out to have a powerful emotional impact...sometimes on entire collectivities, other times, on specific individuals" (Porta and Diani, 2006, pp. 121–2).

An opportunity for political organizing was granted for Andriy upon the conclusion of the "Ukraine without Kuchma" protests. Their group had caught the attention of Serbia's *Optor*, an opposition group that led protests to down Milosevic in 2000. Andriy was contacted by Serbia's *Optor* and he organized seminars for Ukrainian activists, inviting Serbia's *Optor* on two occasions, 2000–2001 and again in 2002–2003 in Lviv. The purpose was for the Serbians to share information about "...how they worked, methods, principles, and timeline history of events" (Ibid., 2007). By 2003, these seminars had produced an effect on Andriy, who had "an idea to create something similar" (Ibid., 2007). During this time, Andriy was motivated by a growing awareness that the country was headed in the wrong direction. The indicator for him was a reawakening of fear among older people of Ukraine's secret service, SBU.

68   *Personalized expressions of activism*

Andriy's participation in multiple groups enabled him to come "...into contact with their activists and supporters" (Porta and Diani, 2006, p. 131). At this time, Andriy was already involved as a member of the civic association, *Moloda Prosvita*, mentioned earlier. His role was to work on cultural projects to reawaken young people. This supported Porta's and Diani's studies on Passy's research that concluded "...participation in a movement's life consists of involvement in cultural and social activities...always with a critical edge and element of symbolic and/or political challenge to some kind of authority" (Ibid., 2006, p. 132). By fall 2003, Andriy was involved in *Opir Molodi* (Young Resistance). His political activities were formative experiences. He explained that "...it was a test for us to see what and why young people would get involved. We found youth were interested in our actions and we initiated contacts with them across Ukraine" (author's interview, Kohut, 2007, Kyiv). In sum, Andriy's activities in *Opir Molodi* had a social effect in that "they produced specific subcultural or countercultural milieus that offer[ed] both opportunities for protest activities and transformation of critical orientations" (Porta and Diani, 2006, p. 117).

Ostap Kryvydk, Lviv, Ukraine

The fourth activist chosen for analysis was Ostap Kryvydk. His path to activism differed from the previous accounts and contributes to the multiplicity of explanations for student mobilization in the period of the "Ukraine without Kuchma" protests. Ostap was a university student in Lviv when he was recruited into a new protest campaign. In his early youth, he participated as a member of a far right organization for ten years (from 1990–2000). Upon entry into the university, Ostap, soon thereafter, ended his participation in the group and, instead, as a student of political science, focused his studies on analyzing far right organizations (author's interview, Kryvdyk, 2008, Kyiv).

In Lviv, Ostap observed the anti-regime protests tied to the "Ukraine without Kuchma" protests, but did not get involved. His reason for not participating was strongly based on a personal sense of identity. He explained that "I am a political scientist and my issue is to study this and not to participate" (Ibid., 2008). Despite his initial objections, Ostap eventually got involved in the movement through his friend, a member of the Committee "For Truth." This friend invited him to attend a protest event in Kyiv. Ostap's decision to participate was strongly influenced by personal concerns. He recounted that "we wanted to make a student conference, but we had no funds at all" (Ibid., 2008). He explained that a university conference scheduled for March had been postponed due to a lack of funds and inability to send their students to Kyiv. The situation had the potential to change if Ostap accepted his friend's invitation to go to Kyiv. The protest provided Ostap an opportunity. He said, "I used that moment to meet Vitali in Kyiv and to talk about what we should do" (Ibid., 2008). Unlike the others, Ostap's recruitment to a protest event was primarily based on personal

Personalized expressions of activism 69

interests, rather than a motivation to advance the social movement goals. As he clearly stated, "...frankly speaking, I didn't believe in that. I just used them to go Kyiv" (Ibid., 2008). Ostap's invitation to protest followed recruitment theories that suggests "several stages from emphasis on individual traits to one on structural availability, and finally toward synthesis of these dimensions" (Goodwin and Jasper, 2003, p. 53).

Given the observed differences in recruitment patterns of Ostap from the others, this created an entry-point into another line of inquiry. Furthermore, it led to an examination of whether or not low interest in the political event had an impact on Ostap's subsequent participation in the movement's events. His protest experience on that first day pointed in the direction of uncertainty as to whether Ostap would remain engaged in the group's activities. In Kyiv, he was assigned to a small group to distribute flyers with messages about the murder of Gondadze and the criminal regime. His initial observations spoke of people's negative reactions to their political activity and accusations made of being paid for their work. He described the atmosphere on the scene in the following words:

> people were taking it [the leaflet] and in two meters, they were throwing it on the ground. Just throwing, throwing. I saw when we went to Kyiv Polytechnic how they treated these leaflets. Students were taking it and there was a garbage bag and it was full of leaflets. And we were saying to these people why are you doing so, there were two answers: I don't care and the second answer, we can't change anything so we shouldn't try.
> (author's interview, Kryvdyk, 2008, Kyiv)

The public's reaction mirrored his. He admitted that "as a political scientist I knew all these things, but did not believe I can change anything too. So, I suppose it was actually not a good point of view. At that moment it was mine" (Ibid., 2008). The key issues of the movement were not sufficient to mobilize the minds of the public, including that of Ostap, who was a participant distributing this information.

This perspective changed with Ostap's next experience of protest in the same group. The protest event took place in Kyiv on 9 March 2001. This event had made an impact on him and he emphasized, "was the day, as we say, which made my roof move" (Ibid., 2008). He had arrived by train to Kyiv on the day of violent clashes between the police and protesters in an event organized by the "Ukraine without Kuchma" movement at the monument to Taras Shevchenko. However, the demonstration had ended when Ostap and others from the Committee "For Truth" arrived there. He remarked that people were gathered in a meeting, and hundreds of people were shouting, "Kuchma, get out!" He and his friends were disappointed that they were not inspired by the speaker's speeches about the 1990s. The event ended at noon, and Ostap and his friends from the movement spent the reminder of the day walking around the city.

70 *Personalized expressions of activism*

In order to capture the sentiment of how Ostap was recruited into the movement as a member, the event that changed his mind about activism is described below. The outcome of the event resulted in Ostap's recruitment and assuming of a leadership role in the Committee "For Truth."

In the late afternoon, Ostap arrived at the train station in Kyiv to wait for his train. He remembered that "I came early and it was a bit cold." He wore "some symbol of the Committee 'For Truth' on me (arm band). It was a triangle and an exclamation mark" (author's interview, Kryvdyk, 2008, Kyiv). When it was time to take the escalator up for his train, someone approached him and said, "Hey you, go away" (Ibid., 2008). Ostap thought, "what a stupid guy. What is he saying?" He continued to walk when "four people [were] standing over here, and they just said to each other, 'HIM.' I was caught by hands and put near the wall" (Ibid., 2008). Ostap cried out to them,

> Hey you guys show your documents, its democracy, you can't arrest me, show me your documents. I was afraid, yep, I got afraid, completely frightened and didn't expect that to happen. They also got frightened with me shouting like a crazy man on the subway. People were just passing me by like nothing was happening.
>
> (Ibid., 2008)

When suddenly, a well-dressed man in a suit tore his armband from him. He heard the man that said it and he reacted in the following way:

> bring him to the local police room on the subway station. I started to go and didn't want to let them do so. At that moment, two people from (OMON) came, the police department of special service. So you know they have such helmets, shields, and rubber to beat people. And they entered from the exit, and one of the first thing[s] that one of the police did was beat me on my face, just directly, not stopping. He showed me what he can do. He did that so I had no trace on my face. Though he did it with a fist and he did it like that. And he said don't you dare to escape. You understand what will happen to you.
>
> (Ibid., 2008)

They took him outside the station and he spotted his friend nearby and described his reaction in the following words: "I saw Slavko standing near Buhovetsky and Taras Chornovil and shouted with all my lungs Slavko. Two [secret service] OMON guys wanted to escape with me but they couldn't bring me. They escaped and left me." (Ibid., 2008). He said, "I wasn't arrested and many were. Slavko got his bone[s] broken. He was so rapidly beaten, he got broken bones" (Ibid., 2008). He credited for his rescue, two politicians "Taras Stetskiv and Taras Chornovil that opened the car door (from the police cars) and brought our guys out" (Ibid., 2008). They returned us to the train station and Ostap felt a sense of euphoria that "we wanted to

Personalized expressions of activism 71

sing, but the conductor for the train car told us that another car is full of policemen and they are going to arrest us at some other station" (Ibid., 2008). He described the fear of police violence as the following:

> If you are in Kyiv, there are police. If they put you out on some regional station nobody will know, um, every Ukrainian man knows what happens when someone who gets into police hands. These people are roughly beaten and many becoming invalids. Many people have strong problems, serious problems with health after that.
>
> (Ibid., 2008)

The protests ended in the arrest of hundreds of young activists. He said that upon returning to Lviv that

> we were crazily afraid and angry. In response, we organized a big protest. We blocked L'viv University, and had about 3000 students participating in that action and the next day we had even more participants. Later, it started getting more organized, but we stopped acting and put more energies into building a structure.
>
> (Ibid., 2008)

It also resulted in the increase in Ostap's activism in the organization. He said that

> I was elected as the chief of the 'For Truth' group at our faculty of philosophy. It was [a] great team, I think there were some 50 people (it is not a large faculty) together with the political science and economics departments. In total, I think up to 70 people. The students were there including many we call chief of academic group, one who is responsible for keeping records of being present or not present during the periods, and to information from the students whether they are ill or not, they have to prove they were ill and not just drinking beer.
>
> (Ibid., 2008)

Ostap also took on a new role in the protest movement, training others on how to effectively communicate the movement's goals. He said, "then we started some training to deliver information to people who were in the Committee 'For Truth,' how to talk to people and to deliver our point of view" (Ibid., 2008). Ostap's involvement into the movement was linked to Jasper's concept of "moral shocks" or personal offenses that have a positive effect on participation and function as a "process of self-recruitment" that results from personal experience. As Jasper explains, "when protesters are entirely rebuffed or even violently repressed by their own government, their indignation may grow even stronger from the shock" (Goodwin and Jasper, 2003, p. 56).

72 *Personalized expressions of activism*

Volodymyr Ishchenko, Kyiv, Ukraine

The last activist I selected to analyze as a case study was Volodymyr Ishchenko. In 2000, he was an 18- or 19-year-old university student in Kyiv when he got involved in the "Ukraine without Kuchma" protests. He volunteered at the organizational structure's headquarters, housed at the NGO "Institute of Economic and Social Problems 'Respublika'" that was headed by the movement's co-founder Volodymyr Chemerys.

Shared values with the movement mobilized Volodymyr into this protest movement. He believed, with other activists, that the UWK was "a revolutionary movement to change the political system of Ukraine" (author's interview, Ishchenko, 2008, Kyiv). He shared the movement's ideology on social change. Among the ideas proposed was to transform Ukraine into a parliamentary republic to strengthen the role of parliament and weaken the president's power. Volodymyr was drawn to Chemerys's ideas published in articles that he read in 2000 and 2001. The articles spoke about how UWK protests would change the system, not just the president in power (Ibid., 2008). Volodymyr's experience followed theories on recruitment, more particularly of "self-recruitment" processes, in those cases, individuals "...actively seek out a movement or movement organization in which they can participate as opposed to being recruited by the movement itself" (Goodwin and Jasper, 2003, p. 56).

As an activist, his political activities included the distribution of leaflets and newspapers in the universities. Although, Volodymyr explained that he did not understand much of the group's strategy beyond the removal of Kuchma's regime, it did not prevent him from participating in the protest movement. Volodymyr expressed doubts about the group's strategy, "it was quite abstract and not very clear. At least for me, it was a kind of belief. We are participating in important events and we will win with truth on our side" (author's interview, Ishchenko, 2008, Kyiv). Ishchenko's shared beliefs with the movement guided his decision to take an active role in protests.

Observing the forms of Volodymyr's activism offered insight into the challenges of how to build networks of protest from university structures. Volodymyr took part in mobilizing students at the university and confronted resistance by the administration. He helped to organize a student strike and attracted a few hundred students, but it was not sustainable. As Volodymyr remarked, "we were not able to make any stable group structure [in the university] it was a failure" (Ibid., 2008). His difficulty in mobilizing students was a problem that the larger movement had confronted, but not resolved. On the whole, the UWK protests struggled for popular support of the movement. As an activist in this protest movement, Volodymyr expressed doubts about how the group should proceed. In his views: "...personally, I didn't have any clear strategy. We were waiting for some support from politicians and waiting for support from the population. We were waiting for more mass demonstrations not several thousands

Personalized expressions of activism 73

or tens of thousands or hundreds of thousands. They were not coming to us" (Ibid., 2008).

Voldymyr's experience was situational. He worked in the NGOs of the co-founder of the UWK movement. It had the effect of predisposing him and creating greater possibilities to participate, especially "if they are connected to people already involved" (Porta and Diani, 2006, p. 119).

Individual approach to activism

I will now revisit the book's problematic, namely, how did individual actors decide when to participate in political activity; and did other people play a determining role in influencing their behavior? Doug McAdam and Paulsen (1993) did a similar study on activism since, at that time, there existed little research that focused on individual decisions to enter a social movement organization. He found that most studies examined activists that had already joined a Social Movement Organization. McAdam wanted to learn, given the multiple social ties of most individuals, how one tie became determinant over all others to motivate an individual into political activism. This research goes a step further to position the individual in a different context than McAdam's social structural view. This differentiation was made to highlight unique, personal experience as a possible driver that may have provided differences in the decision-making processes, which favored more individualized reasons for joining. Furthermore, this raised other questions, such as how did individuals decide to sustain their participation beyond one political event and to make a larger commitment to greater engagement as coordinators or leaders in the protest movement? These types of decisions were personal dimensions, as recognized by Touraine and Jasper. That was the reason why these approaches were applied to the case studies. It enabled steps to further develop an understanding of individual recruitment that transforms a protester. These formative experiences had the effect of transforming the individual into an activist. These case studies demonstrated that for some actors, their participation in civic associations also played an educational role in deepening an individual's commitment to a movement beyond the level of protester. Associational life seemed to produce sociality between unknown people that became acquaintances. This was very evident in the case of Andriy Shevtsiv and his path to activism through a series of youth associations, which enabled him to find like-minded individuals interested in political activism. In turn, his friends in these civic associations were able to more easily recruit from these social groups. This type of sociability had an important role for protest recruitment. In at least one instance, it facilitated the process of placing young people with similar affinities together to support culture and politics.

For others, the mobilizing structure followed friend networks like McAdam's study. These types of personal networks oftentimes engaged

74 *Personalized expressions of activism*

apolitical young people into their first protest experience. However, mere participation, as these case studies have shown, was not always sufficient to guarantee that the individual would sustain interest and continue to participate. As was seen in the example of Ostap, the emotion of anger triggered the individual's action to get involved as a reaction against police brutality on university students, or disagreement in terms of the country's political direction. These emotions felt by young people drove them to commit to the protest cause. In one instance, it produced student solidarity and self-defense against the police forces, which drew some individuals into permanent forms of activism. Most of the activists presented above were young men who started political activity in their late teens or early 20s. This generation's political behavior was detailed in Nadia Diuk's 2003 survey of 16–34 years old, whom she described as "political catalysts of change." Her study found that young people were reacting to the political crisis that developed since Ukrainian Independence, but she concluded their political activity was not effective to reform politics (Diuk, 2012, p. 8). This was reflected in life satisfaction polls taken in 2003 and 2013 that remained stable at 47.1 percent among young people (Ibid., 2012, p. 15), which translated to more than half in this age group who were dissatisfied overall with their lives in Ukraine.

Yet, these case studies went beyond a structural determination to explain the social mobilization of young people, and found more agency in protest recruitment, following Touraine's (2000) theories on social change and individual transformation. In Touraine's approach, the social movement's actor should be examined on his own terms as an autonomous agent of social change (Touraine, 2000, p. 900). He proposed an alternative to the existing social systems structural approaches of sociology by redefining an actor as an "agent of transformation of his environment, his situation, as a creator of imaginary worlds...as [self-reflexive] actors capable of changing their environment and of reinforcing their autonomy" (Touraine, 2000, p. 901). Implied in Touraine's interpretation was the understanding—also put forth by Alberto Melucci, whose theories supported the capacity of actors to act outside of their historical situation—that, when social actors acted, it coincided with the start of social movement activity (Melucci, 1996, p. 13). This also meant that agency existed when these individuals acted outside of their socio-historical conditions. Ostap's experience highlights this transition from far right activist to intellectual, and, finally, to assuming a coordinator role in protests at the university. His experience provides an example of an individual that acted outside of his social structure. Further, the actions taken by these individuals to redefine their socially defined roles as youth, dissatisfied and passive, were necessary conditions for activism to occur. When the individuals decided to take action against the constraining social structure of Ukrainian political life, it had a transformative effect on them. These individuals became dedicated to the overall democratization movement and became permanent fixtures as young leaders in Ukrainian protests that followed in 2004 and 2014.

Bibliography

Author's interview, Andriy Kohut, Committee "For Truth," August 12, 2007, Kyiv.

Author's interview, Andriy Shevtsiv, Committee "For Truth," February 25, 2009, Lviv.

Author's interview, Ostap Kryvdyk, Committee "For Truth," September 10, 2008, Kyiv.

Author's interview, Stanislav Kutsenko, student at the National University of Kyiv Mohyla Academy, September 25, 2008, Kyiv.

Author's interview, Volodymyr Ishchenko, volunteer at NGO "Institute of Economic and Social Problems" Respublika, November 26, 2008, Kyiv.

Diuk, N. (2012). *The next generation in Russia, Ukraine, and Azerbaijan: Youth, politics, identity, and change.* Plymouth: Rowman & Littlefield.

Goodwin, J., & Jasper, J. M. (2003). *The social movements reader: Cases and concepts.* Malden, MA: Blackwell Pub.

Granovetter, M. (1983). "The Strength of Weak Ties: A Network Theory Revisited." *Sociological Theory, 1,* 201.

Jasper, J. (1997). *The art of moral protest culture, biography, and creativity in social movements.* Chicago, IL: University of Chicago Press.

Mcadam, D., & Paulsen, R. (1993). "Specifying the Relationship between Social Ties and Activism." *American Journal of Sociology, 99*(3), 640–640.

Melucci, A. (1996). *Challenging codes: Collective action in the information age.* Cambridge: Cambridge University Press.

Porta, D. D., & Diani, M. (2006). *Social movements: An introduction.* Malden, MA: Blackwell Publishing.

Touraine, A. (2000) "A Method for Studying Social Actors." *Journal of World-Systems Research,* 6(3), 900–918.

4 Professionalization of activists

This chapter builds on the last chapter on individual recruitment to further examine an individual's social movement participation and modes of action. Included in the analysis are considerations of Anthony Giddens's (1991) concept of reflexivity, drawing from Bauman's (1992) concept of individualization, which characterizes modern life and shapes an individual's action in protest movements. The actor's repeated action of participating in new protests reflects what Bennett labeled as "personalized politics" which symbolizes "individually expressive personal action frames in many protest causes" (Bennett, 2012, p. 20). The chapter undertakes an analysis, not of these frames, rather, it investigates the individualized process for frame-making or creating ideas to plan and execute new civic campaigns in newly formed groups. While I do not apply a systems approach in this research, there is knowledge to draw upon that is informative to a theory of individual action and social change. In particular, Schwandt's reconsideration of the social system theories, stemming from Buckley's (1967) concept of "complex adaptive systems," is helpful to describe social interactions in society from the perspective of "interacting and independent agents" who are "self-referential" and "reflexive" in their social environment (Schwandt, 2009, p. 128). This form of agency afforded to the actor provides cognitive conditions to explain change in the social system that occurs through a process of "coevolution" of both agent and society produced through its interactions (Ibid., 2009, p. 128). For our purposes, this phenomenon described in Schwandt's work expands our discussion on agency and social actors, which has explanatory power, as did Touraine's concept presented earlier, to explain why individual actors that act outside of their historical circumstances are capable of making social changes.

In this chapter, I observe the five activists featured in the last chapters and examine their roles in the new protest event. The contributory role of previous protest experience will be considered as the individual's professionalization as an activist occurred in this new round of protest. The majority of the activists presented are members of the Pora campaign. Due to conflicts within the group over the ownership of the Pora name and brand, it divided into two separate campaigns—one black and the other yellow, these colors

Professionalization of activists 77

also incorporated in the group's logos were also important markers to differentiate one group from the other. The Black Pora campaign is responsible for grassroots and more radical actions that mobilize young people. The Yellow Pora campaign is organized for providing information on the national and international levels regarding the presidential electoral process. Both groups cooperate together in shared protest activities in the Orange Revolution. The purpose of this section is to observe individuals and agency in protest-making activities. These experiences, I argue, would have a transformative effect on these individuals' self-recruitment 10 years later in the Euromaidan protests.

Andriy Shevtsiv

Andriy graduated from high school and entered his first year of university at the Ivan Franko National University of Lviv as a history major in fall 2004. His experience in public information in the association, *Opir Molodi* ("Youth Resistance") was the reason that he got recruited in March 2004 to do similar communications work in Lviv's Black Pora (translated as "It's Time!") campaign. In his role, Andriy was responsible for writing press releases and publicly distributing them with the objective "to spread information about us to [reach] people who wanted to join us" (author's interview, Shevtsiv, 2009, Lviv). As Stalder reflects in his analysis of Castell's social movement theory, he says, "social movements are increasingly rooted in ideas, not in places, though these ideas become effective only when embodied in (material) organizations" (Stalder, 2006, p. 83). Stalder's interpretation of social movements can be extended to understand how Black Pora's ideas have social meanings, which distinguished them from other political groups. This could be observed in the group's identity that Andriy described in the following way:

> In the information department [at Black Pora], we were fighting against Kuchmism. This is a figurative notion with which we were labeling all the problems in the country. First of all, Kuchma was accused of journalist Gongadze's murder. That is why we chose the idea of Kuchmism because he was a personification of this regime. In this way, we wanted to concentrate our efforts on the negative.
>
> (Ibid., 2009)

The group's direct engagement with their anti-government identity was publicly transmitted on 29 March 2004. On that day Black Pora launched their first protest action to post stickers with the inscription "Kuchmism—is?" in a few Ukrainian cities. The objective of this protest activity, Andriy explained was to increase the public's awareness on what Kuchmism was. The term Kuchmism was invented by the group. As a concept, it represented the group's values and was meaningful, for it oriented their protest actions.

78 *Professionalization of activists*

Kuchmism symbolized a group's self-consciousness closely connected to the problems in Ukrainian politics linked to President Kuchma. In the group's second action held on 24 May 2004, Andriy described that this protest action was to answer the question on what was Kuchmism presented in the first action. They pasted stickers in the city with the inscription: "Kuchmism is hopelessness, unemployment and corruption" (Ibid., 2009, Lviv).

The political issues presented by Black Pora's campaign had a mobilizing effect, which Andriy perceived in his work. The campaign's ideas attracted outsiders. In Andriy's interactions with them, he met people that had seen their flyers and wanted to join them. In some cases, he said, these people were from other Ukrainian regions. Andriy helped to connect them with activists working for their group in that region. In his words, "I was kind of a mediator. I was receiving a call from a person from Vinnytsya. In Vinnytsya, we had our people and gave contacts to them. This was the way mobilization took place" (Ibid., 2009, Lviv). People also contacted their campaign from the group's website (Kuchimizm.info) and reached Andriy, who managed the online recruitment of volunteers. As Andriy explained, to join the campaign, individuals with Internet access could register for their campaign by completing the online application form and activists from Black Pora would contact them. They also had other means for volunteers to reach them without Internet. For those cases, they established in the office two different phone lines that were manned 24 hours a day to allow those without Internet to call them and to participate in the campaign. He remembered receiving phone calls from the regions such as Vinnytsya, Kyiv, Kirovograd, and many other calls from Lviv. Andriy stressed that "it is important to remember that it [the phone] was one of the important channels of mobilization" (Ibid., 2009, Lviv). This example also served to first highlight Andriy's self-reflexivity on his mediator role and multiple forms of action to recruit. Secondly, it pointed out how the Internet (the group's website) was instrumental in facilitating mobilization in the regions; it supported Bennett who argued that "the pervasive use of social technology enables individuals to become important catalysts of collective action processes" (Bennett, 2012, p. 22). However, this does not discount, in this case, the preference for traditional mode of communications, the telephone, which was determined the more critical method to recruit new members.

In addition, Black Pora's diffusion of ideas also had a negative effect on attracting the government's attention, and a positive effect on gathering the support of journalists, whose published articles resulted in magnifying publicity for their campaign. This phenomenon represents an instance of social and political conflict. Beck described social and political conflict as where "political involvement is increasing at the microcosmic level and subpolitical society is governed from below in more issues and field of actions" (Beck and Beck-Gernsheim, 2002, p. 29). In September 2004, Andriy was promoted to the position of coordinator of the Black Pora office in Lviv. In his role, he confronted the issues with the occasional case of government

Professionalization of activists 79

repression of their activists when their group was not well-known. However, when Black Pora became more popular, Andriy said it became increasingly clear that the government targeted them for repression. At that time, the authorities considered Black Pora activists to be terrorists. The main wave of repressions began in September 2004 with the suspected government's planting of explosives in their four offices in the cities of Kyiv, Chernihiv, Lviv, and Uzhhorod. The activist arrests were connected to the authorities' discovery of explosives in police raids of their offices. On another occasion when Andriy was attacked and escaped, he contacted a journalist who published his story as an article on a popular, online newspaper. With the spread of media information on the Internet, Black Pora was made the object of news. The activists' repressions and arrests were reported as front page news in nearly all the weekly papers. Andriy reflected that the media effect worked for them as a form of "national mobilization action," by reporting on the activists' arrests and giving their campaign media attention (Ibid., 2009, Lviv).

Andriy also experienced repression in the participation in protest activity. He was arrested along with three others in a street performance protest on 8 September during a peaceful protest action near a university in Lviv. For the activists like Andriy, this repression had a positive effect on the campaign. It led to reflexive actions taken by the coordinators of Black Pora to change their campaign's message and to concentrate on the theme of police repression and to pose the question of "why?" in its future protest events. This shift in individual consciousness was important for Andriy since it addressed the key issues that concerned the arrests of 300 activists in their group (author's interview, Shevtsiv, 2009, Lviv). As a result, the theme of "why they did this" appeared in the campaign. Andriy spoke of their change of position in communication strategy in the words below:

> We were a menace and government wanted to fight us in this way. The reason was simple. The government wanted to counteract our force. They were right. They also thought of the experience of Georgia and Serbia that was put into life. They understood that we can repeat it and that is why they tried to stop us. These are reasons of national importance.
>
> (Ibid., 2009, Lviv)

By 27 October 2004, Andriy started to withdraw as an organizer and passed on his responsibilities to other people. He was being followed by the authorities and had difficulties commuting around the city. He was keeping a low profile and working underground for the campaign. When mobilization for the Orange Revolution started, Black Pora stopped recruiting members and focused on mobilizing people for the Orange Revolution. At that time, Andriy said that their campaign became "the center where people came who wished to go to Kyiv. We worked with Our Ukraine. They gave us money for

80 *Professionalization of activists*

the trip. It was coordinated and synchronized" (Ibid., 2009, Lviv). Activists from Lviv Black Pora also went to Kyiv and participated there in the actions of Pora. They had 1,000 of their activists in Kyiv that worked with Andriy Kohut. Their role for mobilization as Andriy recalled, was "to transport people who wanted to take part in the Orange Revolution. They were mostly students. In Kyiv, they joined an organized structure who had concrete tasks" (Ibid., 2009, Lviv). Andriy left for Kyiv on 27 November and there he started to work at the public information department as press secretary of the national office of Pora (Ibid., 2009, Lviv).

Andriy's experience helps us to observe the rise of political participation and trend of personalized politics. It is important in this process to observe Andriy's role in creating political ideas and diffusing them in planned events and press releases. Its effect on Andriy's mobilizing supporters was demonstrated to the campaign. His modes of action in the communications department of the campaign also represented individualized, self-production of printed artifacts that had social meaning for the group and those they recruited.

Stanislav Kutsenko

In 2004, Stanislav was a fourth-year student at the National University of Kyiv Mohyla Academy, and also the chair of student government. At the time of his mobilization into political activity, he attended a discussion held at Yushchenko's "Our Ukraine" political party headquarters to organize a campaign named "Student Wave" (Student'sky Vysha). Stanislav described that event in his words, "I was there and they ['Our Ukraine' politicians] listened to what I was talking about and also what the other students said" (author's interview, Kutsenko, 2008, Kyiv). This led to Stanislav's invitation from Taras Stetskiv in "Our Ukraine" to coordinate the "Student Wave" campaign in cooperation with the political party's headquarters in September 2004. The aim of the "Student Wave" campaign was to create a united, national student movement to support the opposition candidate in upcoming presidential elections (Ibid., 2008). Andriy's experience of political mobilization highlighted the open communication process between two groups, a student and political one, and its effect of rapprochement, which was created between them.

In terms of assessing power and knowledge production in the organizational structure, we consider the example of the system of coordination established between "Our Ukraine" and the "Student Wave" campaign. Stanislav explained that the organizational strategy used for the "Student Wave" campaign was coordinated with the headquarters of "Our Ukraine." This structure of coordination was replicated in other branches of "Student Wave" in every major city. Stanislav's self-reflection on the structure of coordination process was that it worked "like a system, it was because it was not allowed to make hasty decisions" (Ibid., 2008). He described the system developed by "Our Ukraine": it involved developing political actions with achievable objectives outlined in detailed steps for the coordinators of "Student Wave" to follow (Ibid., 2008). This system of cooperation seemed to follow a hierarchical structure of top-down formation, given that the political party ultimately had the power to decide the actions for the coordinators in "Student Wave" to follow.

The terms of the relationship with "Our Ukraine" required Stanislav to follow the directions received from the political party's headquarters. The party employed as tactic the training of the "Student Wave" coordinators (Stanislav included) to follow their strategic methods to mobilize students. Stanislav was trained and spoke of the problems recruiting students using the party's approach. He encountered difficulties recruiting members of student government and student trade unions, since they were not all supporters of Yushchenko or politically engaged. Stanislav spoke about the situation, in this case, the trade unions were dependent on the university deans and these deans in Eastern Ukraine were pro-Yanukovych. This situation complicated student mobilization for him. He continued to persevere with encouragement from "Our Ukraine" who applauded the "Student Wave" coordinators' efforts to increase student participation. This was his work for two months in September and October. Stanislav described the successes of the campaign in the following example. He told the story of buses filled with students going to a political event that were stopped before reaching Kyiv. The students responded by lying down under the bus to prevent the bus from turning back. This incident highlighted the students who were possibly politically awakened by "Student Wave" and its larger felt effects on students' engagement and determination to attend the event in Kyiv despite obstacles to arriving (Ibid., 2008).

Students were learning how to get involved in politics and perhaps "Student Wave's" strategy of empowering them had played a role. A pinnacle event for the "Student Wave" campaign preceding the Orange Revolution was underscored by Stanislav. On 16 October 2004, a student meeting "Student Vichy" (similar to a Student Council) was held on Kontraktova square across the street from the National University of Kyiv Mohyla Academy. On the square, there was a stage. Thousands of students attended the event, including students from different regions of Ukraine. Stanislav attended with "Student Wave" and mentioned the highlight of the event was Yushchenko's speech—this more than a month after his toxic poisoning. Stanislav, like the other students there, was inspired by Yushchenko's courage, and that, for him, "it was a very big point" (Ibid., 2008).

Stanislav's political activity did not end with "Student Wave." He continued his activism with his university, Kyiv Mohyla Academy, during the Orange Revolution. He described his first experience of joining the university's student strike committee, which formed in November before the revolution. In those days, he remembered, the activities of the student committee

82 *Professionalization of activists*

attracted the attention of the authorities. Stanislav reflected that "there were problems when some guys connected to Kuchma tried to come [on campus]. At that time, everything was serious since they could spy on us" (Ibid., 2008). Students were under suspicion and their activities were being monitored by the government. Stanislav attended a student strike committee meeting on the first day of the Orange Revolution where it was announced that students were participating in the protests and would not attend classes. Those days were challenging days for Stanislav and other students involved in these activities. In the morning, the students would walk from one university to another. Stanislav recounted the daily routine for the Strike Committee was to meet early in the morning at 5 AM or 6 AM to decide the next day's activities. They would hold a meeting at Kyiv Mohyla Academy with the university board at 8 AM to decide where to go. After the morning meeting, the day's activities would be communicated to the entire student body that gathered in the courtyard every day. Students were accompanied by the university's rector at all protest events.

The next day's event would have significance for Stanislav and his views on social change. The second day of protest started with a student march from Kyiv's Maidan to the university of Taras Shevchenko. Students there had not gone on strike. Many students skipped class and gathered on the Maidan. Kyiv Mohyla Academy was the first university in Kyiv to go on strike, followed by the National University of Ivano Frankiv'sk in Lviv, which was the second. On this day, 10,000 to 20,000 students, including Stanislav, went to demonstrate in front of the University of Taras Shevchenko. He described observing a group of activists who entered the university and went to the dean's office or university administration to demand that the university's students attend the strike committees. After that day, Stanislav recalled, "big changes started" (Ibid., 2008). The Orange Revolution protests shaped Stanislav's political views. In his words, "I considered it to be very important in the history of Ukraine because a lot of freedom and liberalization came to Ukraine. Of course, maybe not all of Ukrainian authorities used it properly—that's why we have such results now" (Ibid., 2008). While Stanislav's role in the protests changed from coordinator to protester, it resulted in his self-reflexivity on activism and the social change brought about in Ukraine.

Stanislav's experience of mobilization can be further analyzed using Taylor and Van Dyke's (2004) understanding of collective behavior tactics in four categories that they draw from Turner and Killian's (1987) work. Only the first three are of relevance to be examined in relation to Stanislav. They are described below:

> *persuasion*, which appeals to the values or self-interest of the target; *facilitation*, which assists the target group in acquiring knowledge or resources to support the movement, for example, through consciousness raising; *bargaining*, such as when a movement exchanges electoral

and other kinds of cooperation with the target group for support of the movement and *coercion*, which punishes the target group for failure to support the movement's goals.

(Taylor and Van Dyke, 2004, p. 267)

In the case presented, applying Turner and Killian's (1987) knowledge, we can learn a few things about individual behavior and group relations. This enables a better understanding about how tactics actually work to mobilize individuals. Considering Stanislav's experience, we observe how he is persuaded in his interactions in political party meetings. His experience as a student of gaining recognition from a political party shaped his decision to participate as a coordinator. The party was receptive to students' ideas, and that had an impact on Stanislav. The "Our Ukraine" Party was facilitated in its capacity to target students and trained them to mobilize other students, which involved strategies for increasing consciousness. Lastly, implicit in the relations established between "Our Ukraine" and "Student Wave" was an element of bargaining. The student coordinators would help mobilize students for opposition's candidate electoral campaign and in return, elect a candidate to bring more democracy to Ukraine.

Andriy Kohut

Andriy was a founder of the Black Pora campaign, which launched in 17 regional networks on 28–29 March 2004, daylight savings time. This date was symbolic, metaphorically speaking, given its choice of group name, "Pora," translated in English as "It's Time," and its logo of a clock that signaled time was running out for Kuchma. That particular night was meaningful, as it represented a time change to spring forward, and, more significantly, regime change for protest organizers. The coordinators were aware of the importance of beginning their campaign mobilization process early. This permitted, as Andriy said, sufficient time for coordinators to raise consciousness of the group's ideology of Kuchimizm among young people. To achieve the group's objectives, Andriy explained the two phases of the protest that they created. The first stage was to introduce the negative aspects of Kuchimizm. The second phase was to mobilize young people in joyous, playful street actions, which poked fun at the regime, while also introducing an alternative point of view (author's interview, Kohut, 2007, Kyiv). The process of creating Black Pora's campaign illustrated Andriy as part of a group of self-conscious activists, with great knowledge of the political situation in Ukraine and clear political positions that translated into their protest campaign and political activities.

Noteworthy and of interest for further analysis was their political strategy, in particular, the group's use of ideology as a chosen method for mobilizing youth in street performances. To illustrate, Andriy provided an example of a political performance held in Kyiv. Black Pora activists marched in a

84 *Professionalization of activists*

procession in the city center wearing prison hats with their hands tied behind their backs. He explained the protest's message was to make a mockery of Yanukovych's candidacy for presidency since he had a prior criminal record. The purpose was to attract the attention of young people watching their satirical protest and to share a laugh at their joke. The main message Black Pora wanted to communicate using humor with this performance was that if you vote for Yanukovych for president, then you vote for a criminal. In terms of resonance, Andriy saw its effects in terms of an increase in students who watched their political performance and later got involved, as was intended by the coordinators. The group infused their political ideas and translated them into parodies. It was an effective tactic for the mobilization of young people. Black Pora's strategic uses of lively and fun street performance functioned, as Andriy also confirmed, to recruit many volunteers to their protest organization (author's interview, Kohut, 2007, Kyiv).

Andriy's narrative of the construction of a protest movement is situational and represents the underlying conditions of a political culture of young people campaigning against the regime in an election year. This phenomenon also aligned with Bennett's (2012) analysis of the young generation's culture and its role in shaping a "DIY" (Do-It-Yourself) politics (citing examples of the Occupy Wall Street and Indignados protests and its direct democracy practices). He observed in those protests the following: "...large-scale examples of individualized collective action that dot the political landscape... At the same time, the protests displayed openness to individual-level innovation aided by clear avoidance of formal organization, leaders, collective identifications, divisive ideology, or hierarchy" (Bennett, 2012, p. 30).

These novel ideas of individualized protests materialized in Black Pora's organizational structure, which was characterized as non-partisan (not affiliated with a political party), leaderless, and horizontal in its structure of decision-making by consensus. Andriy described Black Pora as an autonomous organization composed of autonomous networks. These overlapping activist networks exercised independence to develop and organize a maximum number of protests under the Black Pora campaign. There was no centralized coordination or approval process for these protests. In addition, it was understood by these activists that involvement in the campaign was under the condition of no personal gain. That is, participation in the organizing of protests was not meant to result in a political career or to benefit a political party.

Oliver and Johnston (2000) studied the importance of ideology for providing a framework for interpreting our social world and explaining individual action. Furthermore, their work provided social scientists with a capacity to question the formation of ideas. In particular, their work pushes researchers to question the structure of an 'idea system.' The purpose is to investigate if ideas properly represent phenomena and to see how they are diffused within populations (Oliver and Johnston, 2000, p. 7). I observed this phenomenon in the structure of communications established by Black Pora. To that end,

Andriy provided an example of internal workings of the group, which help unpack how their group's political ideas came to fruition. Andriy explained the process for sharing ideas and decision-making in the group. Moreover, to propose ideas in the group, an individual would share their proposal with others in the group. Collectively, the group would decide whether or not to accept the proposed idea. This open structure of communication among its activists, Andriy explained, was meant as a way for individuals to freely express their ideas and to feel included in the decision-making process of political activities (author's interview, Kohut, 2007, Kyiv).

From the outset, as Andriy explained, Black Pora's campaign was based on the ideology of resisting the power. Eventually, with the onset of the presidential campaigns, activists decided to make preparations for large-scale protest on Kyiv's Maidan in the event of election fraud. In the summer of 2004, Black Pora activists organized a summer camp to strategize. In attendance, Andriy explained, were representatives from every region. They divided up into two groups with four themes. The third group would combine the final results into a week by week calendar of protest events until the election day. In their meetings, the activists discussed theory about street actions, visuals, election and post elections activities, and mobilizing young people. Decisions on idea proposals were voted by consensus. An example of how this process functioned was provided by Andriy who described the situation where an individual would present an idea, email all the activists, and wait for the majority to agree on the proposed action. At the end of the summer, a list of activities agreed upon were drawn up in a plan and sent out to all the activists. As a group, it was decided among the activists to execute these planned protest events in 17 regions with one or two protest activities planned a month during the summer and one action a week (minimum) planned for the fall (Ibid., 2007).

Ostap Kryvydk

Ostap's activism experience is distinct from the others, since it offers valuable insight into the dynamics within the field of action from the point of view of an activist's actual practices inside a civic campaign. His different activities in a civic campaign represent a multifaceted view of his changing beliefs, which motivates his action of engaging in various political activities. Ostap's narratives also highlight an individual's interactions within a group or an organizational structure as an important process of self-actualization into an activist. In his experience, the organizational structure of Yellow Pora constrains Ostap in his assigned role, but these limits do not have the effect of demobilizing him. Instead, the constraints placed on him from the organization do the opposite, they permit him to engage in ways reminiscent of alter-globalists, as Pleyers describes, that result in the "construction of new forms of sociability" (Pleyers, 2010, p. 42). Ostap is innovative in his approach to initiating new forms of political action. He finds new groups

86 *Professionalization of activists*

and proposes new ideas, which enables him to actively contribute to the protest movement. Ostap's engagement in the Yellow Pora campaign is presented below in a biographical format. It begins with Ostap's retelling of how he was recruited in a new round of political activity.

A few years later, we find Ostap moving from university life into professional life. As a result of his acquired skills and activism, he was hired to work on a new civic campaign. In 2004, Ostap graduated from the National University Kyiv Mohyla Academy with a master's degree in political science and comparative politics. In his thesis, he applied discourse analysis to interpret the ideologies of the Ukrainian far right nationalist parties. Ostap also had experience working for mass media at the Ukrainian television channel 1+1 (until July 2004). During this time, his good friend, Anastasiya Bezverkha, an activist in Yellow Pora, contacted him about the vacant position in the campaign and asked if he was interested in working with them for a monthly salary equivalent to $300. Ostap wanted to participate, since he remained active as an activist following the "Ukraine without Kuchma" protests (author's interview, Kryvdyk, 2008, Kyiv). He was offered some incentives to join Yellow Pora that provided him with sufficient resources to meet basic needs, while also allowing him an opportunity to continue with his activism. He reasoned that their offer, "was enough to pay for a flat and food, so I agreed" (Ibid., 2008). Ostap spoke of his daily life in the campaign, which he expressed in the following words: "Actually, I didn't need much money. I spent all of my time in Pora, I didn't have any holidays. It was a working day from late July until December. There were no holidays, nothing. It was for life, and everybody was working like that" (Ibid., 2008).

In the civic campaign, Ostap was assigned a role as manager of the creative design department for Yellow Pora. Daily life in the Yellow Pora office was a challenge. He cited as an example, his graphic design work on outdated computers. In general, in his words, Ostap described the working conditions in Yellow Pora's office:

> I would say there was a huge economy over what little there was, we did not even have good tables, with the possibilities to hide the documents. All the documents were on the table, the list of activists with cell phone numbers and emails. Everything was there. There was no air conditioner in this flat. It was summer heat. Later on, in September and October, it was 40 C inside the room with no breeze. All activists in separate groups worked in the same shared space, and there were people coming and going.
>
> (Ibid., 2008)

In his interactions with the group, he described the process of decision-making in a non-hierarchical structure. In this context, group meetings were organized following the format of an advisory board with a lead

Professionalization of activists 87

coordinator, Vladimir Kaskiv, and activists to collectively make decisions. Among the activists, there was a plurality of different actors, including individuals representing the Communist or far right nationalist political parties—most of them under the age of 35. Ostap made a general observation that the coordinators of Yellow Pora were intelligent, but they also reminded him of Ukrainian politicians in that, "when they do something, they think that they will get something out of it" (Ibid., 2008). Confirming Ostap's opinion, the organization's structure was later modified. Ostap's group was negatively impacted by the change in the decision-making processes. The group was modified to adopt a hierarchical management structure. This resulted in Kaskiv making all the decisions for the group and delegating tasks to the activists who would create a to-do list from Kaskiv's ideas. This list would trickle down to Ostap and his creative department to design these ideas. Lastly, Kaskiv was in the central position to give final approval before Ostap could print the materials (Ibid., 2008).

The formalization of the campaign and hierarchical structure alienated Ostap. His role in the campaign was in doubt since he no longer felt he could contribute. It ultimately led to his exodus from the creative department (at the first round of the presidential elections and transition to Yellow Pora's coordinator of a group of special tasks on the Maidan during the Orange Revolution). Before the transition in roles happened, Ostap made an individual decision to seek out other opportunities and to continue his activism in other spaces with different groups of people. He moved from office work to the first tent camp established by Yellow Pora in Kyiv's district of Podil near the National University of Kyiv Mohyla Academy. He found activists there "who were sitting there and didn't know what they wanted to do" (Ibid., 2008). So, Ostap went to the tent camp with materials from the creative department and found a way to engage the activists with political ideas. He brought six or so posters with slick slogans. They occupied the public space to show the police that, as activists, they were willing to risk their lives. The activists were no longer just sitting, instead Ostap said, "we are showing our position, we care" (Ibid., 2008). Ostap and these activists had hoped their tent camp would become the heart, the coordination center of the student movement of activists in Kyiv. Unfortunately, he said, it did not happen. Instead, their contributions were reduced to fund-raising. The activists came to the camp and collected funds to pay for those who lived in the tents and provided security for the inhabitants (Ibid., 2008).

Despite its failure, the experience allowed Ostap the opportunity to re-engage himself in new actions. Before the second round of the presidential elections, Ostap received a phone call from a friend working on staff at Yushchenko's "Our Ukraine" headquarters. She gave him a tip that people from a state-owned gas company, Naftogaz, were in the process of

88 Professionalization of activists

committing voter fraud. Essentially, she explained how employees were being forced to vote for Yanukovych by absentee ballot and were being taken by bus to vote again in the Poltava region (Ibid., 2008). She communicated to him that the staff at "Our Ukraine" concluded that they needed to block the buses to prevent fraud. Ostap reflected on what his friend said and drew the following conclusion:

> It seemed to be completely stupid, crazy and on the border of common sense. Starting from primary risk of health, life, and ending up with an arrest for blocking the traffic. This might be seen as administrator or criminal case. There might be both. Basically, it was bothering people the possibility to go vote and there could be another criminal issue in it.
>
> (Ibid., 2008)

Ostap called upon Yellow Pora for support and help. Yellow Pora coordinators told him they were too busy to make preparations for setting up a tent camp on Maidan for the next day. They did not want their activists to participate, since they would be too tired for protest activities planned later that day. Ostap's action required activists to be present to stop a bus from departing at 7.30 AM. When Ostap approached Kaskiv for assistance, Kaskiv declined and told Ostap that it's his health, it's his life, and to do what he wanted. Without support from his group, Ostap sought out help from an activist from Georgia's *Kmara*. This activist had executed a similar action a year and half before in Georgia and agreed to help Ostap to organize the protest. Ostap gathered support from Black Pora activists; his proposal obtained majority consensus for approval. Activists in Black Pora helped with activities such as creating banners, carrying flags, and informing the journalists. Ostap remembered that it was difficult to find anyone to lie under the bus. He volunteered, along with an activist named Alina from the Donetsk region. She was a student at the Kyiv Mohyla Academy and a family relative. In total, there were five activists, most from Black Pora, as participants in the protest event that took place on 21 November 2004. It was the second round of the presidential elections. They arrived 15 minutes early and saw journalists from the television station, Channel 5 were already there on the scene. Ostap informed the media that they would lie under the buses, and the journalist expressed her disbelief (Ibid., 2008). Ostap described the day in the following way:

> So it was a rather cold day, muddy and the road was muddy completely. It was dirty and wet. If I walk there, I would leave it and walk aside. There were two buses. Two buses near the metro station, so we did it. Three people bus blocked the front and the two others laid down on the back of the bus so it could not move.
>
> (Ibid., 2008)

Professionalization of activists 89

The workers got inside the bus and news about their protest action reached other activists on *Maidan's*. There were even some people filming it, Ostap recalled.

> When we saw first bus started to move, it was Alina, Vadim, and me in front and there was Yurko and another standing behind on the second bus. When it started to move, we said to each other, 'Pora.' At that moment, we moved from the front window of the bus, it continued moving, we had no option but to fall down in the mud. Then he pressed the break, and the bus stopped. I felt my trousers went completely wet and cold. We lied under the bus.
>
> (Ibid., 2008)

The activists from Black Pora appeared on the scene with posters. One of them read that the bus was not an administrative resource and that you cannot drive over people, Ostap said. He described the scene filled by activists with megaphones shouting for the people to get off the bus and to freely vote for their preferred candidate. The situation continued and Ostap lost track of the time spent under the bus. He remembered wondering when the police would arrest them. The police arrived and asked the activists to stand up and to let the buses go. The journalists were filming and recording the police officer speaking to the activists. The police responsible for unblocking the traffic got scared and they left, Ostap later discovered. He was told that 10 minutes had passed since they were under the bus, but it felt more like 30 minutes to him. Ostap and the other activists felt cold and soon the workers started to get off the bus. Then they stood up. Ostap remembered that they were muddy and went back to Black Pora's office to clean up. Afterwards, Ostap joined the mobile groups for observing the election polls. He received a temporary journalist ID, and asked questions to voters in some districts. Later in the afternoon, Ostap received word that his action had been recorded by media and sold to Reuters. Soon, Ostap had become, in his words, "one of the faces of the revolution" (Ibid., 2008).

During the period of the Orange Revolution, Ostap had the idea to create another Maidan in Eastern Ukraine in the Donetsk region. He received funds from Yellow Pora, equivalent to $300, two tents as well as some flags, and other equipment. Ostap invited his friends to go to Donetsk and to start a tent city. Their immediate response was an overwhelming "no" and they "chose life," he replied. He said, "it was completely crazy I went to church. I prepared myself to die" (Ibid., 2008). He and four others went by train to Donetsk. They were approached by secret police on the train. They knew if they stayed on the train they would not reach Donetsk. So, halfway there, they got off at the train station in the Dnipropetsk region of Ukraine at 2 AM, as Ostap retold his story. He called a friend there and shared his idea of going to Donetsk. His friend understood the risks

90 *Professionalization of activists*

of being beaten and agreed to go with them. Early in the morning, they took the bus from the train station and split into two groups and agreed to meet in the city at noon. One group took the bus and the others, a taxi to Donetsk. Ostap remembered that the police stopped them at the border of Donetsk for a bribe. He was afraid they were going to be arrested before the protest action was held. They had sent out a fax to notify the city council in advance so their action would be legal. When they arrived, there were media journalists who were contacted and interviewed them. Ostap remembered that they were in the process of setting up the tents when 50 people from a boxing club, he thought, were ordered to scare them and damage their tents. Ostap was slightly pushed and one journalist was beaten and his camera damaged. The police arrived and started to write them up for violations and took information from their identity cards. They spent, as Ostap recalled, the remainder of the day in the police station, and were released at the end of day (Ibid., 2008). The next day, they decided not to return and try again since they were afraid. It was a regret for Ostap. He reflected that

> My biggest fault, we didn't come back the second day. We should have done it. I suppose, also, one of the reasons why we didn't start tent camp, it might have been perceived that we are terrorists...I should have returned on Tuesday, and I felt like I can't, I gave up. I was afraid. I was tired. I was sick of the revolution. I started work in late July and no holidays. I gave up.
>
> (Ibid., 2008)

Ostap's activism did not end yet. He volunteered as an election observer in Dnipropetrovsk, in Eastern Ukraine, during the repeat vote of the second round election. In his view, Ostap did not consider this role as a form a political action, but he received training on electoral laws, he learned what to do, and how to cooperate. For him, it was okay since it posed no risks (Ibid., 2008). When the Orange revolution ended, Ostap reflected,

> I got burned out from revolution. I don't feel that I can survive another campaign like that. I am used material. I don't know if it was efficient or not, it was great. It was bright people who put soul in it. It was a great time. It left a good trace and I am trying to keep contact with these people.
>
> (Ibid., 2008)

Ostap was not disappointed in the Orange Revolution, but felt regret in himself as "revolutioner." He said that not many things have been accomplished since the Orange Revolution when the revolutionary mentality should have been sustained, but he admitted, that they did not sustain it (Ibid., 2008).

Professionalization of activists 91

On one hand, Ostap's lived experience of activism provides an alternative view into how participation took place within these civic groups; it reveals conflict and tensions but also the mechanisms and group processes of consensus and cooperation that occurred between rival groups in the Orange Revolution. His experience expands our thinking on the role of social movement structures that goes beyond claim-making. His personal accounts allow us to conceptualize social movement groups with potentialities in terms of capacities for the individual to develop his/her own political actions. This follows subjectivity theory on alter-globalists from Pleyers (2010) that underscores the important role of lived experiences on influencing individual social change, like in the case of Ostap. Pleyers describes this form of personal transformation as significant, he argued

> Subjectivity and experience being at the heart of the engagement, it does not only play out against an external adversary or system. It is also within the personality of each individual and in each actor of the movement... Activists' subjectivity is immersed in the movement, giving not only their time but their emotions and their very being. It is consequently also a matter of transforming the self, one's relations to others and to one's self.
> (Pleyers, 2010, p. 38)

The result in Ostap's example was social change. This is produced when an individual realizes one's agency and freely engages to produce one's self-creations of protests from a political culture characterized by a decentralized group structure. Perhaps, the initial open structure of the group encouraged Ostap to imagine new types of protests and have the freedom to execute them without the restrictions of a hierarchical organizational structure and decision-making. In the case of Ostap, he was a graphic artist with a role of depicting the civic movement in images, yet his role was greater than that. His experience also demonstrated that membership in a civic movement is more than the performing of tasks. Participation in a civic movement is also about individual contributions to protest-making activity, which is also something significant to consider. Ostap's process of self-fulfillment as an activist was visible when he was in the protest field engaging in self-created initiatives like developing a peaceful action of civic disobedience to stage a sit-in (or rather to lie-down) under a bus or his attempt to create a public space for occupation in East Ukraine. These were experiences that illustrate how an individual's interpretation of a situation and actions create social change from within, and how it materializes in the social world in the context of a protest movement.

Volodymyr Ishchenko

In 2004, Volodymyr was a Ph.D. candidate and an instructor at the Taras Shevchenko National University of Kyiv. Volodymyr was involved in the initial stages of training prior to the creation of the Black Pora campaign.

92 *Professionalization of activists*

He participated in training sessions with Serbians from the *Optor* campaign to learn how to create a similar campaign in Ukraine. Due to his personal convictions, he did not participate as an activist in the Orange Revolution. Instead, Volodymyr contributed self-reflections on the protest groups that existed at that time. Volodymyr acknowledged that the activists he knew from Committee "For Truth" had made progress in continuing the protests in the new civic campaign Pora. He explained that many of his friends from the UWK protests were dissatisfied following the failure of the political actions, and they started something different, which later became the Black Pora campaign. Unlike the UWK, Volodymyr described significant differences that gave Black Pora an advantage—they had more resources, greater capacity to create a civic campaign and to mobilize people using existing regional activist structures. Distinct from the UWK protest, Volodymyr pointed out additional distinctions that set the Orange Revolution apart. For instance, the latest protests were centered on the 2004 presidential elections, and they had a clearer objective, which was to motivate the people to vote. He cited as examples the fact that the opposition political parties had more financial resources for campaigning and distribution of orange materials and creating advertising campaigns to focus on humiliating Yanukovych. The political campaigns also benefitted, he said, from international funds from Europe and the United States. As a result, Volodymyr reasoned that this permitted conditions for protest groups to easily achieve their immediate goals (author's interview, Ishchenko, 2008, Kyiv).

Volodymyr's actions have strong ties to his political beliefs. To further explain, Oliver and Johnston (2000) analyzed the complex process of interaction between the cognitive beliefs of an individual and their personal understandings of events, which underpin social movement behavior. They make a connection between ideology as important to create conditions for individual action in the following description. "The concept of ideology focuses attention on the content of whole systems of beliefs, on the multiple dimensions of these belief systems, and on the ways the ideas are related to each other. Ideologies as sets of ideas can be abstracted from the thought processes of any particular individual" (Oliver and Johnston, 2000, p. 8).

Volodymyr spoke about his direct experiences with protests. He reflected on the Orange Revolution events and the general expectations that the protests would succeed. This sentiment, he remarked, was absent in the UWK protests. In the latter, the student strikes did not have an effect on political change. This time, in 2004, he saw a domino effect with Kyiv Mohyla Academy leading the student strikes that made it possible for students in other universities to attend the protests. The students were some of the hundreds of thousands of people who went to protests on Kyiv's Maidan. Volodymyr compared both student mobilizations, the UWK and Orange Revolution, and concluded the latter's success was not linked to a change in universities policies, rather he speculated the contributory role of Pora in universities as critical to explaining the great mobilization of students in advance of the Orange Revolution (author's interview, Ishchenko, 2008, Kyiv).

Volodymyr was mobilized by political ideas in the UWK protest, but this experience did not have the same effect of recruiting him into activism in the Orange Revolution. He explained the differences for him. In the UWK protest, Volodymyr believed in the protest movement's ideas not only to elect a new president, but to restructure the system in a more fundamental way. Volodymyr was motivated by the group's ideas for profound systematic change of the Ukrainian political system (Ibid., 2008). In contrast to the Orange Revolution, Volodymyr remembered the protests were, in his view, only about Yushchenko. He shared his feelings in the following words: "I had no motivation, I could go to Maidan as any other person to shout Yushchenko. I didn't support Yushchenko, I voted against all. I don't support any–in fact I was right. Not much difference between Yushchenko and Yanukovych" (Ibid., 2008).

When Volodymyr examined his thoughts about the Orange Revolution, he concluded that the Orange Revolution was a continuation of the electoral campaign for Yushchenko. He expressed discontent that there was an absence of discussion of post-revolution strategy in terms of what to do and what they were going to change (Ibid., 2008). His summary of the events was: "It was reduced to elections...What are we going to change in the political system. They were no discussion on what to do change system–people standing in Maydan shouting 'Yushchenko' They were listening to music and speeches, that is all" (Ibid., 2008).

Conclusion

I applied a cultural approach to life histories to depict how social issues linked to a staunch anti-government position unfolded over time from the "Ukraine without Kuchma" (UWK) protests to the 2004 presidential elections. The presidential elections (2004) was an opportunity for veteran activists from the UWK movement to continue the anti-Kuchma campaign to change the regime. This chance at political change was seized by such activists who had spent over a year in preparations for political activities that directly and indirectly impacted the opposition candidate's electability. It also had a spillover effect in influencing the people's choice to favor him as the popular candidate representing them, especially following his poisoning. Both Pora campaigns adopted different methods, one local and grassroots based, and the other followed a PR campaign with international visibility, which placed them in the category, as Touraine defined, as "agents of transformation" (Touraine, 2000, p. 900). In the case of Black Pora, they created what Touraine described as "imaginary worlds" (Touraine, 2000) that functioned to expand the spaces to exercise freedom in their capacity

94 *Professionalization of activists*

to critique the ruling government, to overcome repression and to continue activism, spontaneous flash mob political actions, and expressions of creativity in political performances filled with imagination. The result was that many young people wanted to join the campaign, which transformed the political environment of students. This was highlighted in the experience of Andriy Shevtsiv and mobilization in the region of Lviv.

Considering Touraine's concept of *ambivalence*, there were instances when it appeared, such as in the experiences of Ostap and his proposed ideas to lie under a bus, and also to set up a tent city in Yanukovych's stronghold in the region of Donetsk. For the activists, the proposal to protest under the bus presented a high risk, and a few participated; in both cases around five people went. These few overcame this emotion of ambivalence, fueled by fear to act anyway, despite the fear felt under the bus and fear of violent beatings in Donetsk. They worked through the fear, and in the first instance were successful in stopping the workers on the bus from participating in voter fraud. On the other hand, their cheerful and fun political street theatrical performances helped to overcome students' fear of participation in the campaign. These instances of street performance were reminiscent of the creative strategies of activists in the global justice movement and alter-activism.

Bibliography

Author's interview, Andriy Kohut, [yellow] Pora coordinator, August 12, 2007, Kyiv.
Author's interview, Andriy Shevtsiv, [black] Pora coordinator, February 25, 2009, Lviv.
Author's interview, Ostap Kryvdyk, [yellow] Pora coordinator, September 10, 2008, Kyiv.
Author's interview, Stanislav Kutsenko, Student Wave coordinator, September 25, 2008, Kyiv.
Author's interview, Volodymyr Ishchenko, Instructor and PhD Candidate, November 26, 2008, Kyiv.
Bauman, Z. (1992). *Intimations of postmodernity*. London: Routledge.
Beck, U., & Beck-Gernsheim, E. (2002). *Individualization: Institutionalized individualism and its social and political consequences*. London: Sage.
Bennett, W. L. (2012). "The Personalization of Politics: Political Identity, Social Media, and Changing Patterns of Participation." *The Annals of the American Academy of Political and Social Science*, *644*(1), 20–39.
Giddens, A. (1991). *Modernity and self-identity: Self and society in the late modern age*. Stanford, CA: Stanford University Press.
Jasper, J. (1997). *The art of moral protest culture, biography, and creativity in social movements*. Chicago, IL: University of Chicago Press.
Oliver, P., & Johnston, H. (2000). What a good idea! Ideologies and frames in social movement research. Retrieved January 30, 2016, from http://www.ssc.wisc.edu/~oliver/PROTESTS/ArticleCopies/Frames.2.29.00.pdf.
Pleyers, G. (2010). *Alter-globalization: Becoming actors in the global age*. Cambridge: Polity Press.

Schwandt, D. R. (2009). "Collective Learning as Social Change: Integrating Complex Adaptive Systems and Structuration with Parsons Theory of Action." *A collection of essays in honour of Talcott Parsons* (Christopher Hart Ed.). Cheshire: Midrash Publications, pp. 124–149.

Stalder, F. (2006). *Manuel Castells and the theory of the network society.* Cambridge: Polity Press.

Taylor, V., & Van Dyke, N. (2004). "'Get up, Stand up': Tactical Repertoires of Social Movements." *The Blackwell companion to social movements* (S. A. Soule and H. Kriesi, Eds.). Malden, MA: Blackwell Pub, pp. 262–293

Touraine, A. (2000) "A Method for Studying Social Actors." *Journal of World-Systems Research, 6*(3), 900–918.

5 Activists' self-organization of the Euromaidan protests, 2013–2014

The last chapter considered an actor's subjectivity in relation to the socio-cultural context and intentionality to present alternative conditions for social movements to thrive. This final empirical chapter will return to the book's central interest in explaining an activist's repeat participation, while observing a third case study of political protests in Ukraine. To that end, I once again revisit the original research question of why individuals continue their activism in three protest events. I consider research from Van Stekelenburg and Klandersmans (2010) that drew from social psychology theories for an explanation for this observed phenomenon in social movements. They suggest a possible way to analyze subsequent activism using Simon et al.'s (1998) theory, featuring "dual pathways to protest participation," which combined ideological and instrumental bases as explanatory factors in initiating an individual's action in social movements (Van Stekelenburg and Klandersmans, 2010, p. 8). This social theory was used by Van Stekelenburg and Klandersmans (2010) to argue that protest participation was a product of shared grievances (interest-based) that elicited emotions such as outrage or dissatisfaction when peoples' values were violated and at risk of being lost (instrumental view), which contributed to further political activism. This was important for two reasons: Van Stekelenburg and Klandersmans argued that "instrumental based participation can be purposeful in solving a social or political problem whereas ideologically based participation can be purposeful in maintaining moral integrity by voicing one's indignation" (Van Stekelenburg and Klandersmans, 2010, p. 9). Their theoretical frameworks shape the discussion that follows in this chapter on repeat protest participation by five activists, whom we have already traced in two previous protests. This is considered in the framework of the socio-political context for protest, as well as actor identification with the movement and its contributory effect on participation, which are examined below.

The previous chapters applied cultural approaches of actor subjectivity to examine why some social movements succeed and others fail to recruit individuals to participate. In the case of Ukraine, successful social protest mobilization was attributed to the strength of diverse coalitions cooperating and making personal contributions to social movement making activities, as seen in 2004. The failures to mobilize individuals occurred when the people (including activists) no longer personally identified with the movement, as in the case of the "Ukraine without Kuchma" protests. Previous chapters explored the new strategies utilized by protest actors to seek out training and increase their grassroots campaign's possibility for success. The effect of the new strategies of training was visible in collective mobilization practices seen in 2013–2014. The activists' previous narratives in the earlier chapters described the emotional dimensions of defeat and loss of confidence, as well as their civic practices to regain the social movement's confidence through their interactions with transnational networks (Serbian, Georgian) from the period of 2002–2004. These networks of activists sought out new and creative strategies to develop alternative civic campaigns and to draw new, young members into politics and protest in 2004. At that time, the student activists faced a challenge, given the demobilization of actors from prior movements between 2000–2003, and the apolitical beliefs of young people who were passive in politics. With the aid of transnational activists and international donors, the young actors were taught how to appropriate relevant strategies, like those of the global justice movement and alter-activists, to incorporate into their civic monitoring of the presidential elections in Ukraine's 2004 presidential campaigns. The social effect of their tactics, use of carnivalesque street theater for protests, resulted in an increase in young people's mobilization. This produced a political awakening, which had the consequence of facilitating the rapid mobilization of young people as a group of protest "occupyers" in the city's square during the Orange Revolution. In Kyiv, these lived spaces in the tent cities were like utopias. The spaces of occupation were also places for young people's experimentation with democratic practices, which were, at first, mostly peaceful forms of resistance. This time in Euromaidan, we observe the activists from earlier protest movements' (2000/2004) processes of self-mobilization and social interactions with their activist networks (once again in 2013) to organize new rounds of political dissent. The recent protest resulted in a violent and revolutionary change of regime, which saw the government yield its power to opposing forces of resistance. Detailed further in this section were the historical accounts from veteran activists that described their efforts for social change to reform Ukraine's political system in the direction of transparency and elimination of corruption, for instance. The individual's experience recounted below represents an oral history. These individual portraits of lived histories are valuable to illustrate the mechanisms from which an actor adopts the role of agent and assumes the responsibility for coordinating citizen-generated protests for political change and a European future.

Andriy Shevtsiv

The starting point for an analysis of protest participation is to understand the grounds for an individual's protest activity. After the Orange Revolution,

98 *The Euromaidan protests, 2013–2014*

Andriy decreased his activism and went to work for a tourist agency in Lviv. The situation changed when he realized that Yanukovych would most likely win the 2015 presidential elections. This produced an inner desire to become once again active in political life, but Andriy simply did not know how to defeat Yanukovych. He had hoped that former activists would regroup and coordinate similar civic campaigns, like they did in 2004. But this was 2013, and to his dismay, the activists that he knew from the Orange Revolution were not preparing for the elections (author's interview, Shevtsiv, 2015).

Andriy's experience served as an example to respond to the "paradox of persistent participation" that was raised by Van Stekelenburg and Klandersman (2010), which addressed repeat activism, despite "pessimism regarding the action's ostensible goals" (Van Stekelenburg and Klandersman, 2010, p. 9). Andriy had not participated in much activism since 2004, but then in 2013, he protested again because of his friends, activists from the "Ukraine without Kuchma" protest who helped awaken his consciousness about police oppression. Andriy reunited with these former activists to organize two protests events: 1) local pickets against police rape in Vradiivs'kyi district in Mykolaivs'ka region; and 2) picketing against the police tyranny in Lviv region. In the first demonstration, he reconnected with an activist, Bohdan Solchanyk (who later died on Euromaidan, one of The Heaven's Hundred), whom he had known from Black Pora, and with whom he identified on shared political beliefs. In particular, Andriy spoke about a speech given by Bohdan at the first demonstration, signaling precedents for the revolution to come, which left an impression on him. These demonstrations, Andriy said, were part of larger regional protests reproduced throughout Ukraine. The protests resulted in the arrests of the accused, he explained. This most likely contributed to a sense of empowerment, particularly among the activists involved, and perhaps helped to overcome public pessimism about the pickets. For a third time that year, Andriy, participated in protests—this time it was the Euromaidan for political reasons. He protested again to support Ukraine's accession to the European Union, to protest against the increased influence of Russia in Ukraine and to oppose the tyranny of the police and government corruption (author's interview, Shevtsiv, 2015).

Andriy's history of the protest is included as more context into an actor's interpretation of the situation that precedes his action. His decision-making process that led him to participate in activism is analyzed in relation to his social ties to the former Black Pora group. Many of these activists had been active in protesting against language policy in Ukraine since Yanukovych came to power. Andriy was a part of the activist network, since he was the former coordinator of Black Pora in Lviv. His past activism enabled his access to activists that provided him with information about the Euromaidan protests. Through activist networks, he received the first calls to protest on 21 November from Mustafa Nayyem and Volodymyr Viatrovych (former leader and a founder of Black Pora). These social ties kept him informed about future events that were held on 23 and 24 November and featured

The *Euromaidan protests, 2013–2014* 99

the participation of political parties, which attracted about 100,000 people. His social networks also provided him with insider knowledge about the formation of new activist groups to organize protests events. Andriy was aware of the creation of two Maidans, one for politicians and the other, an apolitical group (Civic Sector of Euromaidan). Their assigned roles were mutually agreed-upon by both groups before the violence of 30 November. The former, the politicians, were the decision-makers, and responsible for mobilization. The latter, a grassroots group of mostly Black Pora activists, were responsible for implementing a strategy of nonviolence and peaceful struggle (adopted from the structure of Black Pora). The group was informed of organizational issues by Viatrovych, and the organizing roles would be divided, more or less, among former activists from Black Pora. The two Maidans shared office space in The Trade Unions Building in Kyiv's central square (Independence Square or Maidan).

Andriy's process of self-mobilization derived from a multiplicity of beliefs, based on future elections, regime change, social networks (employer and activist), and European ideals. This led to another inquiry into the situation surrounding Andriy's participation in new protest events. To that end, Andriy attended his first protest event in Kyiv with the director of his company on 29 December 2013. He arrived on Kyiv's Maidan with the expectation that the protest against Yanukovych's refusal to sign the EU Association Agreement (AA) would resemble the "Ukraine with Kuchma" protests, which it did not. On his arrival, Andriy met his friend Bohdan to discuss participation in the Civic Sector of Euromaidan (in Kyiv). Andriy's initial impression was that this group used spontaneous forms of organization, but was effective. Together, they discussed the coordination of protest actions with former Black Pora activists that had already joined the Civic Sector of Euromaidan. Andriy was surprised at how many of these activists from Black Pora had returned to protest once again. He had wrongly assumed that the group's activism had ended with the Orange Revolution. Instead, he discovered that the core members of Black Pora remained active in civic life. As contributors, they supplied professional skills to the group, and were among the most organized activists. The following day, Andriy arrived in Lviv to obtain news that the police had beaten students on Kyiv's Maidan and as foreshadowing, he remarked that "it seemed that it was only the beginning" (Ibid., 2015). His group, Civic Sector of Euromaidan, announced a meeting for 1 December in Kyiv. In his personal circles, he already had a family member and his director from work going to Kyiv. This prompted Andriy to seize the moment to self-mobilize. He posted on Facebook that he would go to Kyiv with a friend from Black Pora. He arrived later that day (1 December) and gathered with other people on St. Michael's Cathedral in Kyiv. This meeting, Andriy admitted, was not well-organized. Despite the lack of organization, he shared the group's emotions, and reflected in the moment "if we do not go out, it will be worse... we must do something" (Ibid., 2015).

100 *The Euromaidan protests, 2013–2014*

The actor's ground for protest was examined through individual accounts of action taken. In the Civic Sector of Euromaidan, Andriy was assigned the role of organizing the protesters and keeping them together. In his early days with the group, he observed a lack of organization and activists were not prepared. He described the group as being small with about 30 active members. Andriy spoke about the dynamic of the group's activism as reactive to the situation like a reflex. He observed that organizing occurred under conditions where "people's response was a reaction to what happened" (Ibid., 2015). To improve coordination, he worked together with political parties that had greater access to technology and financial resources that improved the group's organization of protests. In particular, he coordinated the protests with deputy Ihor Vasyunyk from his district, in his role, "he [Ihor] was organizing people from the margins–his assistants were around– he was involved" (Ibid., 2015). The activists were well aware of the benefits of cooperation with politicians and as a result, they, including Andriy, made efforts to minimize disputes with them (Ibid., 2015). While Andriy was from Lviv, he would return on the weekends to Kyiv to organize large-scale protests for the Civic Sector Euromaidan to take place every Sunday. This would include the organization of mobile teams (called Automaidan) that would drive around the city, spreading the group's main message by megaphone to the public. Andriy gauged the Automaidan's effectiveness by the public's reaction, which he described as being in control with no outward expressions of indignation directed towards them (Ibid 2015). Besides protest organization activity, Andriy's participation also included picketing, a speaker role on the Maidan stage, and the role of moderator of the group's meetings with activists in the Euromaidan Civic Sector. Andriy's protest activities underscored the multiplicity of roles performed by an activist in the protest movement. His main function can be interpreted, on the one hand, as a communicator for protesters of information on the protest event. On the other hand, Andriy's role can also be analyzed as actualizing the group's message of protests in material form as actions in terms of location in relation to specific targets.

Political actions amplified the communication of the group's protest message. Examples of how it worked in the Civic Sector of Euromaidan are examined below. To illustrate, Andriy, with megaphone on hand, organized a demonstration march with several hundred protesters from Kyiv's Maidan to the European Union Embassy. He explained that the main purpose of the protest was to air their grievances about President Yanukovych to EU countries and to advocate that the EU adopt tougher policies against his government. The outcome of their protest actions was interactions with a representative of the EU Embassy that spoke with them. The demonstration held near the EU Embassy ended in mid-December 2013. In another instance, Andriy explained that there were additional means for the group to spread information about their group and their key messages through protest events, public speaking, group promotion

The Euromaidan protests, 2013–2014 101

in flyers and banners, and media coverage. To further illustrate the spread of protest messages through political events and effect, Andriy provided the example of his participation in a protest at the end of December with the Parliament deputy Yuriy Derevyanko. It was a staged protest against Vitaliy Zakharchenko, the Minister of Internal Affairs and his attempts to repress the protest movement. Igor Lutsenko, a journalist and activist (who was later kidnapped and violently beaten), was responsible for the organization of the program for the protest event. To contribute, Andriy's group created slogans to shout aloud with a megaphone in the action, and made and distributed flyers on Khreshchatyk Street. Andriy's participation also included making speech announcements about the Civic Sector of Euromaidan's mission and activities on Maidan's stage throughout the day. In the evening, he gave a speech on stage at Maidan. In attendance were representatives from the EU Embassy. This resulted in the filming of their activism by Ukraine's television Channel 5 and free publicity for their group (Ibid., 2015). The protest actions that Andriy helped organize were also examined as a group's responses to the political situation. To demonstrate further, Andriy received information about the possibility of Prime Minister Nikolay Azarov resigning and a tentative date of 2 December for the Ukrainian Parliament to vote its approval. Andriy conducted media research and passed his findings to Volodymyr Viatrovych, who shared the information with the other activists. This initiated, Andriy explained, the coordination of protest actions (7 December 2013) to partially block access to the government administration buildings off Sadova Street, adopting strategies that they used as activists in 2004. The protesters arrived by bus and were greeted by Andriy and his director. They used megaphones to provide information to the protesters (Ibid., 2015).

There were marked differences to note between this recent protest and comparisons with the Orange Revolution, when considering the conditions for protest. Firstly, in 2004, Andriy reminded us that civic organizations received funding from Western sources, and in 2013–2014, most civic groups used their own resources. Andriy received a stipend for living expenses in 2004, and in 2013, individuals paid their own expenses. One reason for the difference, Andriy believed, was that activists did not know how long the protest would last. He was under the impression that "many times...[it] will end" (Ibid., 2015). Another key difference to note was the organizational structure for protest, which also took on different forms. In 2004, Andriy was trained with politicians and civic activists from Serbia and Georgia in nonviolent resistance. This was in contrast to 2013, where protest strategies, for instance, use of barricades on Maidan, were organized by the Civic Sector of Euromaidan, and not by the political parties, Andriy explained. In his view, there was a major difference between the political party and civic organization. He pointed out that the "political leaders were not in tune with what was happening" on the ground (Ibid., 2015). As example, he mentions an encounter with Oleh

102   *The Euromaidan protests, 2013–2014*

Tyahnybok and Arseniy Yatsenyuk. They were organizing peacekeeping patrols in Kyiv. He and the activists "had a sense that the situation could spiral out of control" (author's interview, Shevtsiv, 2015).

In the Euromaidan protests, violent conditions served as contributory factors for an activist to exit the protests, which happened with Andriy. When the nonviolent phase ended, in late December, he grew conscious that, "I was not ready to go under bullets" and he left the capital city for Lviv (author's interview, Shevtsiv, 2015). During this time, Andriy's health deteriorated, since he was not eating properly. There was a plan among activists to create an organization based on the structure of Civic Sector of Euromaidan. Many agreed that they wanted Andriy to head a branch office in Lviv. His enthusiasm for participating decreased since he would have to resign from his current job to do it. Before his departure, he attended an assembly meeting (of the Civic Sector of Euromaidan), but he reflected that there had been no changes in strategy to respond to the violent turn in protests. He thought it might be useful if they did more physical labor in the tent camps to raise morale. The activists were demoralized and fearful in a stressful situation where the police were in place and ready to attack. Andriy would leave Kyiv before the protesters were killed. In retrospect, he reflected on the achievements of the protest action. The success in the removal of Yanukovych was, in his view, "a big win–otherwise it would be worse" (author's interview, Shevtsiv, 2015). He reasoned that Russia was absorbing Ukraine, and the situation might make them a colony. The activists he knew protested for reasons of self-preservation, and, he said, "to live without police interference" (author's interview, Shevtsiv, 2015). He explained the outcome of the protests and the feat of many activists who came to power. He provided names of activists like Igor Lutsenko (was a possible candidate for mayor of Kyiv) and Anna Hopko (member of Civic Sector of Euromaidan) who had an opportunity to work on Ukraine's reform package. Viatrovych heads the Institute of National Memory. Since January 2014, Andriy had not been in contact with the Civic Sector of Euromaidan—it no longer exists. It was reorganized, and now focuses on donations to Eastern Ukraine, immigrants, and the residents of Crimea. He hopes that revolution can be avoided in the future. For now, Andriy's activism focuses on the protection of the rights of Ukrainian language speakers (author's interview, Shevtsiv, 2015).

Volodymyr Ishchenko

This form of activism reflects Volodymyr Ishchenko's experience in the Euromaidan protests. Presently, Volodymyr is a sociologist, lecturer at Kyiv Polytechnic Institute, deputy director of Center for Social and Labor Research, and member of editorial boards for *Commons: Journal for Social Criticism* and *Left East* webzine. He contributed articles on Euromaidan protests for the UK's *The Guardian* newspaper, *New Left Review,* and others, mostly intended for a Western audience, covering topics such as

The Euromaidan protests, 2013–2014   103

Yanukovych's regime, political corruption, and issues related to the protests, like participants in far-right groups and the regional population mobilized in the anti-regime/pro-Europe protests.

Perceptions are important reflections of personal opinions and may assist in interpreting the forms of action taken by an individual. To probe further, in the movement's first days of protests, Volodymyr remained a skeptic about the Euromaidan. His difficulty accepting the situation was rooted in his belief that "I couldn't be so uncritical of the EU" ("Volodymyr Ishchenko," 2014). Although he observed the support and participation in the protests from the Ukrainian left, he had doubts about European integration, given that "the EU has precisely been destroying the welfare states established in previous decades" (Ibid., 2014). His views aligned with those people who believed that the "EU could be a dangerous thing for Ukraine" (Ibid., 2014). After the police brutality against students on 30 November, he reflected, the "character of the protests changed—this was now a movement against police brutality and against the government" (Ibid., 2014). Volodymyr's beliefs in the protest's cause seemed to explain his activism at the university. His participation behavior follows a social psychology theory summarized by Van Stekelenburg and Klandersmans (2010) that says people protest because of group efficacy, grounded in, "beliefs that individual actions have the potential to shape, and thus change, the social structure" (Van Stekelenburg and Klandersmans, 2010, p. 3). Volodymyr participated in the early stages of the student strike meetings at the National University of Kyiv Mohyla Academy. At that time, he "believed that it had some chance to create an alternative center and to propose another tactic for the struggle against Yanukovych after the 16 January laws had been passed" (author's interview, Ishchenko, 2015). When the protest on Kyiv's Maidan entered its violent phase with the increased presence of extreme rights groups, his activism ended. He did not cooperate in any activities with these groups (author's interview, Ishchenko, 2015).

Voldymyr's understanding of the situation enables us to see his perception about patterns of identification that underlie protest behavior in the Euromaidan. He categorized the protesters as middle-class residents from Kyiv, students, who identified with a European future, or, rather, "a European dream" for an improved life (Ishchenko, 2014b). He also found support for the Euromaidan movement was a minority view among people from eastern and southern Ukraine (Ishchenko, 2014a). Voldymyr explained that a large segment of the protesters originated from western and central regions of Ukraine. Their self-organized forms of protest, he described as resembling a "mass rebellion" (Ibid., 2014a). This was in reference to the lack of organization characteristic of the first days of protest, and described the participants who were self-mobilized by their beliefs in European ideals. He illustrated the protest dynamic in the following words: "The level of civic self-organization in the protest camp is impressive and the mass rallies are bringing hundreds thousands of people not involved in any political parties,

104 *The Euromaidan protests, 2013–2014*

or even civic organizations, hoping to win fundamental change towards European dream" (Ishchenko, 2014b).

His interviews also provided an interpretation of the context on the ground from which the Euromaidan protest over principles changed to one of interests. Van Stekelenburg and Klandersmans described the process when "people are more inclined to take an instrumental route to protest to enforce change" (Van Stekelenburg and Klandersmans, 2010, p. 2). The protests restructured into a conflict of interest when the Euromaidan became organized by two principal groups, one that Voldymyr called "civic Maidan" (Civic Sector of Euromaidan) and the other "party Maidan," which was composed of three parties: Tymoshenko's Batkivshchyna, Vitali Klitschko's UDAR, and the far-right Svoboda party. In the early days, Voldymyr noted the distinctions in protest actions from the two groups. The first group— the civic one—was locally organized and grassroots. Voldymyr compared it with the Occupy Wall Street movement or Spain's *Indignados* movement, since "it was pro-neoliberal, pro-nationalist in orientation" ("Volodymyr Ishchenko," 2014). Whereas the latter, Tymoshenko's and Klitschko's parties were more comparable to political machines, he said, "designed to bring certain people to power," their methods focused on the personalities of political leaders not ideologies (Ibid., 2014). Eventually, he said, these groups coalesced together into one group, thus changing the context of protest.

This had a visible effect on the protest strategy. This was demonstrated in Volodymyr's account of the events. He spoke about the organization by the two Maidan groups of Sunday rallies with political speakers on stage for tens of thousands of people. In January, Voldymyr observed a decline in public interest and attributed it to a lack of strategy for removing the president. By the middle of the month of January, he saw fewer participants on the streets. His impression was that "people wanted progress in the campaign; they wanted some action" ("Volodymyr Ishchenko," 2014). Their desires were rendered difficult, he said, when the Parliament approved of the "turbo-laws" that limited protests on 16 January, and protesters felt the government's repression. The laws were to restrict freedoms of assembly and speech, as well as, he said, "an NGO law requiring Western-funded organizations to declare themselves as foreign agents" (Ibid., 2014). More restrictions, he observed were placed on the activists. They were prohibited from wearing masks and banned from car processions—the latter directed to the Automaidan; their protesters were targeted by the regime in attacks. This phenomenon supported findings from Van Stekelenburg and Klandersmans (2010) that "people who experience both personal deprivation and group deprivation are the most strongly motivated to take to the streets" (Van Stekelenburg and Klandersmans, 2010, p. 2). The protesters felt their rights had been violated and this produced activism to make demands on Yanukovych. To illustrate, Volodymyr described protests organized on 19 January to fight against this law, and altercations with the police that broke out. It marked the period when violence was introduced as a tactic in the protests. As a result, he concluded that the general assemblies lost their importance as a strategy for organization. This was reflected in demographic surveys he read that discussed the change of participants in this period of protests. The majority of protesters, he learned, were no longer from Kyiv; the majority came from rural areas from central and western Ukraine ("Volodymyr Ishchenko," 2014). He described features of this new group of protesters in the following way:

> People from these regions are obviously very much in favour of European integration, of being allowed to go to the West freely and work there. They also had clear social grievances against Yanukovych, and not much holding them back—that's why they were prepared to join the Maidan self-defense forces and go up against the police.
>
> ("Volodymyr Ishchenko," 2014)

Volodymyr's reflexivity presents a historical account of protests that evolves from issues of grievances and interpretations of the logic for Euromaidan's organization via two groups.

Andriy Kohut

In comparison, Andriy's experience was connected with civil society initiatives at a national and international level since the end of the Orange Revolution. His direct engagement in these issues will provide the basis for his participation in the Euromaidan protests. Andriy Kohut is a member of the Center for Research on the Liberation Movement that focuses on national memory policy. He helped to draft the Ukrainian Bill #2540 to open the communist archives. He is director of an online, open source digital archives of a KGB documents project, including the release of information on the resistance movement in Ukraine ("Staff," 2015). Previously, he was involved as secretary of the Organizational Committee of Network of Public Organization "Public Assembly of Ukraine." This organization was created by the European Union on 18 February 2010 to promote dialogue between members of civil society in Ukraine. Its objective was to establish cooperation on Ukrainian civil issues with corresponding pan-European platforms with representatives in Brussels (author's interview, Kohut, 2015).

Andriy's mobilization process exemplified the idea that "consciousness raising takes place within social networks" (Van Stekelenburg and Klandersmans, 2010, p. 6). To describe further, listed below are civic projects and networks in which Andriy participated. They are featured to show the sequence of events in which Andriy got involved in civic work, which explained the context which produced his disappointment, since his involvement in the preparatory work on the Associated Agreement—and subsequent activism—had stalled. To illustrate, in mid-November 2011, Andriy worked with the Laboratory of Legislative Initiatives, a legal and political research center located in Kyiv. They submitted an open appeal of Ukrainian NGO leaders to advocate for proceedings to begin work on the Association Agreement between Ukraine and EU (author's interview, Kohut, 2015). He attended with this group, the National Platform of the Eastern Partnership Civil Society Forum with other Ukrainian representatives from NGOs, trade unions and other associations. The goals of the forum were to identify shared values from the Treaty on European Union (article 2), highlight Ukraine's European identity, and take stock of the EU-Ukraine initiatives that had been completed for the Association Agreement ("The EU," 2015). On 19 December 2011, the Civil Society Forum "EU-Ukraine Summit 2011: Civil Society Dimension" was held in Kyiv. The organizers were the Ukrainian National Platform of the Eastern Partnership Civil Society Forum, the Laboratory of Legislative Initiatives, the Civic Expert Council, and the European Program of the International Renaissance Foundation ("The EU," 2015). He explained the goals of the meeting were to prepare Ukraine for the signing of the Association Agreement, including EU assistance programs for reform, transparency, and self-governance, as well as assisting members of Ukrainian parliament with following EU policies for the agreement. Lastly, he participated in a Ukrainian assessment of democratic governance with the International Renaissance Foundation from May 2012 to October 2013. As a participant in the Eastern Partnership Roadmap to Vilnius Summit, Andriy was in Vilnius when Yanukovych refused to sign the EU partnership agreement and expressed his disappointment (author's interview, Kohut, 2015).

Andriy got involved in activism because he identified with the students who had been brutally repressed. This was similar to what Van Stekelenburg and Klandersmans (2010) concluded about the role of identification in protests, moreover, they said, "the more one identifies with the group, the more weight this group norm will carry and the more it will result in an 'inner obligation' to participate on behalf of the group" (Van Stekelenburg and Klandersmans, 2010, p. 5). A defining moment that convinced Andriy to personally get involved to coordinate the protests happened after the students were brutalized by police. He recounted that he was in Kyiv a few days earlier with the student protesters to execute an action. Late in the month, on 30 November, the students were violently beaten by the authorities, which made an impact on him, leading him to get involved. Those students were against Yanukovych's policy and they knew he was not going to sign the EU agreement, he said. The following Saturday, he went to St. Michael's Square and saw friends from different NGOs. They were civil society experts. He observed a lack of organization and decided on the spot, with 20 to 30 friends who were core activists, to coordinate the protests. They met with other friends to start a working group to assist the protesters to better organize the protests. Among them were former activists from both Pora campaigns, now affiliated with different civic groups. They appropriated shared values of nonviolence from the Pora movement, but they also incorporated new tactics of a business-like approach to mobilizing people in their

The Euromaidan protests, 2013–2014   107

principles for organizing. He said modestly about the group assembled, that "we must call them informal organizations, civil society from 2004" (author's interview, Kohut, 2015). The Civic Sector Euromaidan was created by Ukrainian civil society organizations that united in this effort (Ibid., 2015). "If each citizen sees that something is wrong and realizes how it can be fixed, he fixes it. This formula united Maidan from the beginning to this day. Everyone was doing what he found important to do here and now–without any instructions" ("Maidan is," 2014).

Andriy participated in the Civic Sector of Euromaidan. He was quick to point out the differences in terms of readiness and preparations that he observed. In 2004, he was active with other activists in making preparations in advance with NGOs for election monitoring and voter political drive campaigns. In contrast, this time, in 2013, he was working again with an organization that adopted a similar nonviolent approach to protest. The difference from earlier protests was that the Euromaidan protests were unexpected and self-organized by Ukrainian civil society organizations, which united in the civic sector, he said. The international NGOs were not prepared to help, and interacted with them to obtain updates on the ever-changing protest situation. He remembered that these offers to assist arrived too late after Yanukovych had fled Ukraine and the protested had ended. Another difference from 2004 was that Kuchma understood the Ukrainian political culture and did not use violence on the Maidan during the Orange Revolution. He said that Yanukovych inflicted violence on students since he was under the influence of a Russian advisor that used tactics used in Moscow (author's interview, Kohut, 2015).

Andriy's narrative provided an understanding of how the protest movement functioned and mobilized people through the lens of his participation as a coordinator in the Civic Sector of Euromaidan. He described that the protest movement was dynamic and their volunteers changed all the time throughout the protests. As a response, Andriy explained how they were able to achieve continuity in numbers of volunteers in terms of replacements. This aspect is seldom considered. In his case, his group mobilized young people using tactics of flash mobs. He explained that students were attracted to them because of their nonviolent approach. The group also organized activities for the young people on Kyiv's Maidan. Andriy provided logistical support, such as bed, food, showers, and clothing for protesters. He saw that there was no coordination, so he decided to take charge of logistics and to establish an information center on Maidan (author's interview, Kohut, 2015).

> ...[A] strong informational support and social media coordination was organised with a published newsletter, appeals and active spread of information through Facebook and Twitter. This was especially important, when after the events of the 30th of November many activists have disappeared and required urgent medical help.
>
> ("Organisations of," 2014)

108   *The Euromaidan protests, 2013–2014*

Over time, the efficacy of the protest was in question and Andriy's experience shows the dilemma presented to his group and efforts to respond by changing its forms of actions. In January 2014, Andriy did not see any visible effects from their two-month campaigns of nonviolent protests on the government. He felt that "our government doesn't hear us," and then he saw people responding to police brutality with violence (author's interview, Kohut, 2015). This division on use of violence also he said divided the political opposition and civic groups on Maidan. With more wounded protesters and their turn to violent action, he responded by redirecting efforts in the Civic Sector Euromaidan in January to include humanitarian assistance in a makeshift hospital for the injured on St. Michael's square (Ibid., 2015).

In the aftermath of protests, Euromaidan activists focused on creating institutional reforms in the political realm, and electoral laws. Andriy participated in an archiving of Yanukovych's documents that proved corruption and money laundering on his estate in Mezyhirya; the property had been seized by the State ("Organisations of," 2014). "[W]e are communicating with the parliamentary deputies; besides, we also are contacting ministers for implementing the reforms. We do what we can; and let's see how the authorities are going to correspond to the suggestions and conditions set by Maidan and citizens" ("Maidan is," 2014).

Civil society is working with political decision-makers to bring out much needed structural reforms. Andriy's interest remains concentrated in structural political reform. His priorities are stated in the following: "the reform of the legal system, the reform of the public prosecutor's office, [and] the reform of the ministry of domestic affairs, decentralization of power, delegating authorities to local agents" ("Maidan is," 2014).

Ostap Kryvydk

Ostap Kryvydk belonged to a group of Ukrainian political actors who worked on European integration issues. His story of protest comes from the perspective of a politicized actor with national interests in pro-Europe reforms, which involved direct interactions with the state for social change. Ostap's choice of work as a consultant aligned with his political desire for a European future, which preceded the Euromaidan protests. To illustrate, Ostap worked as a political consultant for a politician on a project called Euro Advance, supporting Euro integration for Ukraine. Ostap's role was an advisor in charge of international communications for the foreign embassies and EU representatives. The group, he recalled, was confident that the Association Agreement would be signed, and set up activities to support its success. At the time, Ostap believed that support for the agreement was universal since its objective was to restructure Ukrainian politics. As an example of the group's initiatives, Ostap described a project to reform Ukrainian politics through the preparation of a checklist with 12 issues for Ukraine's government to complete in order to fulfill the requirements for signing the EU Associated Agreement. The group drafted a list of laws for each government institution to address with a specified deadline. This was done, he said, so they could track the progress and identify the areas of violations. His experience found that some of the politicians were open to these ideas, and depending on their position, they would cooperate. He said that their interactions with political actors functioned like a "political game," especially on the part of those who did not like this action plan that they formulated to follow. He regretted that the Euro plan was not upheld by the EU Commission and Ukrainian government at that time. He had believed in assurances that Yanukovych would sign. When the agreement was in danger of not being approved, his group grew afraid that the whole process would get cancelled. In fact, he said, "and that is what happened" (author's interview, Kryvydk, 2015).

To trace Ostap's route to protest, it seemed to be the direct result of his social networks ties to political and civic groups, which got him involved doing similar work in a different protest structure. His recruitment experience seemed to align with Van Stekelenburg and Klandersmans' (2010) discussion on the role of groups in the identification process, which conditions an actor's action in the direction to join a protest. Moreover, in their analysis, they described the function of an individual to group interactions in the following terms, "the more one identifies with the group, the more weight this group norm will carry and the more it will result in an 'inner obligation' to participate on behalf of the group" (Van Stekelenburg and Klandersmans, 2010, p. 5). That is to say, social obligation is a factor to consider when an individual is involved in groups. In Ostap's case, group ties may have contributed to his mobilization into protest activity. To illustrate, before Euromaidan, Ostap worked for Andriy Parubiy, a Ukrainian Deputy in Parliament (who became the chief of the Maidan Self-Defense Forces). Andriy would combine both his interests of activism with his role in the Euro Advance campaign. Ostap started his protest activity in earnest in mid-November within the context of the Euro Advance campaign. He explained that, through a petition campaign, the group collected a million signatures nationwide in support for EU integration and brought it to the Presidential Administration. Ostap described that on Kyiv's Maidan, people were using the space for advocacy activities and the Trade Union building had set up a big screen to broadcast the news on its building. He and thousands more were mobilized through a message asking them to protest, sent out on Facebook by Mustafa Nayyem, whom he knew personally. Ostap went to the protest with his Euro Advance campaign group. They brought the first microphone and EU/Ukrainian flags to the Maidan. Additionally, it was his group's idea to rent time on the big screen to introduce their protest initiative that they named Euromaidan. This was the first reference made to Euromaidan in the protests. His group was credited for naming the protest (Euromaidan). His group's political actions were combined with Nayyem's. At the peak of the protest event (that day), Ostap recalled that there were 1,000 people and

110   *The Euromaidan protests, 2013–2014*

30 students who spent the night in the city's square. The next day, the police prevented them from keeping their tents there, so they dismantled them (author's interview, Kryvydk, 2015).

A turning point in Ostap's activism occurred during the protest's phase of radicalization, which happened after the students' forced removal from their occupation of the city square on 30 November. He described the event; in his words, "I was present that day and this was the day when Maidan Self-Defense emerged. Since the police had beaten the protesters, this was the reason to organize Maidan Self-Defense as a protector's militia. They weren't armed except for maybe sticks. They didn't have helmets; that came later" (author's interview, Kryvydk, 2015). The wearing of helmets became standard because the police would target their heads for the beatings, he clarified. In terms of its group's logics for organization, Ostap detailed the structure of Maidan Self-Defense; he explained it had two major groups. The first was the Euro Advance network of 500 people nationwide from 15 regions. It was the outgrowth of the "Renewal of Ukraine" campaign. This group was composed of the core members. The second group came from the private sector. It was extremely diverse with units created from Cossacks, Afghanistan war veterans, Svoboda party, and UDAR party. They were connected to units from western and eastern regions. In this group, there were people with a criminal past. They were helpful, he said, since they thought in non-orthodox ways and stayed for the length of the protests. This diverse group of protesters included rich people, poor people, celebrities, and those with a basic education, he observed. In the beginning, Ostap volunteered and later he was assigned to manage communications for the Maidan Self-Defense, including its publications.

In his role, Ostap was responsible for communicating the group's main issues to a large audience, including internationally. He explained his strategy of communication. In one instance, he obtained information that the tent cities might be dismantled. In response, he felt the urgency to diffuse his message about these dangers of repression to an international audience. He understood that if there was violence, the victims would be known around the world. In order to make these links, Ostap traveled many times abroad to cities such as Berlin and Brussels to spread his message about the Euromaidan protests. He feared there would be violence and felt it was necessary, in the meantime, to gather international support for the protesters before that happened. This was the moment when Ostap observed that the Maidan had grown in importance and strength as the numbers of people increased in the tent camps. Once the tent camps reached 3,000 inhabitants, Ostap described that they had eight major barricades set up and manned by guards both day and night. Students and graduates from the National University of Kyiv Mohyla Academy came to Maidan at night. They served as critical mass when the numbers mattered until 4 or 5 AM. This protest experience was different from the Orange Revolution in size, time, and scale, he explained. The demands of camp life soon began to take a toll on Ostap. He spent several nights at Maidan in November. Eventually, Ostap decided that he was more efficient when he worked during the day and slept at night. He changed his routine and instead spent the entire day at Maidan, from 10 AM to 11 PM. To facilitate accessibility to the Euromaidan's key events, he was given an all-access badge to all areas, including the backstage on the Maidan (Ibid., 2015).

Motivation for Ostap to continue his activism in the group was explained by Van Stekelenburg and Klandersmans (2010), they reasoned that "for the perception of the possibility of change to take hold people need to perceive the group to be able to unite and fight for the issue and they must perceive the political context as receptive for the claims made by their group" (Van Stekelenburg and Klandersmans, 2010, p. 3). This was the context that Ostap engaged in the Euromaidan protest until its completion. Two events, which were pivotal for Ostap's sense of efficacy, fed into his desire to take an active role in the protest's final days. The first episode took place on 18 February 2014, which was declared as a day of violence in the Euromaidan protest. That morning, Ostap went to the Trade Union House, headquarters for Euromaidan. He learned of the organization of a peaceful march to Marinsky Park, which later erupted in fights and massive bloodshed inflicted by riot police. The police burned down the protesters' tent cities and their belongings. The people who stayed there were credited, he said, "with keeping Maidan standing" (author's interview, Kryvydk, 2015). Ostap was several hundred meters away from the violence at the time and had been given the orders to hide three or four laptops. The computers had sensitive data, which, if it fell into government hands, he reasoned, might result in the arrests of hundreds of thousands of activists. The next day, he was streaming the protests on the Maidan from his home computer. He felt he was assigned an important role as the guardian of laptops and data for the movement. But his wife said he should participate because he was a man. He felt ashamed and went to Maidan. He had two children at home; this was not an easy decision for him. The following day, he wore a bulletproof vest for protection. He was ashamed to be the only one wearing it in the meeting with ambassadors and Parubiy. Parubiy told him that the police snipers were targeting the head and a vest did not make any sense. Parubiy was very popular. Ostap credited him as "born to have a Maidan, one of best revolution managers in Ukraine; he still is" (Ibid., 2015). The second event took place on 21 February, the day when Yanukovych left his residence to go east. He remembered that no one prevented Yanukovych from fleeing, not even his security guards. Ostap recounted that at 6 PM the Maidan Self-Defense units came to the presidential administration and the presidential guards of the official buildings handed them the keys and said "goodbye." Ostap described that period as when "people were tired and there were hundreds of casualties" (author's interview, Kryvydk, 2015). Before leaving, the guards told them there were state secrets in the building and it cannot be opened to the public. They assigned the responsibility to the Maidan Self-Defense to stay inside the

112 *The Euromaidan protests, 2013–2014*

building and to close the doors to the administrative offices before exiting to stand guard outside. Ostap described the distribution of roles to guard the administration buildings, "three of our people are there inside protecting all the infrastructure, secret documents in co-operation with the presidential guards so that there will be no ransacking, so that everything will be proper" (Olearchyk et al., 2014). The Maidan Self-Defense also closed the whole area to the public for the first few days. Ostap was introduced to the chief of the guards and given permission to take journalists to the stairs of the presidential administration (author's interview, Kryvydk, 2015).

When the Euromaidan ended in early March 2014, Ostap contacted Parubiy to work with him as a political advisor in the new government. He continued to work there after Parubiy left. Working as a political advisor has resulted in Ostap having less time available to work on the Euro Advance civic campaign and the National Roundtable Initiative (author's interview, Kryvydk, 2015).

Stanislav Kutsenko

While there may have been two main actors of mobilization on the Maidan (the political side and the Civic Sector of Euromaidan), Stanislav Kutsenko's experience reminds us of the plurality of other smaller actors (and groups) also on Kyiv's Maidan who organized independent protest actions for their networks. This was the social movement model followed by Stanislav's civic group. In this case, his mobilization to protest operated in the context of an existing civic organization's norms. In his group, they were already involved in related issues of democracy development and the Euromaidan values resonated with its members. The group's beliefs provided a basis for organizing protest actions that reflected the group's European values. Stanislav's activism, that is, the process involved for Stanislav to join the protests, is presented here. Prior to the Euromaidan, in September 2014, Stanislav was elected chairman of the Ukrainian Youth Forum, a civic union that unified all student organizations in Ukraine. He felt the public's indignation over Yanukovych's failure to sign the agreement, and it became his motive to protest. This was empirically observed and built upon Van Stekelenburg and Klanderman's previous research, which concluded, "anger is seen as the prototypical protest emotion" (Van Stekelenburg and Klandersmans, 2010, p. 6). This sentiment of outrage was expressed in Stanislav's following words, "I thought we, the Ukrainian people, were tricked, because we thought, finally, we have a chance to join the European Union" (author's interview, Kutsenko, 2015). When he discovered that this was not true, everyone that he knew became distressed. It was also the primary reason that he thought the Euromaidan happened. Before the shooting of police snipers started, he said, "the atmosphere was very friendly, everyone was inspired…it was really, really emotional" (Ibid., 2015).

The Euromaidan protests, 2013–2014   113

Stanislav's contributions to the organizing of protest events included the expansion of protest to international participants. The inclusion of a diversity of actors served to provide legitimacy to the movement, and also amplified its message on a larger scale to European actors. Stanislav's role in the protest was to mobilize the Ukrainian Youth Forum's representatives from the regions of Ukraine to come to Euromaidan; it encompassed five to seven regions with five to ten people from each region. Stanislav also coordinated street protests with the Ukrainian Student Association, a civic association. Their shared objective, he said, was "to protect the choice of the people to enter the European Union" (Ibid., 2015). Stanislav's first visit to Kyiv's Maidan was in December 2013. He recounted the day's activities; his group helped to build barricades from snow and he distributed water to the protesters (Ibid., 2015).

Particular to Stanislav's experience was the inclusion in the protest of in-group international networks to disseminate the protest movement's key messages. The Ukrainian Student Association was a member in the European Democrat Students (EDS) organization, a pan-European student organization based in Brussels. Ukrainian Student Association proposed several motions to the European Parliament to increase attention on the Ukrainian situation, he said. His association also prepared articles in the European Democrat Students (EDS) newsletter (*BullsEye*) "to share our perspectives from the student point of view, to European politicians" (Ibid., 2015). In that same vein, he organized the visit of a delegation from EDS, and the EDS Chair Eva Majewski prepared a speech to deliver on the Euromaidan on 24–26 January 2014 (Foinska, 2014, p. 8). In interviews, she spoke about her experience at Euromaidan. She spoke about her participation at the Euromaidan as a "call of duty" since EDS, the organization she represents, upholds European values of free speech and human rights. She observed how Yanukovych's decision went against the will of the majority of the population. As a result, her organization, EDS, has been vocal in its support of a European Ukraine (Foinska, 2014, p. 8).

The in-group interactions had an inspiring effect on Stanislav. These social ties with international actors were also sources of support for the movement and contributed also to providing greater recognition of the Euromaidan's protest issues on the European level. This appeared in Stanislav's reflections, which is appreciative of the EU's support to Ukraine in his following words:

> I am deeply impressed how much the EU is supporting Ukrainian citizens these days. I support the opinion of European colleagues that only imposing particular sanctions from the European Union to the oligarchic clans who are holding Ukraine in their hands [over] several years would lead to effective results in the long lasting struggle of Ukrainian people.
>
> (Foinska, 2014, p. 8)

114 *The Euromaidan protests, 2013–2014*

Stanislav continued activism into the following month (of February) to protest against Russia's occupation of Crimea. These forms of actions can also be analyzed to determine mobilizing issues for the protest organizers and protest demands. To illustrate, Stanislav created protest actions to communicate their group's grievance. In one case, it was about Russia. He described how his group and the Ukrainian Student Association demonstrated in front of the Russian embassy to protest against the occupation in Crimea. Their demands were directed at Russia. The protest's objective was to communicate a clear message about Crimea and their perceptions of Russian interference in Ukrainian politics. (author's interview, Kutsenko, 2015).

With Stanislav's reasons for protest identified, another question to ask was how did he evaluate his contributions to the protests? Overall, he thought the Euromaidan was successful, but he regretted the war. He reflected that for young people, the Euromaidan was an important event to shape their activist experience. Considering his group's civic initiatives on Euromaidan, he responded that "we had a chance to change a lot in our country" (Ibid., 2015). He hoped the war would end and Ukraine could have a chance at development like other countries. After the Euromaidan, he continued the activities with EDS. Unfortunately, by 2015, he regretted that the "European partners were not so much interested in our activities anymore" (Ibid., 2015). As a result, Stanislav turned his attention to work in the Ukrainian Youth Forum (after the Euromaidan). He said their group's mission was to make inroads to implementing European standards in youth policy in Ukraine. To that end, the group created a delegation to address youth employment since young people continued to struggle to find good jobs in Ukraine. He pointed to the brain drain problem in Ukraine. In general, post-Euromaidan, he described a situation where people feel dissatisfied. He stated that the reasons for their dissatisfaction were because "people don't have possibilities to run a business, people can't afford to buy things, people want to leave Ukraine, and corruption is too high" (Ibid., 2015).

Conclusion

These activists presented portraits of what the Euromaidan looked like from the internal perspective of experienced contributors involved in different initiatives. They demonstrated how the Euromaidan was hastily created by activists, themselves, on Facebook as a peaceful, nonviolent protest. The nature of protests changed with the authorities' repression of unarmed students, which escalated the conflict in December. It also produced a public response of volunteering with the veteran activists taking on the role of coordinators. This newfound community of activists and volunteers undertook daily protest actions, projecting an image of freedom and creativity in their art and slogans. Communal life was also displayed in the Maidan with a food kitchen tent supplied by local restaurants to feed its protesters free of charge. In the course of protests, the activists were able to identify needs, and, in one case presented, to organize logistical support for the distribution of donations. It was winter, and that meant a need to set up distribution centers for warm and dry clothing for the activists. During that period, it was also common for residents of Kyiv to offer shelter and housing for protesters. This was coordinated by the information center set up by the Civic Sector of Euromaidan. While the protest started as a makeshift one with little advance preparation for a long duration and large-scale numbers of protesters, the experienced activists were able to respond and to organize based on needs. The Civic Sector of Euromaidan held nightly meetings with its core members to update them on political events, and to determine the next day's activities. The civic group's ad hoc planning showed their high-level capacity to self-organize as experienced coordinators from successful protests, namely, the Orange Revolution.

However, the problem activists confronted from 30 December was the militarized police aggression against their peaceful activists. Members of the civic initiatives were concerned for the public's support and its international image to maintain nonviolent protests. In one example, Andriy Kohut spoke about how he saw activists attempting to upturn a public bus, and his role of talking to them to persuade them from violence was captured in a YouTube video that went viral. This main issue organizers of protest began to confront was a struggle to redirect activism efforts to advocate alternative practices of nonviolence as a defensive tactic in the face of police brutality against their student volunteers. Despite all their efforts, eventually their strategy of nonviolence was ineffective and unable to reach the radical activists that turned to violence as a protest tactic for regime change. As a result, in some cases studied above, it meant the end of participation of activists in the violent phase of the protests.

Bibliography

Author's interview. Andriy Kohut. Skype interview. August 13, 2015.
Author's interview. Andriy Shevtsiv. Skype interview. Translator Katya Bondar. July 22, 2015.
Author's interview. Ostap Kryvydk. Skype interview. August 6, 2015.
Author's interview. Stanislav Kutsenko. Skype interview. August 7, 2015.
Author's interview. Volodymyr Ishchenko. Facebook messenger. 29 July 29, 2015.
Foinska, E. (2014). "The Situation in Ukraine." *BullsEye*. No. 55: (Feb 2014) ISSN 2033–7809.
Heritage, T., & Polityuk, P. "Ukraine Protesters Seize Yanukovich Office; Jailed Rival Free under Law." *Reuters India*. Retrieved November 18, 2015, fromhttp://in.reuters.com/article/2014/02/22/ukraine-crisis-idINDEEA1K01J20140222.
Ishchenko, V. "Ukraine Has Not Experienced a Genuine Revolution, Merely a Change of Elites." *The Guardian*, February 28, 2014a, sec. Retrieved December 1, 2015, from Comment is free. http://www.theguardian.com/world/2014/feb/28/ukraine-genuine-revolution-tackle-corruption.

116   *The Euromaidan protests, 2013–2014*

Ishchenko, V. (2014b). "Support Ukrainians but Do Not Legitimize the Far-Right and Discredited Politicians! | LeftEast." January 7, 2014. Retrieved November 17, 2015, from http://www.criticatac.ro/lefteast/support-ukrainians-but-not-far-right/.

"Maidan Is Undergoing Transformations, and Even More Surprises Are to Come." Retrieved November 18, 2015, from http://cet.eurobelarus.info/en/news/2014/03/20/maidan-is-undergoing-transformations-and-even-more-surprises-are-to-come.html.

Olearchyk, Roman, & Neil Buckley. "Uncertainty in Ukraine as President Goes Missing." *Financial Times*, February 22, 2014. http://www.ft.com/intl/cms/s/0/69b57a22-9baa-11e3-afe3-00144feab7de.html.

"Organisations of EaP Civil Society Forum Perform Key Functions in Euromaidan Activities." Eastern Partnership Civil Society Forum RSS. 2014. Web. 22. Nov. 2015. http://archive.eap-csf.eu/en/news-events/news/organisations-of-eap-civil-society-forum-perform-key-functions-in-euromaidan-activities/.

Simon, B., Loewy, M., Sturmer, S., Weber, U., Freytag, P., Habig, C., et al. (1998). "Collective Identification and 12 Van Stekelenburg and Klandermans Protest Social Movement Participation." *Journal of Personality and Social Psychology, 74*(3), 646–658.

Staff, About the Source Euromaidan Press. "Defending Decommunization: Expert Answers Criticism -." *Euromaidan Press*. Retrieved November 18, 2015, from http://euromaidanpress.com/2015/04/14/defending-decommunization-expert-answers-criticism/.

Stekelenburg, J. van, & Klandermans, B. (2010). "The Social Psychology of Protest." *Sociopedia.isa* (e-journal), 1–13.

"The EU Will Cooperate with Ukrainian Civil Society." Retrieved November 18, 2015, from http://www.irf.ua/en/knowledgebase/news/the_eu_will_cooperate_with_ukrainian_civil_society/.

Tytysh, Galina. "'Я дівчинка. Я не хочу сукню, я хочу змінити цю систему': молодь, яка творить мирний протест." *Українська правда _Життя*. Retrieved November 19, 2015, from http://life.pravda.com.ua/society/2013/12/19/146507/.

"Volodymyr Ishchenko: Ukraine's Fractures. New Left Review 87, May–June 2014." Retrieved November 17, 2015, from http://newleftreview.org/II/87/volodymyr-ishchenko-ukraine-s-fractures.

6 Conclusion

The previous chapters detailed the life histories of five Ukrainian activists who lived and participated in three protest events that occurred since Ukraine gained its independence. Their life stories provided new insights, including an alternative perspective of activism as a process, which was largely individualized in the cases studied. It also represented examples of individual contributions to protest-making activities. Additionally, these narratives demonstrated the important role that individual actors played in starting a protest movement and/or initiating its organization through friend networks. Using ethnographic methods, this book made inroads to redirect scholarly focus once again onto the actor as a mobilizing agent for protests. The earlier chapters demonstrated that Ukraine's protest movement activity was oftentimes initiated by single actors with previous protest experience, who were in a position to decide to react to a political crisis situation. This involved an actor recruiting through friend networks, which would provide mobilizing structures and resources to expand the protests into campaigns, and to include the broad participation of citizens. This recurring tendency of protest-starters in Ukraine was also mirrored in the global waves of protests seen in the Spain's 15 M movement and many others. The activists behaved the same way during the third wave of protest action (Euromaidan). In this instance, single actors self-mobilized to organize the protests once it had started. This newfound role adopted and self-initiated by former activists was also unstudied. I hope that this research will contribute to the field of social movement studies by generating more interest in analyzing individual actors who take it upon themselves to organize ongoing protests, which had already been launched, but were not being organized by any civic group or organization. In this case, what was of particular interest was how the individual actor decided to take responsibility for organizing existing protests. A second aspect of interest, was how that actor used personal networks as a base for mobilizing activist friends in the construction of new groups (such as Civic Sector Euromaidan) to aid in these efforts. More comparative studies on this phenomenon are needed to characterize this type of "actor" who puts out that first call to protest, which proceeds the networked movement, as well as the single actor who takes it upon him/herself to organize the protesters.

118   *Conclusion*

Social change and transformation of individuals

Moreover, this book's contribution was to extend the explanatory power of cultural theory to place a greater importance on the social meaning embedded in the individual's choice to protest. This had profound effects on social change transformation based on a citizen's participation in Ukrainian politics. This micro-study on the political culture applied ethnography and case study approaches to demonstrate the dynamics of democratization processes in an ever-growing self-conscious and self-organized citizenry. The catalyst for deciding to partake in protests varied from personal accounts of government repression, informal networks connected to civic or political activity, or personal beliefs. The life histories' narratives revealed the complexity of ways in which individuals transformed into activists. This was in direct relation to their past social protest experiences and their continued participation in civil society. This activism was attributed to the older generation of political dissidents' personal, democratic visions for Ukraine's future development. Among the new, post-Soviet generation of activists, some of them, like Ostap Kryvdyk, had entered political life as political consultants, following the end of a protest cycle. This was very much in line with what the founders of their alma mater had hoped for and envisioned for the new generation of graduates from the National University of Kyiv Mohyla Academy. The university's graduates' entry into civic and political life was a fulfillment of the university's objectives for new leadership to drive national development in Ukraine. As stated earlier by the former university president (Bryukhovetsky), this university was modeled to meet the higher education standards of Western democracies. Its graduates contributed to the emergence of Western-style educated Ukrainians, whom, it was envisioned, would help to reform Ukrainian politics from the inside. This university had a reputation for cultivating free minds, and it attracted many students who were critically-minded, including some activists who went on to produce a type of samizdat of *Maidan* magazine on campus that helped politicize students there in the years preceding the Orange Revolution. In that revolution, students from the National University of Kyiv Mohyla Academy participated in large numbers in youth movements, including both Pora campaigns, as coordinators. This was illustrated in the case studies that presented the National University of Kyiv Mohyla Academy at the center of political activity for "Our Ukraine" political party, as well as positioned as the first group of mobilizers in the 2004 and 2013 protests.

In the recent protest, these individuals active in 2004 reemerged and self-mobilized to assume leadership positions as coordinators in the organization of the Euromaidan protests. In this instance, the activists were working under more constraints—they had not prepared in advance and possessed limited resources as compared to the 2004 civic campaigns. However, they called upon their friends from the Orange Revolution to contribute their talents to a new round of citizen-led protests. Individuals reactivated their

Conclusion 119

old activist networks from a group of volunteers from 2004 (or later), and integrated them into a core group to address the immediate needs of the Maidan as was the case of the Euromaidan Civic Sector. For example, this group of individuals drew from their past experience in the large-scale information campaign of Pora from 2004 to establish another communication center (i.e., PR Maidan) to provide information about the Euromaidan protests at the national and international levels. These individuals were able to draw from their past experiences, and now as adults in their 30s, they had matured, and were capable of assessing the protest situation like their predecessors had done during the 1990s student protests. As adults, in the Euromaidan, they were able to self-organize based on on-the-ground needs in order to supply logistical and humanitarian support to the protesters with local outreach to the community for donations. In addition, their grassroots mobilization efforts included the indoctrination of a different generation of university students into activism, as was the case in the 2000 and again in 2004 and 2013.

Furthermore, the last objective was to redirect attention and provide final comments on three critical areas that were revealed in this study on the individualized nature of protests in contemporary Ukraine. The first was to address the evolving forms of activism that were observed in the changing roles of the individual as a protester, volunteer, and eventually, co-ordinator of protest actions. The individual's tendencies to accept more responsibility represented a process of transformation into an activist. These experiences in multiple protests reflected building blocks of knowledge that accumulated from each subsequent wave of protests, which had an effect on an individual's long-term involvement in civil society or democratic reform initiatives. Also noteworthy, was the fact that this book drew a distinction among different types of activism for a first-time protester. Among such individuals, attendance at a single protest event was not sufficient to determine whether they would continue to participate in the protest movement. Repeated participation in ongoing protests seemed to lead, in some cases, to an individual's willingness to assume greater responsibility in the organization of future protest actions. Greater implication required more effort on the part of the individual, to sign up as a volunteer or connect with friend networks for a coordinator position. For the individual as volunteer, it meant a greater time commitment, skills to contribute, and self-initiative to get involved in the organization of protests. The latter was facilitated by networks, which worked as a source of information. Individuals close to protest activists were not only informed about actions, but invited to take a pre-defined role in the organization of protests in campaigns or civic initiatives. The individual's experience gained in the organizational structure of protest also contributed to a greater likelihood that they would continue to work in civil society on related issues after the protest ended. Some actors presented in the case studies remained part of the activist network, while others who were not active, had friends who reached out to them, since they possessed valuable skills to apply to future protest events.

120 *Conclusion*

On the other hand, the role of networks in politicizing an individual remained less clear. As some cases revealed, a few individuals were introduced to protest through friends, but it was not a sufficient condition to politicize them. Some of the cases, e.g., Kryvdyk's, showed how an individual who did not understand the forms of collective action, or see an immediate result of their activity, remained a skeptic. He attended the "Ukraine without Kuchma" protests, more out friend loyalty than out of an actual belief in the protest's ability to bring political change. In his case, it was not necessary to have political convictions in order to participate in the actions, rather, friend loyalty meant more involvement for him. Kryvdyk was ambivalent about his activism, but returned to participate due to his social ties to his friendship groups. His story involved personal transformation that materialized as a result of repression inflicted by the police. The violation of citizens' rights at that event angered and politicized students to support the protests at that time. His experience of self-defense and declaration of his civic rights had no effect on the authorities that violated them. Simply knowing his citizens' rights was not enough to protect himself, but the experience of violence worked in effect to mobilize him as an active member in the protest movement. He understood through his experience that his Constitutional right to protest was not safeguarded by the authorities. When it was clear that a risk was being posed to lose his civic rights, it had an impact on his decision to react and to join the protest as an active member of a civic group—thus to become a political actor. This was an example of the concept of *individualized collective action*. The politics got personal when Kryvdyk was threatened and aggressed by the secret police at the train station; he witnessed the authorities representing law and order violating his civil liberties. This was the turning point in activism to motivate Kryvdyk from his non-committal stance as participant into an active organizer for the "For Truth" protest movement at his university.

In the case of Volodymyr Ishchenko, who came from a family of Left activists, his personal ideology as a Socialist was shaped by his social structure and ideological beliefs, which drove his mobilization. In "Ukraine without Kuchma" his social ties to the organizer Volodymyr Chemerys put him to work in the NGO Institute of Economic and Social Problems "Respublika," in the center of activities, and in contact with activists. His beliefs also put him on the sidelines and he was not active as an activist in the Orange Revolution. Instead, he adopted a critical perspective on the Orange Revolution. He modified this point of view a bit in the Euromaidan, where he was engaged in early activities at the universities. Again, when the protest movement took a violent turn, he rationalized his withdrawal from collective actions. So, ideology for Ishchenko both enabled—and at the same time, constrained—his level of engagement. However, in the case of the Euromaidan, although Ishchenko stopped activism on the ground, it did not mean withdrawal from public debates. He would publish numerous articles in his journal and for international media, such as UK's *The Guardian*

Conclusion 121

newspaper, as well as become known as an expert to be featured in several international media interviews. His ideas explaining the Euromaidan found a local and global audience. Ishchenko's contribution was linked to an intelligentsia class, his critical views also served to provoke national debates with those who disagreed with him. To illustrate, in Ishchenko's words, he spoke about public opinion on his published articles about the Euromaidan and its public response as the following, "writing from a critical position is not something to be widely appreciated in turmoil times. For some hysterical idiots I've succumbed to the fascists, for others–betrayed the Fatherland" (Ishchenko, 2014). In other words, his interchangeable roles of activist and intellectual positioned him on one side as a critic featured in critical articles about radicalization from the right sector. His words had consequences in terms of stirring controversy in Ukraine. It produced an unintended effect, as Ishchenko pointed out in the following statement "Ukrainian comrades, let's think what we could do. It's clear that signing up in the Right Sector [which has issued a call for mobilization] is not an option" (Ishchenko, 2014). Therefore, Ishchenko's personal conviction drove his action off the street and instead, redirected his contributions to an intellectual role, stirring public debate over topics such as the extreme right party's rise to power.

The second point to underscore was the interaction between the individual's decision-making and preference for collective action of nonviolent protests, and its effect of increasing participation as observed in the protests studied. In the instance of the Euromaidan, the Kyiv's Maidan was divided into three camps as mentioned earlier, one of them, the Civic Sector Euromaidan, was run by former Orange Revolution activists following the same strategies of nonviolent resistance as they did in previous protests. This differed from the "Ukraine without Kuchma" protests. In that case, the organizers were unable to keep the protests peaceful, and suffered a negative effect of dissonance, which resulted in the loss of legitimacy and public support. Instead, in preparation for the 2004 presidential elections, these same activists wanted to learn from their failures, and analyzed the recent successful protests in Serbia and Georgia, to arrive at the conclusion that peaceful resistance worked to overthrow the authoritarian regimes. It was for that very reason that these individuals, with social ties to democratic civil society, reached out to the Serbians and Georgians for training in new strategies of nonviolence. As a result of Serbia's success, the Ukrainians decided to incorporate nonviolence into the new civic campaign. In the case presented of the Pora campaign (yellow/black), the protestors applied nonviolent practices. The activists employed strategies based on Gene Sharp's (from The Albert Einstein Institution) book *From Dictatorship to Democracy* (1993). This was the main manual for protest used by Serbia's Otpor campaign, and transferred in joint training seminars to Ukraine's civic campaign, Pora, which was applied to successfully down authoritarian regimes. As a strategy of resistance for Pora, their nonviolence also helped to attract a volunteer network and establish connections with the international

122 *Conclusion*

community, including the media. The appropriation of such tactics by local activists and volunteers had an indirect effect of increasing their popularity among university students; perhaps it provided a sense of security to participate. Students wanted to join their campaign even more so after the activists who were already well-liked were subjected to unfair government reprisals. As a result, Pora's campaign garnered the students' support and solidarity for their activists—so much so that there was more interest than available positions in the campaign. It also generated a shift in greater overall public support when the students of the civic campaign were accused of terrorism and the regime targeted them in repression. Moreover, the three-week, nonviolent protests of the Orange Revolution inspired its citizens to exercise autonomy from the State. Further, the massive numbers on the Maidan were the outcome of the early mobilization efforts of civic campaigns such as Pora, which produced massive turnouts on the street, and helped bide time to overturn election results, to the advantage of the political opposition.

As Andriy Kohut's narratives presented, within the Civic Sector Euromaidan, there were discussions among leaders concerned about the radicalization of the protests and the movement's evolution into violence. Andriy and others were aware of its negative effects in terms of public withdrawal of support for their protest actions and providing a cause for government crackdown on the protesters. Moreover, the question raised to Andriy and many others, was how to maintain nonviolent protests and also how to prevent protesters from initiating violence. As discussed earlier, the peak in student mobilization occurred following the student repressions on 30 November. Their participation as a group would fall sharply as the nonviolent phase ended in January with the outbreak of street violence. The next phase of protest begun in January 2014. There were changes in terms of the population of inhabitants on the Maidan and a decrease in young people in the tent camps. This partly explained why the support for violence won over nonviolent resistance methods, which resulted in the alienation and withdrawal of many young people from the space of occupation in the city's square. Within this context, Andriy Kohut's experiences pointed to the struggles within the Civic Sector of Euromaidan to maintain the peace among frustrated protesters resorting to vandalism. He recounted in our interview his response when he saw activists committing an act of destruction by overturning a public bus. In the video, he played an important role in convincing the violent protesters to reconsider their actions and to maintain peaceful protests. His action was recorded by an unknown person and diffused throughout social media networks. This video of the incident and Kohut's involvement in the mayhem went viral on the Internet. Its diffusion through social media networks had the effect of demonstrating the extent to which personal convictions (i.e., nonviolent resistance) played a role in influencing an individual such as Kohut to get involved in the madness of mayhem to stop violence from the part of aggressive protesters. Kohut's personal belief of nonviolence was put to the test, and, in reality, he put it

Conclusion 123

into practice that day, by dissuading the protesters from committing an act of destruction. For the others like Ishchenko and Shevtsiv, they retreated from the actions when the violence on the Maidan began in January. Even Kryvdyk took precautions and wore body armor to protect himself when he went to Maidan after the peaceful phase of protests ended. This suggested that even among a group of activists, there were limitations, and that their engagement seemed to be conditional and oftentimes linked to personal beliefs. A greater commitment to participation on Maidan was conditional, i.e., more likely to occur when it aligned with their personal preferences for nonviolent resistance actions. These individuals, like the university students, retreated from the battlefield of the Maidan to return to ordinary life or to work in a different capacity for the movement, but at a distance, like in Kryvdyk's and other cases presented when violence erupted on Kyiv's Maidan.

The third point to highlight was the social change effect of individual activists and their efforts to institutionalize civic campaigns into political structures following the termination of protests. Observing the situation following the Orange Revolution, there were two groups to underscore, which derived from the former Pora campaigns. One group of [black] Pora activists entered public life and became a non-governmental organization (NGO) (politically and financially independent) and in 2006 changed their name to Opora. They worked as a kind of watchdog organization to improve "...public participation in the political process by developing and implementing models of citizens' influence on the activities of state and local government in Ukraine" ("About us," 2015). They focused on areas of municipal and education policy, and monitoring of the process of elections. Their organizational structure followed a decentralized network, bottom-up management, and consensus-based decision-making among others ("About us," 2015). In their work to observe presidential and local elections of 25 May 2014, as part of a civic network, Opora reported that the elections were free and fairly conducted ("Civil Society," 2014). In local elections on 26 October 2015, Opora was active to report over 1,000 electoral violations ("Opora," 2015). This example represented how civic campaigns can be transformed into new civic organizations, which work towards social change, as was the case with Opora and the legacy of many activists tied to [black] Pora.

In the second example, it demonstrated how a civic campaign entered the legislature to push for political reforms as a new political party. [Yellow] Pora's leader Vladyslav Kaskiv officially registered as party leader, the Civic Party Pora as a political party on 23 March 2005. It was an offshoot of the [yellow] Pora campaign from 2004. During the 2006 parliamentary elections, the party was invited to run as part of a civic bloc PORA-PRP (Reforms and Order Party, headed by Vitali Klitschko) and received 1.47 percent of votes. Kaskiv attributed their success to the alliance: "...we strongly believed it would be a fair proposal. We would have failed, had we offered

124 *Conclusion*

money, or anything else to Vitali. We didn't offer anything but our agenda and our solutions to key problems" (Kaskiv, 2006). Their success attracted Klitschko, in his opinion. Kaskiv replied that, "I dare say that Pora also knows the taste of success and how to attain it. Because where Pora is, there is always victory" (Kaskiv, 2006). In Kaskiv's view, Vitali represented the principles of Pora, as "a young and successful representative of the new generation" (Kaskiv, 2006). By the next elections, this alliance with Civic Party Pora ended because of differences in priorities. For the special parliamentary elections in 2007, the Civic Party Pora ran under "Our Ukraine bloc- People's Self-Defense" and obtained 14.15 percent of the votes ("Громадянська," 2011), winning three seats in the 2010 local elections in Lviv ("РЕЗУЛЬТАТИ," 2010). It became part of the rise of new parties, but without much popular support. Following 2010, it was no longer active as a political party in national elections. In 2011, Kaskiv had been assigned as the head of the state agency for national projects management in Ukraine. By 2013, Kaskiv submitted his letter of resignation and expressed his desire to work in the private sector ("investment agency," 2014).

Kaskiv's transformation from civic activist to politician also illustrated the conflicts over newfound fame presented to a charismatic protest movement's main coordinator when he got transformed into a political party politician. Following the end of the [yellow] Pora campaign, the leaders in the group envisioned a future civic party Pora that would become "a new political force…[it] will draw talented young professionals into the realm of politics and administration…The civic party PORA is to be an independent political structure based on a clear prioritization of national interests over corporate ones" (Kaskiv et al., 2005, p. 27). On one hand, Kaskiv was heralded by activists like Ostap for the success of Pora. Without Kaskiv and his networks from the Freedom of Choice coalition, Ostap admitted that Pora's campaign would not have been able to gain international recognition as a central brand. As Ostap put it, there would have been no Pora. Instead, Ostap imagined that Pora would have been composed of a few small activist communities to coordinate with each other. On the other side, there were activists that vocalized their disappointment that Kaskiv's networks coopted the success of the [yellow] Pora campaign for personal interests. This was in opposition to the campaign's ideals of an apolitical campaign and shared understanding among the activists that participated in the campaign with no intent to advance political ambitions. While activists from [yellow] Pora, like Yuriy Polukhovych, did not critique Kaskiv's rise to political power, Polukhovych questioned Kaskiv's decision to promote his close circles of friends in his political party. They disapproved of Kaskiv's decision to make "a career for some people who were not involved in [the] process" (author's interview, Yuriy Polukhovych, 2007, Kyiv). For Polukhovych, this was not normal and he had difficulties accepting it. He observed when the Orange Revolution was about to finish, some of Kaskiv's networks: "they became leaders, they were in TV and newspapers" (Ibid., 2007). Like Kaskiv,

Polukhovych was well known on television, but the difference was that "I didn't want to be so famous. That was not the goal" (Ibid., 2007). The problem that he perceived was a case of the *political formation and its usurpation* and its usurpation by outsiders from the protest movement. He expressed his reactions as the following: "We had problems with this because people used Kaskiv to come to political society with good starting positions. We didn't like to feel like you were used by someone. We didn't want to be used by someone. But at the end of the revolution, we felt that Kaskiv was going to be a big boss" (Ibid., 2007).

The activists like Polukhovych that worked with Kaskiv defended him and considered him as a coordinator, not the group's leader. Polukhovych recalled that Kaskiv did not appoint himself the leader. However, Kaskiv was older and more experienced than the others, and capable of performing the tasks demanded of him. It was okay for him to assume more of a leadership role, in Polukhovych's view. While Polukhovych accepted Kaskiv's work in the campaign, he expressed that not all activists had a good relationship with Kaskiv. He recalled that 50 or 60 percent of the management in [yellow] Pora changed since their first protest actions, some of them went to work for [black] Pora campaign. The activists left because it was difficult to work surrounded by careerists, not activists. Most students were volunteers and not paid for their participation in [yellow] Pora campaign. Other activists departed from the campaign based on principles. Activists like Olha Salo illustrated the internal conflicts, wondering, "how can one person receive salary for his activity [in the campaign]?" (author's interview, Salo, Lviv, 2009). This idea of activism for pay went against her principles.

This also represented a type of struggle for recognition among activists. Polukhovych considered the internal conflicts in the organization normal and thought that it happened in every revolutionary situation (author's interview, Yuriy Polukhovych, Kyiv, 2007). Polukhovych observed that Kaskiv became more powerful as the time passed in 2004. He saw that Kaskiv was responsible for many things in [yellow] Pora, and he took on more risks as a leader with money, influence, and power in Polukhovych's view. That also put him in danger, had President Kuchma decided to kill their leader, he said (Ibid., 2007). In terms of its effects on his personal views activism and its limits on activating him beyond the protest, Polukhovych at the end of the Orange Revolution, went back to the university because

> [p]olitics is so dirty. I know I will go back in five, ten or a year, who knows. I tried to balance two people. I hate to be a leader. If you are leader, you need to balance between people. It is not enough to be in the field alone without people. I kept it in my mind, it helped. It was a difficult time. I don't want to give a prize to myself. In 10 or 15 when it is legend [Orange Revolution], this will be the golden seed...This will be its own seed, what we did and didn't do.
>
> (Ibid., 2007)

126 *Conclusion*

In sum, for those who stayed in the [yellow] Pora campaign until the end of the Orange Revolution, there seemed to be overall acceptance of the coordinator Kaskiv and his network connections who brought visibility to their campaign brand on the international levels—something that would have been unthinkable without him. The change of organizational staff midway through 2004 pointed to disagreement linked to Kaskiv's management style. Notably, his techniques of promotion of outsiders to the campaign caused rifts in the organizational structure of activists. They took issue with the fact that others from outside the protest movement would benefit from the risks assumed by the coordinators and land a career from others' sacrifices. The activists disliked the fact that once the violence had passed that these so-called "fair weather activists" stepped into their campaign to reap the rewards of its success. This was in terms of political careers from individuals that were undeservedly receiving praise for activism that they were not a part of in terms of long-term participation. This was a good illustration of the *personal action frames*. In this case, it was members of a coordinator's friend network reaping the benefits of a political career following the end of protests. There is no doubt that other unpaid activists would perceive this as unfair promotion of latecomers to the campaign. These newly incorporated individuals received pay and a career start by being a celebrity of sorts through association with the successful [yellow] Pora campaign. For these reasons, the process of turning a civic campaign into a political party alienated many of the activist coordinators, many of whom retreated to civic life or back to school at the university ending their political activism until the next round of protests would reactivate them. This presented complications that hindered focus on actual political reforms by including a new generation of activists into the political structure.

Lastly, activism and politics were approached differently ten years later following the conclusion of the Euromaidan protests. In a third example, a network platform got established as a vehicle to drive reform in direct relations with international, civic actors in concert with Ukrainian lawmakers. This represented a contrast with the ideas of the Pora campaign for reform, which was limited in its method chosen to institutionalize the civic campaign through the creation of a new political party, and its selection of a single leader with civic ties (as well as allegations of corruption against him) to represent the values of the Orange Revolution. Given the difficulties to win electoral seats and make change from within Parliament structures, Civic Pora party efforts were shadowed by their leader's "colorful" reputation, which further hindered their ability to make actual inroads to reforming politics with a new generation of thinkers. In the case of Kaskiv, the blurred configuration of power and corruption walked a fine line between offering something new and reproducing old political structures' way of doing. However, more recently, civic activists following the Euromaidan protest introduced an alternative to reform by working with existing civic structures to build relations with political structures. The best example presented was the Reanimation Package of Reforms (RPR) initiated by the Euromaidan activists following the end of protests. They created a platform for civic organizations (NGOs) from national and international levels, including groups such as the Civic Sector of Euromaidan, OPORA civil society network, Hromadske radio, Open Society Foundation, European Youth of Ukraine, EU Information Centre at the National Academy of Public Administration, and International Renaissance Foundation ("Who are we?" 2015). Their objective is "to implement key reforms, that would strengthen open society, government's accountability, new relations between a citizen and the state, security and prosperity of Ukrainian people" (Ibid., 2015). To date, their experts have participated in drafting or amending 59 Ukrainian laws ("Laws," 2015) and outlined a roadmap for reform, highlighting 24 areas, as well as providing a detailed action plan, to accomplish their objectives. This plan includes public discussion, and is meant to be an open and transparent process. So far, they have met with constraints since the government and Parliament have not set up a constitutional commission for making these reforms. Two of their draft laws dealing with members of Parliament (MP) immunity were delivered to Parliament, but none were about actual constitutional reform. In 2014, the president submitted their draft law on amending Ukraine's constitution; it was later withdrawn from the agenda since the MPs could not reach consensus. To address these challenges, the RPR group has proposed to set up a working group, involve civil society, and submit draft laws to Parliament to amend the law to permit Constitutional amendments ("Roadmap of Reforms," 2015).

By the end of 2015, RPR experts wrote a progress report detailing the accomplishments of the "RPR in drafting laws on reforms, cross-cutting areas such as constitutional, anticorruption, judicial, public administration, media, tax, and educational. The RPR also played a key role in advocating relevant legislation. To highlight, the Parliament has passed several important laws, among them, on corruption reform, Law of Ukraine on the National Anticorruption Bureau (NABU), legislation to ensure transparency in the funding of political parties and election campaigns ("Reform under the microscope"). More specifically, to illustrate, I present an example of recent tax reform. There were legislative and executive struggles to agree to amend the tax law. The atmosphere among these politicians was described by RPR as "...unwillingness to listen to the arguments of different parties and the wish to lobby a particular draft law, resorting to manipulations and distortion of facts, lead[ing] to public distrust of [sic] this reform" ("Statement of," 2015). They presented a rational debate to politicians advocating for the adoption of these laws; the outcome of their appeals is still pending.

The new form of activism of the RPR involved decentralized processes as the strategy for political change by involving multiple actors into the decision-making process. It also built in openness and transparency as part of its structure, to permit a wide reach of participation and information

128   *Conclusion*

networks. It also functioned using democratic methods to determine the course of reforms and to coordinate among experts of civil society and NGOs. The RPR appealed to lawmakers to stop political conflict and to balance the tax budget. Theirs was a collective effort to provide the rationale for improving the situation, and to identify the beneficiaries of the draft law. Lastly, they appealed to ministries to implement changes. This draft law (Reg. No. 3357) would contribute to decrease "the share of expenditures of the public sector in the structure of the gross domestic product by 10 percent" ("Statement of," 2015). They also contributed arguments to politicians to encourage them to implement changes in the law to the public benefit. Jack Duvall captured the essence of what the RPR was attempting—to transform the civic structures from precedent movements, such as Civic Sector Euromaidan and others in RPR. He wrote that, "no participant in a movement can 'become the change you want to see' unless he or she takes action that is consistent with the political values and social vision held by the movement" (Duvall, 2010). An examination of the case of Civic Sector Euromaidan and their anticorruption platform that followed revealed that it was representative of the protest movement's power to integrate its political beliefs on reform representing new structures of cooperative civic networks driving political change.

Bibliography

About Us. (2015). Retrieved December 7, 2015, from http://www.oporaua.org/en/about-us.

Author's interview, Olha Salo, April 16, 2009, 3rd year university student at Ivano Frankiv'sk University, [black] Pora, Lviv.

Author's interview, Yuriy Polukhovych, Nov. 12, 2007, Kyiv, history student at NaUKMA, Yellow Pora coordinator of Kyiv Branch for Pora civic campaign before Revolution until we finished the campaign, origins: Ternopil, Western Ukraine.

Civil society election: observation mission presidential and local election, 25 May 2014 Ukraine. (2014, May 25). Retrieved December 7, 2015, from http://www.epde.org/tl_files/EPDE/RESSOURCES/Election reports/Ukraine Presidential Elections 2014/EPDE_finalPC_en_fin.pdf.

Duvall, J. (2010, November 19). Civil resistance and the language of power. Retrieved January 11, 2016, from https://www.opendemocracy.net/jack-duvall/civil-resistance-and-language-of-power.

"Intentions of Ukraine"-results of conjoint nationwide sociological survey kiis and socis. (2014, February 1). Retrieved December 6, 2015, from http://www.kiis.com.ua/?lang=eng&cat=reports&id=227&page=15.

Громадянська партія "Пора" - Центр политической информации "Дата" (2011, December 29). Retrieved December 7, 2015, from http://da-ta.com.ua/mon_mainnews/916.htm.

Investment agency head Kaskiv ready for resignation and work in private sector. (2014, March 5). Retrieved December 7, 2015, from http://www.kyivpost.com/content/ukraine/investment-agency-head-kaskiv-ready-for-resignation-and-work-in-private-sector-338479.html.

Ishchenko, V. (2014, March 2). I hate! On war in Ukraine. Retrieved December 6, 2015, from http://www.criticatac.ro/lefteast/i-hate-on-war-in-ukraine/.

Kaskiv, V. (2006, March 4). The Goals of Parties that Formed Orange Coalition in 2004 Are Different. *Civic Party "Pora"*. Retrieved December 6, 2015, from http://pora.org.ua/eng.

Kaskiv, V., Chupryna, I., Bezverkha, A., & Zolotariov, Y. (2005). *PORA-Vanguard of Democracy: A case study of the civic campaign PORA and the Orange Revolution in Ukraine*. www.pora.org.ua.

Laws. (2015). Retrieved January 11, 2016, from http://www.rpr.org.ua/en/achievement/laws.

OPORA NGO registers 1,118 violations of election law by Oct. 26 morning. (2015, October 26). Retrieved December 7, 2015, from http://www.kyivpost.com/article/content/ukraine-politics/opora-ngo-registers-1118-violations-of-election-law-by-oct-26-morning-400646.html.

Reform under the microscope. (2015). Retrieved January 11, 2016, from http://www.rpr.org.ua/uploads/files/source/z_briefs_web_eng.pdf.

РЕЗУЛЬТАТИ МІСЦЕВИХ ВИБОРІВ. ПОПЕРЕДНІ ДАНІ. (2010, November 8). Retrieved December 7, 2015, from http://www.pravda.com.ua/articles/2010/11/8/5552584/.

Roadmap of Reforms. (2015). Retrieved January 11, 2016, from http://www.rpr.org.ua/en/achievement/roadmap-of-reforms.

Statement of the Reanimation Package of Reforms Regarding the Situation Around the Tax Reform. (2015). Retrieved January 11, 2016, from http://www.rpr.org.ua/en/news/2015-11/0/420.

Who are we? (2015). Retrieved January 11, 2016, from http://www.rpr.org.ua/en/about-us/khto-my.

Index

activists' self-organization,
Euromaidan protests: conclusion
114–15; introduction 96–7; Ishchenko,
Volodymyr 102–5; Kohut, Andriy
105–8; Kryvydk, Ostap 108–12;
Kutsenko, Stanislav 112–14; Shevtsiv,
Andriy 97–102; summary 13
actors, opposition 4–6
Adamkus, Valdas 52
advocacy/participatory 10
"agents of transformation" 93
Alina (activist) 88
"All Ukrainian Public Resistance
Committee for Truth" 21
ambivalence 94
amnesty deal 58
Amnesty International 55
Arab Spring 40
arrests *see* police action and violence
Ashton, Catherine 58
Association Agreement (AA) 8, 30, 38,
99, 105–9
associational life 73
Automaidan 100, 104; driving
protest 100
Azarov, Mykola 58
Azarov, Nikolay 101

bargaining 82
"Bativshchyna" party 21, 104
Bauman's individualization concept 76
Bennett and Segerberg's theory 6–9
Bessmertny, Roman 3
Bezpective website 36
Bezverkha, Anastasiya 86
Black Pora movement: basics 24, 93;
Ishchenko, Volodymyr 91–2; Kohut,
Andriy 83–4; Kryvydk, Ostap 88;
Opora 123; party leader registration

123–6; professionalization of activists
76–7; Shevtsiv, Andriy 77–80
Bromley's research strategy 11
Bryukhovetsky, Vyacheslav 25–30, 118
Buckley's "complex adaptive system"
concept 76
Bullseye newsletter 113

campaign strategy for mobilization 52–3
case study method 11
Castell's social movement theory 77
CEC Central Election Committee
Center for Research on the Liberation
Movement 105
Center for Social and Labor Research
102
Center for Social and Marketing
Research (SOCIS) 39
Central Election Committee (CEC) 3,
52, 56
Channel 5 television station 3, 30, 34, 37,
88, 101
Chemerys, Volodymyr 2, 21, 44, 47–9, 72
Chernobyl nuclear plant 45
Chervona Ruta event 19
Chornovil, Taras 70
Christian association 18
civic associations 73
Civic Expert Council 106
civic nationalism 22
Civic Party Pora 123–4, 126
Civic Sector of Euromaiden: changes in
law 128; concern about radicalization
122; Euromaidan protests 99–104,
107–8, 112, 127; mobilizing friends
117, 119; strategies of 121
"Clean Ukraine" 55
clientelism practices 31
CNN media outlet 49

Index

coercion 83
"collection" action theory 6–8
Committee "For Truth": Ishchenko, Volodymyr 92; Kryvydk, Ostap 68–9; mobilizing new generation 22–3, 54; new initiative 44–5, 49; Shevchenko, Andriy 64–5
Committee of National Salvation 26
Committee of Voters of Ukraine 51
communal life 114–15; *see also* tent cities
Communist Party (KPU) 4–5, 20, 25
Communist Party of Ukraine (CPU) 20, 25; "competitive authoritarian regime" 31
"complex adaptive system" concept 76
Confederation of Student Organizations of Ukraine 19
"connective" action theory 6–9
Constitution Day 33
constructivism 10
Cossacks 110
Creswell (John) methodology 10
Crimea 113–14
criminal past 110
Crotty (Michael) methods 10
cultures of networked belonging 40
CyberBatalion 30

defections 58
democratization processes 17
Derevyanko, Yuriy 101
Derkach, Leonid 45, 47
"digitally mediated action" movements 8
digital technology 6–8, 24
Diomin, Oleh 47
Dnipropetsk region 89
Do-It-Yourself (DIY) politics 84
Donetsk region 89–90
Donii, Oles 20–1
Dubko, Taras 18, 19

Eastern Partnership Roadmap to Vilnius Summit 106
egg incident 54–5
election fraud protests 3, 28, 51–2, 54–6, 88
elites 31
E-Maidan 30
emergence of an actor: campaign strategy for mobilization 52–3; election fraud protests 54–6; Euromaidan protests 56–9; "For Truth" protests

44–5; introduction 44; launch of protests 45–50; "Our Ukraine" 50–2; summary 12–13; "Ukraine without Kuchma" protests 44–5
EU Information Centre 127
Euro Advance project 108–10, 112
Euromaidan protests: analysis of event 12; emergence of an actor 56–9; hastily created 114; Ishchenko, Volodymyr 120–1; model of organizing 7; Orange Revolution comparison 39–40, 77; risks 7; social media integration 40
European Democrat Students (EDS) 113
European Program on the International Renaissance Foundation 106, 127
European Union (EU) 4; *see also* Association Agreement
European Youth of Ukraine 127
EuroRevolution 30
"EU-Ukraine Summit 2011: Civil Society Dimension" 106

Facebook 4, 12, 40, 107
facilitation 82
failure 50, 92, 97
"fair weather activists" 126
Fartukh, Iryna 28
Fatherland Party 58
fear 67, 94, 102
Filenko, Volodymyr 3
force, use of *see* police action and violence
formative experiences 73
"For Truth" *see* Committee "For Truth"
fraud in elections 3, 28, 51–2, 54–6, 88
"Freedom of Choice" coalition 54, 124; of Ukrainian NGOs 21
friend loyalty 120; networks importance 117
From Dictatorship to Democracy 121

generational approach 2–3
Generation Orange 23
Gidden's reflexivity concept 76
glasnost 17, 21–2
Gongadze (Heorhiy) scandal 1–2, 5, 44–9, 69, 77
Gorbachev, Mikhail 17, 25
Greenjolly band 28
Green Party 5
grievances, shared 96
Gryzlow, Boris 52

Index 133

heartbeat method 53
hierarchical structure, Yellow Pora 87
Hopko, Anna 102
Hromadske radio 127
Hromadske television channel 3–4
Hryhorovych, Liliya 31
humor use 24, 83; *see also* satirical
  performance
hunger strikes *see* student hunger strikes

ICTV 34, 46
"idea system" structure 84–5
"imaginary worlds" 93
Independence Square 2, 20–1, 46, 55, 57,
  99; *see also* Maidan
Indignados movement 84, 104
indignation 40
Individual Advanced Research
  Opportunities (IARO) Program
  xii, 11
individualization concept 76
individualized nature of protests 13
individual transformation 118–28
inductive approach 10
Institute of Economic and Social
  Problems "Respublika" 72, 120
instrumental based participation 96
International Renaissance Foundation
  106, 127
Internet 35, 36, 78, 115, 122
IREX/Individual Advanced Research
  Opportunities (IARO) Program 11
Ishchenko, Volodymyr: approach to
  activism 72–3, 120–1; interview
  12; professionalization of activism
  91–3; retreat from activism 103,
  123; self-organization, Euromaidan
  protests 102–5
Ivan Franko National University of
  Lviv 18–19, 82

Jasper's theories 45, 65, 71, 73, 93
journalist harassment 51; *see also*
  Gongadze (Heorhiy) scandal

Kaskiv, Vladyslav 21, 54, 87–8, 123–6
KGB (Committee for State Security for
  Soviet Union) 18, 105
Khreshchatyk Street 56, 101
Kiev International Institute of Sociology
  38, 39
Klitschko, Vitali 58, 104, 123
Kmara 88

knowledge claims and gaps 6–10
Kohut, Andriy: approach to activism
  67–8; concern about radicalization
  122; professionalization of activism
  80, 83–5; self-organization,
  Euromaidan protests 105–8, 115
Komsomol organization 17, 20
Kontraktova Plosha 55
Kontraktova square 81
Kravchenko, Yuri 45, 47
Kravchuk, Leonid 47
Kravchuk, Viktor 26
Kryvydk, Ostap: approach to activism
  68–71, 74; friend loyalty 120; Pora's
  campaign 124; professionalization
  of activism 85–91; self-organization,
  Euromaidan protests 108–12;
  social change and individual
  transformation 118
Kuchma, Leonid: demands against
  45; denunciation, protests and
  activists 49; election fraud 52;
  kidnapping and murder charges 1, 3,
  77; oligarchs support 5; unification
  process 32
'Kuchmagate' 23
"Kuchma Kaput!" 45, 48
Kuchmism 77–8
Kutsenko, Stanislav: approach to
  activism 66–7; professionalization
  of activism 80–3; self-organization,
  Euromaidan protests 112–14
Kvit, Serhiy 29
Kwasniewski, Aleksander 52
Kyiv for Kyivities 6
Kyiv Mohyla Academy *see* National
  University of Kyiv Mohyla Academy
  (NaUKMA)
Kyiv Polytechnic Institute 102
Kyiv Strength 6
Kyrylenko, Viacheslav 21

Laboratory of Legislative Initiatives
  105, 106
language policy 6
launch of protests 45–50
Lenin Square 21
Levytsky, Oleh 2
logos, removal of 34–5
Lukianenko, Levko 45
Lutsenko, Igor 102
Lutsenko, Yuriy 2, 21, 34, 44, 47, 49
Lytvyn, Volodymyr 47

134 *Index*

Maidan: international attention 45–6; renovation closure 48; students protesting together 28; symbolic tent 48; website 2; *see also* Independence Square
Maidan newspaper 27, 29, 118
Maidan Nezalezhnosti 2
Maidan Self-Defense Forces 109–12
Majewski, Eva 113
marches: Kutsenko, Stanislav 82; Maidan to European Union Embassy 100; as protest activity 35; Sumy to Kyiv 37
Marinsky Park 111
Marxism 17, 18
Masol, Vitali 20, 46
mass public support, mobilization 20
Matvienko, Anatolii 45
McAdam (Doug) view 65, 73
media 3, 30, 34, 37, 46, 86, 88, 101
media bias 46, 51
Medunytsia, Oleh 32
Melnyk, Leonid 32
Melucci (Alberto) theories 74
Members of Parliament (MPs) 127
Moloda Prosvita 65, 66, 68
"moral shocks" 71
Moroz, Oleksandr 44, 45, 49, 50
motivations 24

Naftogaz company 87–8
Narodnyi Rukh Ukrajiny 25
National Academy of Public Administration 127
National Anticorruption Bureau (NABU) 127
National Platform of the Eastern Partnership Civil Society Forum 106
National Roundtable Initiative 112
National Salvation Forum (NSF) 50
National University of Kyiv Mohyla Academy (NaUKMA) 25–30, 55, 81, 92, 118
Nayyem, Mustafa 3–4, 39, 40, 98, 109
Nedryhailo (General) 20
negative political ads 51
networked belonging, cultures of 40
networks, personal friends 117–20
New Citizen organization 6
new generation and their subjectivities: 1990 events 19–21; 2013 events 38–40; activists 21–4; Ivan Franko National University of Lviv 18–19; National

University of Kyiv Mohyla Academy 25–30; overview 17; spaces for subjectivities expression in universities 25–38; summary 12; SUMY University 31–5
New School for Social Research (NSSR) xii
nomenklatura 4–5
Non-Governmental Organization (NGO) 6, 106–7, 123; *see also specific organization*
non-violence strategies 23, 101

Occupy Wall Street movement 7, 40, 84, 104, 117
oligarchs (business clans) 5
Olson (Mancur) theory 6–8
online organizing *see* digital technology
open-ended interviews 10–11
Open Society Foundation 127
Opir Molodi 66, 68, 77
Opora 123, 127
Optor 67, 92
Orange Revolution: analysis of event 12, 52; Black Pora, mobilization of people 79–80; changes in society for backdrop 23–4; collective decision 38; Euromaidan comparison 39–40; first phase 52–3; friend networks 118–19; Greenjolly band 28; Ishchenko, Volodymyr 120; Kutsenko, Stanislav 81–2; Kyiv Mohyla Academy 29; mass mobilization 52–3; new protests 3; Pora's campaign and groups 77, 122; re-apppropriated tactics 30; risks 7; second phase 53; surveys 5–6; Taras Shevchenko National University of Kyiv 28; tent cities 56; training 52–3
"Our Ukraine": development of 5; emergence of an actor 50–2; Kutsenko, Stanislav 67, 80; mobilization strategy 52–3; police action against students 34; press center 27; support from 37; voting fraud 3

Panorama newspaper 34, 35
paradox of persistent participation 98
"partial delegative democracy" 31
participation 74, 96
Partnership for Transparent Society Program 32
"Party of Reforms and Order" 21

Party of Regions 37, 51
Parubiy, Andriy 109, 111–12
patronage with politicians 31
People's Democratic (NDPU) party 5
People's Movement of Ukraine for
  Reconstruction 22
Peresiedov, Konstyantyn 27
perestroika 17, 21
personalization of politics 76, 120, 125;
  personal action frames 8, 9
personalized expressions of activism:
  2000–2003 events 64; individual
  approaches 73–4; Ishchenko,
  Volodymyr 72–3; Kirovohrad,
  Ukraine 66–7; Kohut, Andriy 67–8;
  Kryvydk, Ostap 68–71; Kutsenko,
  Stanislav 66–7; Kyiv, Ukraine 72–3;
  Lviv, Ukraine 64–71; political
  mobilization 64; Shevtsiv, Andriy
  64–6; summary 13
personal networks 117
persuasion 82
petitioning 35
Plast 20
Pliusch, Ivan 47
police action and violence: arrests
  during elections 27; atmosphere before
  violence 112; awakening toward 98,
  106; Black Pora 79; Euromaiden
  protests 57–8, 99, 102–10, 115; fear
  71; impact on activists 123; Kryvydk,
  Ostap 70; Orange Revolution 89–90;
  politicians' protection of tent cities
  45; survey results 38; tent cities 33–4,
  38, 58; Tymoshenko imprisonment 49;
  violation of citizen's rights 120
political awakening 5
Pology, Eugene 34, 35
Polukhovych, Yuriy 124–5
Pora movements 31, 38, 93, 121–4
PORA-PRP (Reforms and Order Party)
  123
post-positivism 10
pragmatism 10
Presidential Election campaigns
  (2004) 11
"Prison for Bandits" 48
professionalization of activists:
  conclusion 93–4; Ishchenko,
  Volodymyr 91–3; Kohut, Andriy 83–5;
  Kryvydk, Ostap 85–91; Kutsenko,
  Stanislav 80–3; overview 76–7;
  Shevtsiv, Andriy 77–80; summary 13

protest events: activities of 35; anti-
  regime protests 4–6; Euromaidan 3–4;
  Orange Revolution 3; timeline 12;
  Ukraine without Kuchma 1–3; Great
  Laundry 55–6
"psychological warfare" 49
"Public Assembly of Ukraine" 105

radicalization 23
rational choice, organizations 6
Razom Nas Bahato, Nas Ne Podalty 28
Reanimation Package of Reforms
  (RPR) 127
reflexivity concept 76
regrets 90
"Renewal of Ukraine" campaign 110
reciprocity 50–1
research design 10–12
research framework 6–10
resource mobilization 6–7
"Revolution on the Granite" 2, 20–1
ridicule use 24; *see also* satirical
  performance
"Rise Ukraine" campaigns 5
risks 7, 64
Rukh activists 22, 25
Rushchyshyn, Markian 21
Russia's occupation 113–14

Sadova Street 101
safety against violence 110–11
Salo, Olha 125
satirical performance 55–6, 83–4;
  see also humor use
Schwandt's social system theories 76
Scientific Communism class 18
Security Service of Ukraine (SBU)
  55, 67
self-mobilization 9–10
self-organization: of citizens 6;
  personalized expressions of activism
  64–74; professionalization of activists
  76–94; understanding 9–10
self-recruitment process 72–3
Sharp, Gene 121
Shevchenko, Andriy 37
Shevchenko Square 33
Shevtsiv, Andriy: approach to activism
  64–6; associational life 73; interview
  11–12; professionalization of activism
  77–80, 94; retreat from activism
  123; self-organization, Euromaidan
  protests 97–102

136   *Index*

Shurma, Ihor 55
Simon's theory 96
Slavko (friend) 70
smowball sampling approach 11
Snow (Bedford) theory 65
sociability 73
social changes 118–28
Social Democratic Party of Ukraine 32
Social Democratic Party (United;
    SDPU(O)) 5, 47
Socialist Party 4
social media integration 40
social psychological theory 103
societal fragmentation and individualism 8
Solana, Javier 52
Solchanyk, Bohdan 98, 99
"space of autonomy" 40
Spain's *Indignados* movement 84, 104;
    Spain's 15M protests 7, 40
Spivoche Pole 53
St. Michael's Cathedral 99
St. Michael's Square 108
state-owned gas company 87–8
Stetskiv, Taras 3, 44, 50, 52, 54, 70, 80
Stop Fake 30
street performances 83–4, 94; *see also*
    satirical performance
Student Brotherhood 17–18, 19–20
student descriptions and
    characterizations 34
student hunger strikes: Independence
    Square 20; Masol's resignation 20, 46;
    Rukh activists 25; Shevtsiv, Andriy 65;
    Ukraine without Kuchma 21; use of 2;
    youth associations activation 17
student mobilization 92–3
"Student Wave" campaign 53, 55, 67,
    80–1; "Student Vichy" 81
Studio 1+1 television channel 46, 86
Sumy National Agrarian University
    (SNAU) 32
SUMY University 29, 31–8
surveys 5–6, 38–40, 74
Svododa party 104, 110
Svystovych, Mykailo 2, 21, 45
Symonenko, Petro 45

Taras Shevchenko monument 69
Taras Shevchenko National University
    of Kyiv 28, 91
tax code (Tax Maidan/Tax Maidan II)
    5–6
technology *see* digital technology

telephone importance 78
television stations 3, 30, 34, 37, 46, 86,
    88, 101
tent cities: center of movement 23,
    87; communal life 114–15; Orange
    Revolution 56; participation in 23;
    police action against 33–4, 58, 110;
    politicians' protection 45; resistance
    front 38
"territory of freedom" 56
The Association of Independent
    Ukrainian Youth (SNUM) 19
"The Chrysler Imperial" 22
The Faces of Protest 23
The Guardian newspaper 102, 120–1
The Heaven's Hundred 98
*The Logic of Collective Action Public
    Goods and the Theories of Groups* 6
"The Party of Regions" 3
The People's Movement of Ukraine 25
The Trade Unions Building 99
"time-series analyses" 11
"together we are many, we will not be
    defeated" 28
Tomenko, Mykola 3
Touraine's theories 35, 73, 74, 93
Trade Union House 111
Trade Union of Market and Commerce
    Employees and Entrepreneurs (Tax
    Maidan II) 5–6
training 52–3, 71, 81, 90, 92
transformation of individuals 118–28
"Traveling Egg" 54–5
Treaty on European Union 106
Tsarenko, Oleksandr 32, 37
"turbo-laws" 104
Turchynov, Aleksandr 59
Twitter 40, 107
Tyahnybok, Oleh 102
Tymoshenko, Yulia 3, 21, 26, 49, 104

Ukraine Crisis Media Center 30
Ukraine Students' Union 19–20
Ukraine with Kuchma 7
Ukraine without Kuchma (UWK):
    analysis of event 12; Bryukhovetsky,
    Vyacheslav 26; Civic Sector
    Euromaidan 121; emergence of an
    actor 44–5; Ishchenko, Volodymyr 72;
    Kohut, Andriy 67; Kryvydk, Ostap
    68, 86; Kutsenko, Stanislav 67; lack
    of identification with 97; planning
    and organizing protests 2; reasons

Index 137

for failure 50; Shevtsiv, Andriy 64–6;
 student hunger strike 21; summary
 12–13
Ukrainian Bill #2540 105
Ukrainian Democratic Alliance for
 Reform (UDAR) 104, 110
Ukrainian Helsinki Union (UHU) 19
Ukrainian Inter-Party Assembly 19–20
Ukrainian Language Speakers 102
Ukrainian Nationalist Union (UNU) 19
"Ukrainian Truth" 1
Ukrainian Youth Forum 112–13
Ukrainska Pravda 1, 3
United Kingdom (UK) 102
unification process 32–5
Union of Ukrainian Students 19
Union of Ukrainian Youth (SUM) 32
Union Treaty for the republics 25
Union Treaty with Moscow 20
Unite Kyivites! 6
USSR (Union of Soviet Socialist
 Republics) 18

Vadim (activist) 89
Vasyunyk, Ihor 100
Vesnych, Oleksandra 33
Viatrovych, Volodymyr 98, 101–2
violence, day of 111; *see also* police
 action and violence
virutal spaces 7; *see also* digital
 technology
voting fraud *see* fraud in elections
Viatrovych, Volodymyr 65
Vyvykh-92 festival 22

watchdog organization 123
"Wave of Freedom" program 54

"way of subjectivity" 40
websites, as protest activity 35, 36
Western culture, connection to 22
Western-funded organizations 104

Yanukovych, Viktor: election assurance
 51; failure to sign EU AA 30, 38,
 112–13; removal of 58; seizure of
 estate 108; Social Democratic Party
 of Ukraine 32; voting fraud 3;
 Yushchenko differences 93
Yatensnyuk, Arseniy 58
Yatsenyuk, Arseniy 102
Yellow Pora movement: basics
 24; election fraud protest 54–5;
 Kryvydk, Ostap 85–6, 89;
 party leader registration 123–6;
 professionalization of activists 76–7,
 93; Stetskiv, Taras 53
"Young Enlightenment" 65
Young Resistance 66, 68, 77
Your Right 32
Youth Nationalist Congress 32
youth organizations 17
"Youth Party of Ukraine" 21
YouTube video 115
Yurko (activist) 89
Yushchenko, Viktor: denunciation,
 protests and activists 49; dioxin
 poisoning 51, 55; election 5;
 lack of political leaders support 50;
 "people's president" 53; requests
 for resignations 47; support for 26,
 51, 65; voting fraud 3; Yanukovych
 differences 93

Zakharchenko, Vitaliy 101